Joh. Seb Bach

BACH

by

EVA and SYDNEY GREW

With music examples in the text

McGraw-Hill Book Company

New York • St. Louis • San Francisco • Düsseldorf

Mexico • Montreal • Panama • Rio de Janeiro • Toronto

First published 1947

First McGraw-Hill Paperback Edition, 1972
07-024678-5

1 2 3 4 5 6 7 8 9 MU MU 7 9 8 7 6 5 4 3 2

TO

SIR ADRIAN C. BOULT

IN FRIENDSHIP AND IN ESTEEM
AND WITH REMEMBRANCES OF MANY HAPPY HOURS
WITH BACH TOGETHER—HE AT THE DESK, WE IN THE
AUDITORIUM

No poet in the world is greater than Johann Sebastian Bach. No art but music could have given artistic shape to the Christian religion, for it alone could catch up and reflect the glance into the soul. . . . There are chorales by Johann Sebastian Bach—and not only chorales, but I name these to keep what is best known—which in the simple, literal sense of the word are the most Christ-like sounds ever heard since the divine voice died into silence upon the Cross. . . . I could name a prelude from the *Wohltemperierte Klavier,* in which the words, "Father, forgive them, for they know not what they do"—or rather, not the words but the divine frame of mind which gave birth to them—have found so clear, so touching an expression that every other art must despair of every attaining this pure effect.'

HOUSTON STEWART CHAMBERLAIN.

'Herzlich tut mich verlangen'

To JOHANN SEBASTIAN BACH

Thy art is thought which proves
  The mind a treasure of God
Towards which ever moves
  Music's divining rod.

E. M. G.

PREFACE

IN a small book on a large and an involved subject a good deal has to be left out. The writer of such a book is generally aware of the omissions. Of the things that may be included a choice can be made between saying a little about each of a large number of them and saying a fair amount about a specially selected and representative few. The choice here has been the latter. Therefore in the present book a picture is attempted of Bach's life and work, and of the conditions prevailing in the towns where he lived. Something, but not much at times, is said about the music he wrote in each place. Some particular attention has been paid to the cantatas, which are not well known, and to the organ works, which are well known, though in one section only, which is that of the compositions on free subjects. Both cantatas and organ works are dealt with chiefly as forms of music that are concerned largely with the use of chorales, this being a matter vital in the composer's art.

The following are some of the things that would have been discussed if there had been room: (1) adaptations, as from one sacred work to another, and from a secular work to a sacred one; (2) Bach's phrasing, as recorded in the not inconsiderable number of works he did phrase; (3) his methods of teaching; (4) his reform of fingering on keyboard instruments; (5) his help in the victory won by the believers in equal temperament; (6) his knowledge of the construction of instruments and his inventions in that direction; (7) his orchestration; (8) his harmonic style, which is a blending of the old and the new, and makes D minor and E minor, for example, as near one another modulatorily as D major and B minor, and allows a piece in A minor to settle in its middle into F sharp minor (and this without A minor having previously been discarded for A major); (9) his fugues—what they are, and

what they are not; (10) his vocal declamation and his understanding of metres, syntactical constructions, accents, cadential
rhythms and the other matters that belong to declamation; (11)
his speed in performance, and especially the *tempo rubato* that was
employed in his day; (12) the difference and the absence of
difference between his secular and sacred styles; (13) the difference
between his clavier and organ styles; (14) his humour, that ranges
from a sly allusion to a donkey's song to jests at the clumsiness or
futility of the wiles of Satan; (15) his dramatic style—how nearly
it may come to suggesting action, but how far it remains from
actually depicting it; (16) his powers of characterization, in
music that to the untrained eye and ear seems all alike; (17) what
may be called his metaphorical powers, since by a rare gift of
imagination he can see the connection of things apparently unrelated and so express the one by the other: which is why it is
often not altogether easy to decide his reasons for doing this, that
and the other; (18) his religion, and how it comes about that
persons of a different religion are often good at interpreting his
expression of his articles of faith, while those who hold what he
held are not; and (19)—to make an end—why Bach's music is so
frequently dull and tiresome *in performance* for lovers of it, and
irritating and disgusting to persons who are not by nature in
harmony with it.

The larger books on Bach that are available in English (Spitta,
Schweitzer, Parry, Sanford Terry, etc.) will provide the present
reader with information on some of the foregoing matters, and on
others not enumerated. It can be asserted that for students of
the essential Bachian kind the one indispensable book is Spitta's,
because of Spitta's elevation of spirit, his knowledge of his subject, in the whole and in its parts, and his capacity to see below
the surface of things. The seventy years that have passed since
his work came into existence, with all the discoveries they contain
and the various theories they have seen formulated, have not
radically affected its value. But the work must be recommended
with a few warnings. One is that Spitta was very emotionally a
German of the generation of Bismarck. He can therefore say of

his musical hero such things as this: 'He was a typical German; at once a hero and a child, untamed and yet impressionable and tender.' Another is that this great author and critic had a few ideal fads and fancies: these a reader can detect and allow for himself. A third is that Spitta often goes so minutely and so profoundly into matters that one cannot understand what he says until one knows as much about the subject as he does. A fourth is that at times his translators of the 1880's, not knowing what he is talking about, render him wrongly into English. Sometimes, indeed, they make material mistakes. One such may be described here. It occurs in vol. i of the translation, on page 207. The subject is a chorale work of Georg Böhm's. Spitta speaks of this and that 'versus' in the work. The translators take 'versus' to mean *verse* in the sense of *line*, and so render it as *line*. But 'verse' also means 'stanza': the first *verse* of a hymn is its first stanza. In arrangements of chorales it has the significance of *movement*. Thus the translation is hopelessly confused. And the confusion is worse confounded by the circumstance that the translators get some of the numbering of the verses wrong. It may be said in defence of the translators that such a mistake is excusable: a person cannot know everything. But in the present case there are musical quotations; each quotation is of the first line of a movement, and consequently all the quotations display the same phrase of melody; yet the translators still call that phrase the 'next' *line*, the 'third' *line* and so forth: they did not perceive that something was wrong by realizing that one phrase of melody cannot form the melody of six successive lines of verse; they should have perceived that, and so their mistake is not excusable. Elsewhere paragraphing is not determined by subject, and an occasional sentence is misplaced. But on the whole the translators did a noble piece of work, and often they render Spitta's loftier utterances in terms that are themselves adequately lofty. It has been the custom during the past generation to disparage Spitta. But no book has been written without his aid. In fact, one or two of the smaller books of the time consist of little but borrowings from him, often in the direct words of the English translation.

And in 1911 Sir Donald Tovey made this remark: 'Spitta's biography superseded everything written before it and has not since been approached: with corrections in the light of Rust's *Bachgesellschaft* prefaces it contains everything worth knowing about Bach, except the music itself.'

EVA MARY AND SIDNEY GREW.

ROMSLEY HILL, WORCS.

1st July 1945.

CONTENTS

CHAPTER I

THE BACH FAMILY

BACH was a member of a family of professional musicians who lived in Thuringia in the seventeenth and eighteenth centuries. As a musical family it began, strictly speaking, with his grand-father and grand-uncles, and he was therefore of the third genera-tion. But his ancestry is known a couple of generations farther back, and his great-grandfather was what might be called a semi-professional.

The original Bach in the records was a miller of Wechmar, a village near Gotha and Arnstadt. He was named Veit, after St. Vitus, the local patron saint. Nothing is known about him, except that he played the zither and that religious intolerance com-pelled him at one period of his life to live in Hungary. His son, Hans, the semi-professional musician, was a carpet-weaver by trade. He was musically a fiddler, and he is generally referred to as 'Hans der Spielmann': that is, John the fiddler. His engage-ments were casual, and they took him all over his part of central Germany. He was clearly very popular as an outside occasional member of town and other bands, and he seems to have been especially welcome at weddings. He died in 1626.

The three sons of Hans the Spielmann were Johannes (1604- 73), Christoph (1613–61) and Heinrich (1615–92). Christoph was Sebastian's grandfather. He played violin and was a member of the bands at Arnstadt. Johannes was both organist and violinist: his chief position was that of head of the Erfurt town band. Heinrich, the most gifted of the three brothers, was organist at Arnstadt.

Each of the three had three sons who became professional musicians of one kind or another. Thus Sebastian's father had two brothers and six first cousins in this walk of life. The family was opening out well.

Sebastian himself had three brothers in the profession, ten or a dozen first cousins, and several second cousins. Moreover, Veit the miller had a second son, from whom sprang eventually a family of musicians. The members of this were distant relatives of Sebastian, but they were still relatives; and so in his time the Bachs of his generation numbered between thirty and forty.

It was the peculiar constitution of Germany at that time which enabled the Bachs, and thousands of other men, to live by music. The land was owned by princes, dukes, counts and the like, most of whom maintained something of a band in their establishments. And nearly every town of any importance had a municipal band. These were never large. Leipzig, for example, had in Sebastian's time one of eight performers only. Their civic functions were mostly ceremonial, but it was their duty to supply whatever instrumental music was wanted in the chief local church. The many churches, moreover, required organists and cantors.

There was thus no need for the Bachs to seek work outside Thuringia; and since their natures were against wandering, the great majority of them stayed where fate dropped them. Sebastian himself never saw the Alps. He went north, to Lüneburg, when a boy. Later in life he paid a few professional visits to Hamburg, Lübeck, Berlin and other towns. But for the rest he lived in a piece of land that could be circled by a motor-car in a summer day.

Because of Johann Sebastian there is, for most people, a kind of halo about each member of his family. It is fancied that they must all have been a little like him at least. This is a mistake. Two sons of Heinrich's were good composers for their time and place. Two of Johann Sebastian's remote cousins had some creative ability. One of his sons, the eldest, inherited some of his genius, but failed to develop it. His second son is an important figure in the new school of music that led to Haydn and Mozart. Two other sons made a mark on the fashionable world during their lifetime. But for the rest, all that is to be said of them is that they were useful practical musicians. They were organists of parish churches, members of the band in ducal establishments and members of municipal bands. A few were cantors, that is, directors of music, in endowed schools and in universities: these were the teachers of singing, the trainers of choirs and the occa-sional composers of cantatas and motets. Thus the Bachs were, in the main, the seventeenth- and eighteenth-century German counterparts of such twentieth-century English musicians as church organists and choirmasters, conductors of bands at holiday resorts, conductors of municipal police bands and members of the same. They piped and fiddled, and fingered organ and clavier, well enough to do their work and to keep their engage-ments, and they wrote pieces much as a modern A.R.C.O. or F.R.C.O. writes an anthem once in a while. But they were not interested in music otherwise than as craftsmen. It was for them a simple practical matter: it was there, as was the air they breathed and the language they spoke. They experienced little, if anything at all, of musical ecstasy. They had none of the fine pride of the artist in his art. They knew nothing of the spiritual exaltation that makes a man regard his art as a mission. The conditions and circumstances of their life and work, indeed, were such that if they had brought more to it than they did bring, it would have been a nuisance. The Bachs in general were therefore men of whom history takes no account, any more than it does of such other men as the counts and princes, the church councils and the burgomasters, who employed them. But for the accident of Johann Sebastian's appearance among them, the mass of them would be known merely as an example, interesting but by no means unique, of hereditary occupation in a family that persisted for three or four generations.

When times were good they earned just enough to live on from week to week. When they were not they were rapidly on the verge of destitution. This happened frequently. A church, a town council or the establishment of a count or duke often found itself temporarily without funds. Employees were then not paid their salaries. More than one Bach had to explain to the author-ities that he and his children were literally starving. The same thing happened if a Bach lost his post and was without work for a period. There was, however, a splendid charity in the family, at least up to the generation Johann Sebastian belonged to: those who had at the moment helped those who had not. And no orphans lacked a home and an upbringing.

Salaries were low, and a Bach added to his income by work in other directions than that of his official position. An organist or cantor would teach some general subject in a school of his town. A member of a town band might also be one of the watchmen of the town. A musician in a ducal establishment might also be an official of the domestic kind—a clerk, or a lackey: Johann Sebastian's grandfather, for example, was both footman and fiddler to the Duke of Weimar. Those who could tilled little gardens attached to their houses and grew no small part of their food. They taught music, of course; and when they were established they had resident pupils, called apprentices, who paid a premium for their instruction. A few whose work ran without interruption all through their lives saved a little money to leave to their children. An uncle of Johann Sebastian's was one of these; and he could even pay to have his portrait painted in oils. But on the whole this long-continued and extensive family, lifted high in the knowledge of the world by the greatness of one of its sons, lived as artisans do—carefully, humbly and always with anxiety as to what the immediate future might have in store for them. Johann Sebastian made good money. His income at Leipzig amounted to something between £65 and £70 a year. He left an excellent estate, the value of which was no less than £126 5s. But within two years of his death his widow had to apply to the authorities for relief; she lived her last years in an almshouse; and she was buried in a pauper's grave.

CHAPTER II

EISENACH (1685-95)

BACH's birthplace, Eisenach, is famous in general history as the town wherein Luther hid himself from his enemies in 1521, in the period of his greatest danger. It was in the Wartburg that he was secreted; and there he made his translation of the Bible and created some of his hymns. The Wartburg, the great castle of the ancient landgraves of Thuringia, was in medieval times the gathering-place of the Minnesinger, who held their contests there: when Elisabeth in Wagner's *Tannhäuser* cries 'O Hall of Song, I give thee greeting,' she addresses the hall in the Wartburg.

The ruling family during the seventeenth century maintained a first-class musical establishment. Johann Pachelbel was attracted there, though he remained as court organist only a year. Johann Christoph, son of Heinrich Bach, 'organist well-appointed of all the churches here,' was content to live and work in the town for the last thirty-eight of his sixty-one years. Telemann, the most popular and best-acclaimed church musician during Bach's lifetime, belonged for a while to Eisenach. And so did Neumann, the poet-clergyman who created the new form of cantata libretto that Bach was to adopt for some hundreds of cantatas. Eisenach had great pride in its musicality past and present. Indeed, its annalist in 1698 discovered that its musical glory was declared anagrammatically in the Latin form of its name—*Isenacum* containing in its letters *en musica*, 'See! Music!' and also (a little less perfectly) *canimus*, 'We sing!'

The 21st of March (Old Style) 1685 was the day on which Bach was born. One of his godfathers was a member of the ducal establishment, whose work lay with the woods and forests of the estates. The other a town musician from Gotha. The former, Johann Georg Koch, gave his godson a name that fifty or so of the family bore, had borne or were to bear. The latter, Sebastian

Nagel, gave him a name that was unique in the family until his children began to have children. The name is, indeed, unique in musical history, so far as our observation goes, except for a Johann Sebastiani of the seventeenth century (1622-83). This man was born at Weimar, and he worked as cantor in Königsberg. He is famous for his Passion music; and a believer in such things might fancy that his spirit, released from the flesh a few months before Johann Sebastian Bach was conceived, was one of the many spirits that reincarnated themselves in the person of the child that was to be. Two of Bach's grandsons were named Johann Sebastian: one was a son of Philipp Emanuel (born 1748), who was a painter and who died at thirty; the other was a son of Bach's married daughter (born 1749), whose coming into the world was nugatory, since he died in the year of his birth.

Bach came into no small household. There were four sons there, aged respectively fourteen, twelve, ten and three, and two daughters, aged eight and five. There were assistants and apprentices, probably to the number of four. Thus with the father and the mother the establishment contained twelve persons. Nor was it a quiet one. The three elder sons were already learning instruments: that of the boy of twelve was the trumpet, which is a thing that cannot be worked secretly in a corner. The father and the other professionals practised and rehearsed, singly and together, for coming performances in court, town and church. And the children were clamorous in the ways and degrees natural for their varying ages.

The material changes that took place during the ten years Johann Sebastian was to have his parents were two only: when he was six the eldest brother left home for Ohrdruf, and in the same year died the brother who was a trumpeter; he had left home some time previously for work at Cöthen. This death of a brother was Sebastian's first contact with death. It could perhaps signify little to so young a child. Yet something there might be to carry forward to the effect the death of mother and father had upon him when he was in his tenth year. And from these experiences would come some of his future understanding of this great and universal theme, of which he was to sing as wisely and movingly as other musicians sing of that other great and universal theme, love between man and woman.

Sebastian went to school at eight. The Gymnasium, as it was called, provided an eight-year course for those who were to proceed to a university, and a shorter course for those who had to go early in life into some practical apprenticeship. Sebastian was put into the fifth class. His brother, Johann Jakob, the future oboist in the King of Sweden's band, was already in that class; and he was eleven. Therefore the 'mental ages' of the two were equal, either because Johann Jakob was slower than usual or Johann Sebastian quicker. Moreover, they were next each other in the grading. Together they went up into the fourth class; and there, at Easter 1695, their schooling at Eisenach ended. What they learnt was Bible history, the Catechism, some of the psalms and the elements of Latin grammar. School hours were from six to nine o'clock and from one to three o'clock in the summer, and an hour later in the winter. Boys with good voices were trained by the cantor for the chorus that perambulated the streets, singing for alms: Sebastian was for certain one of these. The school records show that he missed a considerable number of attendances—more than fifty hours in his first year, and more than a hundred in his second; but nothing is known of the childish illnesses that may have been the cause of this.

At home Sebastian learned the violin, his father teaching him. By the time he was ten he was probably more than a fair performer for his age; but he said nothing relative to such matters in the family chronicle he started about 1735, and Philipp Emanuel said nothing about them in the necrology of the Bachs he prepared for publication in Mizler's periodical in 1754: Bach's sons had no interest in the story of their father's earlier years. Things being what they were, it can be taken that Ambrosius, the father, planned a professional musical life for his youngest son, with the violin and viola for his instruments and his aim a court or town appointment. Johann Christoph, the father's cousin, organist of the great church of St. George, may have had occasion to think that

7

the child might become an organist: he may have been led to the idea by something in the child's manner as he listened to his playing—his rapt, concentrated attention, his calculating, ruminating expression, with head already held slightly aslant, and his questions, curious, intent and searching. Perhaps Sebastian wandered with the tuner and repairer inside the instrument, getting first elements of the knowledge that eventually was to make him an authority on organ construction. The assistants and the town bandsmen may have let him experiment with their instruments, so that he learned to make a scale on flute, oboe and trumpet—an activity that his father, easy-going and friendly, would never hinder. All this is surmise. But it is reasonable surmise, since the child is father of the man, more especially when the man is such as Bach was.

The mother died on 3rd May 1694. The father married again and died on 27th or 28th January 1695. The widow was left with her daughter, aged ten, and with four, perhaps five, step-children. The eldest, Maria Salome, aged eighteen, was to marry soon and leave home. The next sister, Johanna Juditha, aged fifteen, was to live not much longer. A son of twenty, named Johann Jonas, was alive; but nothing is known about him—whether he was at Eisenach or away elsewhere in a trade or profession: it is believed, however, that he also died not long after. Johann Jakob, aged thirteen, and Johann Sebastian, aged ten, remained, and they were disposed of in the simple manner of the Bachs, which was to transfer an orphan to the care and keeping of a relative.

The relative in this case was the brother Johann Christoph, organist at Ohrdruf, aged now twenty-four, and married a few months. The boys were taken to him shortly after the Easter o₁ 1695, Johann Jakob to stay with him a year, Johann Sebastian five years.

CHAPTER III

OHRDRUF (1695–1700)

Eisenach and Ohrdruf are thirty miles apart. A river flows through the latter town, which in Bach's time was very quiet and remote, and essentially provincial. It was an ancient place and had a school (the Lyceum) that was famous throughout central Germany, but it was musically inactive.

Johann Jakob and Johann Sebastian were sent to the school as soon as they reached their brother's. The former was put into the third class, the latter into the fourth. But after the August examinations Sebastian went into the third, and the brothers were together again. Jakob left the next year (1696) to start his apprenticeship with the town musician who succeeded his father; for he was then fourteen. It took a boy two years to work through a class, and in July 1697 Sebastian was top scholar in the third. He went into the second, and by July 1699 he was top but one. He was then transferred to the first: as a rule boys did not enter this highest of all classes until they were sixteen or seventeen, and Sebastian was only a few months past his fourteenth birthday. He did not remain for the full two years, but left in March 1700.

The school subjects were like those of Eisenach: Bible history, psalms and the Catechism, some arithmetic, some rhetoric and the 'humanities'—this last a little Latin and less Greek, the Latin embodying Cicero's epistles, the Greek the New Testament. There was nothing of general literature, except a small measure of poetry—nothing of history as it relates to nations and lands—nothing of foreign languages and foreign culture. One wonders if in their playtime the children played in harmony with the curriculum—gravely, heavily and with unanimated countenances.

The school had its perambulating chorus, which sang in the streets four times a year and collected money that was divided among its members. It was trained by the cantor, a man named

9

Elias Herder (or Herda). The chorus also sang at weddings and funerals, of course for a fee, which again was divided among the members. All in all, the sum that came to a boy like Sebastian from this source was not insignificant, and it went a fair way to help his brother to feed and clothe him. For Sebastian was one of the solo singers, and his share in the earnings would be more than the average.

It is expressly stated in the family records that Johann Christoph taught Sebastian the clavier, and that he was his first master for the instrument. He himself was probably a safe and sound performer, since his master for some years had been Johann Pachelbel, but it could hardly be that he stood in anything of a lofty rank. Sebastian, however, must have been a swift learner. Once his technique was in shape—and with his knowledge of music and his capacity of intense application that would take but a year or so—he would be able to play any average clavier piece of the time in a few hours. Fugues in three or four parts would hold him back only in the degree of their requiring larger hands than a boy of eleven or twelve has: and as Bach's hands are reported to have been exceptionally large when he was a man, it may be that when he was a child they were on the same scale. For the rest, little more is wanted in the playing of the contemporary music than nimble fingers and a sense of time and rhythm. Thus it can be imagined that the pupil was a bit of a trial to the teacher: first the teacher would be hard put to it in the matter of finding pieces to feed his voracious appetite, and secondly he would see him advancing quickly to the condition where the child was the better performer of the two—whereupon he would have to say, as more than one master has said of a pupil of genius: 'I can teach him no more!'

Whenever one thinks of Bach's childhood the picture that thrusts itself uppermost in the mind is that of a boy secretly making a copy for himself of a manuscript volume of clavier compositions that his brother did not want him to know anything about, at the moment. The forbidden music was in a latticed bookcase. Sebastian found how to work it through the mesh. No artificial lights were available. But there were every month a number of bright moonlight nights. And on those nights Sebastian copied the music. His paper was probably plain paper that he ruled himself: he could take no printed music paper from what stock his brother had, and if he bought any in the town news of the trans, action would have come to his brother's ears. Weeks and weeks were spent on the task, until in six months it was accomplished. It was really a most unwise undertaking, as any one who has tried to read even written or printed words in moonlight would at once say—as unwise as Schumann's attempt to overcome the intractable third finger by a special piece of mechanism. And as Schumann ruined his finger, so Sebastian may have strained and weakened his eyes, thus preparing them for the blindness that came half a century later. And then Johann Christoph discovered what Sebastian had done and took the copy from him.

As one contemplates this, one lives again some of the anguish the boy must have suffered when the laboriously made transcript of the music was taken from him. Other people have suffered the torture of losing similar treasures. Warburton's servant lit a fire with irreplaceable manuscripts of Elizabethan plays. Carlyle had the manuscript of the first volume of his *French Revolution* burned up—the fruit of five months of toil. To be doomed to rewrite the pages was, he said, 'like half-sentence of death.' But these losses were endured by grown men, and Sebastian was a child; and though the grief of children may be less lasting, while it does last it is often more intense than anything older people can experience.

Why did Johann Christoph deny his brother this music? It could not be that he was jealous of him. Rather would he be proud of him. Nor could it be that the music was something private that must be kept from the possibility of the rest of the world knowing about it; for the music was by well-known com, posers and was owned by scores of musicians, both professional and amateur. It must simply be that he had made a ruling, that Sebastian had disobeyed him and that disobedience must be punished. As for Sebastian, he wanted these works in order to know about them, to study them as examples of composition and to use them as models in his own experimental attempts at music-making; he could not want them to play, at least not yet, since if he played them his brother would hear him, and then—alarum!

Nothing is said in any of the family records about Sebastian and organ-playing at this time of his life. There is no reason to think that his brother denied him access to the instrument in his church or hindered his learning to play it. Sebastian, who was a good organ player at eighteen and a supreme master of the instrument by the time he was twenty-two, must have felt the call of the instrument irresistibly before his eighteenth year. It must have risen in his regard and in his ambition as the instrument of all instruments. It would have been blind, cruel and heartless of Johann Christoph to thwart his desires and yearnings in this direction. He was not the man to act so. If he had been, he would have been no Bach. Therefore it is to be taken that Bach learned organ as well as clavier at Ohrdruf, and that before he left he had for some considerable time given his brother a hand in his church work, and so learned how to take a service.

Long before he was fifteen Sebastian was tired of Ohrdruf and eager to be away. He was tired of it because he had exhausted it. He wanted to be away much as boys of the sea-going temperament get restless to be off to sea.

Bach's life is divided into stages, each higher and more spacious than the one before it. His advance from one to another was necessitated by his need for change: *here* he had done all that opportunity allowed; *there* was a fresh opportunity that allowed something further; in this place he has mastered all there is to master; in that place new models await him, a new atmosphere for the breathing, new spiritual influences to inspire hitherto undeveloped elements of his nature, new artistic conditions. And by good management on his part, or by good fortune, or by a combination of both, exactly the right opportunity came to him at exactly the right moment.

It was so here, at the end of his period at Ohrdruf. He was

still a student, if a very advanced one. He was to be a student—that is, a learner and a copier—for some years yet to come. But he could go farther only in some place where the work was being done that he must learn and copy, and where the men lived who were doing it. Around him was central Germany, occupied mainly by musicians of the class and calibre of his brother, more or less static therefore in art, more or less closed to external in' fluences, and concerned with things in music of which he already knew enough: for at fifteen we can be sure he could write a little tonic-and-dominant fugue, or arrange a chorale with a running contrapuntal accompaniment, as well as Johann Christoph could, or any other pupil of the famous Johann Pachelbel, or even Pachelbel himself. On his right hand was the south—Italy, Austria and the German lands bordering on them. There indeed was an art as yet known to him only slightly, and it was a very fine and beautiful art. But for a central German the south was an exceedingly foreign land. A youth could get into it only with the help of some rich patron. Moreover, it was Catholic, and Johann Sebastian was natively Protestant. On his left hand was the north—a land connected by business with all the world, and therefore cultured and cultivated; with towns and cities that were metropolitan, not provincial: Hamburg, Lübeck, Lüneburg and the rest; with many great and famous musicians living in it; and, above all, warm and glowing and romantic in its musical inclinations and qualities.

It was the north that drew Sebastian, since 'dark and true and tender is the North,' and as such in absolute harmony with his nature. And it was at this precise moment that the north gave him opportunity to enter it; and to enter it, moreover, with an assured means of livelihood.

The opportunity was revealed to him by Herder, the cantor of the school at Ohrdruf. Certain school and church estab' lishments in north Germany liked to have, in the ranks of their choirs, boys from central Germany, because those boys were naturally good musicians and exceptionally fine singers. They attracted them by offering education both musical and general, free feeding, something in the way of a salary, a chance to acquire musical experience and a kind of prestige that was helpful to the boys when, as grown men, they competed for professional appointments. Herder had been one of these boys. He heard now that his old school at Lüneburg wanted a couple of new choristers. He recommended to the school two of his Ohrdruf pupils, Johann Sebastian Bach and Georg Erdmann. They were accepted on his recommendation, and in the spring of 1700 they made their way to Lüneburg.

It was a journey of something over 150 miles. No Bach since the family was established musically in Thuringia had ever gone half that distance from his native locality. The boys would perform it mostly on foot, since the money they—or at least Johann Sebastian—would have could not have been enough for them to stage-coach it all through. But they would enjoy it all the more for that. Carefree and hopeful they went through lands strange to them and entirely different from the wooded loveliness of their homes, meeting different types of people, tasting novel kinds of food and delighting in the fun of picking up lifts on vehicles of every kind going their way. And thus Sebastian hitch-hiked his way into this fresh stage of his life and passed another milestone on his journey.

He would carry with him a few pieces of music he had written under his brother's guidance and in the style and spirit of his time and place, yet already marked by individuality and daring. Perhaps among them was a clavier Fugue in A minor (Peters edition, 212, No. 5). Perhaps among them also was a working for the organ of the chorale 'Vom Himmel hoch' (Breitkopf No. 140). The following is bars 21–30 of the organ piece. It contains the cantus presentation of the first line of the tune, and part of the prelude to that of the second, the melody of which is:

(2nd line)

In the prelude the two lines (*a*) and (*b*) are worked together: a device very nearly of the boy's own inventing, since nothing quite like it could have come his way in other music:

(1st line)

Observe the finish of the piece, with its sturdy, high-spirited giving forth of the first line again—without warning, and with no authority from prevailing custom:

CHAPTER IV

LÜNEBURG (1700–2/3)

I

LÜNEBURG was one of the chief north German towns of the Hanseatic League. It was the great store place for the merchandise that came from other parts of Germany for shipment from the mouth of the Elbe. It is about thirty miles south of another such town, Hamburg, and about fifty south of yet another, Lübeck. All these places enter vitally into Bach's story. So does another local town, Celle, which is some forty-five miles south of Lüneburg.

In each of the three Hanseatic towns there was a famous organist and composer of organ and other music: at Hamburg, Johann Adam Reinken (1623–1722); at Lübeck, Dietrich Buxtehude (1637–1707); at Lüneburg, Georg Böhm (1661–1733). Reinken was born in Holland, Buxtehude in Sweden and Böhm in Thuringia. They all count as north German musicians, and the first two are among the supreme representatives of the romantic school of music which they founded. Böhm was trained first in Thuringia, and then came north to study under Reinken: the influences forming him were therefore dual—those of central Germany and those of north. He was less gifted than Buxtehude and perhaps than Reinken; but by the accident of circumstance he was of more immediate effect on Bach as a writer of music. There were, of course, other great organists and organ composers in this land: for example, Vincentius Lübeck (1654–1740), another pupil of Reinken's, who worked in Hamburg from 1702; but there is no record that Bach associated with them personally, though he would naturally seek out and study their works.

There were three churches at Lüneburg. Böhm played at St. John's. At St. Nicholas's the organist was Johann Jakob Loewe (1628–1703), born in Vienna of a father who was born at

16

Eisenach. All that is known of the organist of the third church, St. Michael's, is his name: Christoph Morhardt.

At Celle the ducal court was a brilliant copy of the French court, and French music was greatly favoured there. The ducal band was famous: the majority of its members were French.

Thus for Sebastian Lüneburg was a centre of quite exceptional variety. To its musical personnel contributed Holland, Den-mark, France and Germany, north, central and south. Its organists were mostly men of advanced age and vast experience. And his church of St. Michael had one of the largest and most representative musical libraries of all in Germany.

St. Michael's had two choirs. One was called the Symphoniac Chorus, because it sang in works that were for orchestra as well as voices. Its descriptive title of 'symphoniac' preserves an old meaning of the word 'symphony,' which is simply that of 'in-strument': players of instruments were called 'symphonists,' and the instrumental parts of a piece of concerted music (the prelude and the postlude, and the middle interlude or interludes) were called the 'symphony.' By Bach's time, however, the use of the word in these significations was dying out: symphoniac music was generally called 'concerted' (the cantata was called the 'concerto,' even by Bach at Leipzig), and the passages where the voices were silent were called the 'ritornelli.' The term survived at St. Michael's traditionally; for the church had been one of the first in Germany to adopt the 'new music'—the music of voices and accompanying instruments—that arose after 1600, and a custom nearly a century old dies hard. The St. Michael's library was rich in both old and new music. Its larger chorus (this 'symphoniac') performed each kind, and it is likely that Sebastian could not have heard the two kinds done better any-where else in Germany.

The other choir was a small affair of boys and youths only; tenor and bass were provided by youths whose voices had broken and then settled into adult pitch. The choir was called the Matins Chorus because it sang chiefly at the ordinary morning services. To secure admission a boy had to have a good voice, to be able to sing part-music and to be in need of earning his living: for the members of the Matins Chorus were paid for their services. They also received free meals.

The payment made to a soprano in Sebastian's position was about 16s. a year. The choir sang at wedding and funeral ser-vices, also in street perambulations. The money received from fees for the services and from collections in the streets was divided among the members, and Sebastian's share was about 15s. a year. This particular boy was useful as accompanist at rehearsals. In addition, he was fit to play as a violinist in the band. He received payment for work in both these directions, and it may have amounted to something like 25s. or 30s. a year. Thus from the start of his life at Lüneburg Sebastian earned nearly £3 a year, and his food cost him nothing. Nor did his lodging, since he lived in the school that was attached to the church. Three pounds seems very little when contemplated with English eyes in the twentieth century, but it was a not inconsiderable matter in 1700. Indeed, the deacon of the church had a stipend that was less than £11 a year.

Sebastian's voice broke when he had been about a year in the choir. It is said that it broke while he was actually singing in a service. But with one thing and another his earnings probably remained the same, if indeed they did not increase, since after a while he trained the choir in the singing of new pieces of music.

The Matins boys attended classes in the school. Sebastian was put into the first class and learnt more Bible history and psalms, more Latin (this time represented by a few odes) and more about such impregnable theological doctrines as election, penitence and the like. He was, from start to finish of his life, an absolutely orthodox Lutheran—a devout, untroubled Christian. Devoid of spiritual pain, he questioned nothing, doubted nothing, ad-mitted no change or expansion of view, conception or idea. He was an opponent of pietism, which is a character and conduct of religious life and belief that is emotional rather than intellectual: that is, enthusiastic in the eighteenth-century use of the word (the English poet William Cowper was a pietist of the extreme kind: his 'O for a closer walk with God' expresses the very soul of his religion). His library of books at the end of his life was composed largely of theological treatises, a fact that proves him to have been unbrokenly interested in the argumentative exposition of his faith. He was thus, as a normal individual, orthodox by nature as well as by early training. But there was something operative in or upon him as a creative artist that was superior to his mind and intellect. It was a rapture essentially emotional in kind, a 'possession' literally *enthusiastic*, that brought him face to face with God and filled him with a sense of the closeness of God. When this rapture seized him—and it seized him whenever his theme gave occasion for it—it lifted him to the production of music that is holy. He was not then the orthodox Lutheran. He was the universal man. No creed functioned. Or, rather, all creeds functioned, from that of the mystic of any age or place to that of the earnest atheist or freethinker of the nineteenth or twentieth century. And he became the artist before whom one would bow, were it not that he takes us by the hand and bids us stand upright and calm in the presence of insoluble and otherwise terrible mysteries. He probably did not suspect this himself. He might have brushed aside impatiently any attempt to explain it to him. His generation, and the generation following, had no idea of it. Perhaps Goethe was the first to discover it, or at least to express the discovery in words. But it is there, and it is the quality by which he stands alone in musical art except for the companion׳ship of Beethoven, who climbed equally 'the mystic stair.' And it is the quality that he found here in the music of some of these north German musicians; expressed weakly, intermittently, sometimes fumblingly, yet none the less certainly, and living still in their works for those of a later day who have eyes to see and ears attuned to hear.

II

There are no records of contact between Georg Böhm and Sebastian, the one a man of forty and organist of an important church, the other a boy of fifteen or sixteen, and chorister and

general help in another local institution. We know that Sebastian developed as an organ player while at Lüneburg, and we
believe—critically, on internal evidence afforded by the music—
that he wrote some of his first pieces of organ music there. He
certainly practised largely on a pedal harpsichord, which was a
favourite instrument of the time. A number of his first pieces
are, indeed, as 'apt' for the pedal harpsichord as they are for the
pedal organ. But the essential spirit of the organ is so marked in
practically all this early music of his, and he was so conspicuously
good an organist before he was twenty, that he must for certain
have had free access to an instrument at Lüneburg and spent much
time at it. Now if Böhm's character can be determined by his
music, he was a genial, friendly man, widely experienced in music
and filled with a living curiosity about anything and everything
connected with it. Such a man would be interested in a boy
like Sebastian. Sebastian, for his part, would not be shy of
approaching him. In such a matter, indeed, he was exceedingly
forward, though the reverse of pert. The two can therefore be
reasonably pictured as in close and frequent association; the more
so from the circumstance that there does not seem to have been
any one else at Lüneburg from whom Sebastian could receive
the help and opportunity he did receive there.

Bach as a student always wrote at once in a style that he had
just encountered and that was promising. Such a style was
Böhm's; or, to speak more correctly, such styles: for Böhm as a
composer was a most versatile man—classical in the Italian
manner, brief and bright in the French, quiet or grave in the
central German and romantic in the north German. His music
was the first novel music that Sebastian could meet at Lüneburg.
He would at once proceed to exercise himself creatively upon
it. The extracts on page 21 show the kind of indebtedness of
the youthful Bach for models he must have found in Böhm.
And among the things that survive of those produced under this
influence are the arrangement in E minor of 'Christ lag in Todesbanden,' the partita on 'O Gott, du frommer Gott' (especially the
first and last numbers) and the partita on 'Christ, der du bist der

'helle Tag' (especially the first number). The music here is
juvenile. It is that of a student-copyist. It is loose, as is its
pattern. But it is already music of character. There is a poetic
vision in it that twenty-five years later was to perceive and express
the themes of the Passion of Jesus. And there is in it the fancy
and the invention of art. (Another work possibly of this time is
the working of 'Christus, der uns selig macht' published in
Peters 2067: the second part is quasi-dramatic; in the first the
tune is played on the pedals, the bass by the left hand.)

It was probably in the summer of 1701, his second in the north,

that Sebastian began to make journeys abroad from Lüneburg.
There was little to do in church and school during the vacation
period. Moreover, Sebastian had a way of asking for time off
and getting it, and indeed of taking it if his petition was hum'd
and ha'd at. He would not hesitate to miss a lesson in the school
if the hour happened to coincide with an interesting or valuable
bit of practice or composition; and it was his good fortune in all
the earlier part of his life to have superiors who either understood
him and sympathized with him, or were too easy-going to trouble
about the matter. It may be that those lost school hours at
Eisenach came about just from this cause.

His chief journeys were to Hamburg. There he heard Reinken
play the organ, also Reinken's pupils. And he heard them play
their own compositions and those of other members of the north

German order. This would be at the church services. An
English cathedral service would afford little material for observation to a student in his position. In a German service things
were very different. There were the opening and closing voluntaries: these might be on the scale of the opening and closing
numbers of the third volume of his *Clavierübung*—numbers that
have been abstracted and brought together as the Prelude and
Fugue in E flat major (the fugue that is nicknamed in England the
'St. Anne'). Before most of the hymns was a prelude based on
fragments of melody from the tune of the hymn, and sometimes an
organ interlude as well between certain verses. There was the
accompanying to the actual singing, which might be as free and
as elaborate almost as anything written for the orchestra in 'symphoniac' music. Above all, there were the *sub communione* pieces:
organ solo compositions based on chorale tunes, often very long,
that were played while the congregation partook of the sacraments
at Holy Communion. Before the sermon there was frequently a
cantata, and early in the service there was a motet: vocal
compositions that revealed further aspects of the art of the
land.

Since shyness and diffidence were not part of Sebastian's constitution, he would not hesitate to make himself known to the old
organist and his pupils. And the force of his personality, even
at sixteen or seventeen, his obvious knowledge and ability, apparent
one may believe in the first sentences of a conversation on a musical
subject, these qualities would win him attention. And with
attention won, all would follow as Sebastian desired it: permission to play on the organ, to play even to Reinken himself, and
advice and commendation as to his attainments and prospects.

An incident of one of these foot journeys to and from Hamburg
became an anecdote that Bach in later years told over and over
again. He was on his way back to Lüneburg. Tired, he sat
down to rest outside an inn. Hungry, he sniffed the pleasant
odours of food from the inn, where some travellers were taking a
meal. Hungrier still, he turned over the few pence in his pocket,
debating whether to spend them on something to eat or to trudge

on and save the cash.   Suddenly through a window of the inn
sailed a couple of herring heads, thrown by one of the feasting
travellers.   The crumbs, as one might call them, fell near Sebastian from the table of the rich men.   They brought the smell of
cooked fish more penetratingly still to his nostrils.   He picked the
heads up and began to extract from them the edible bits of warm
flesh.   And in the mouth of each he found a ducat.   The ducat
was a coin of variable value.   Its lowest seems to have been
between 3s. and 4s.   Whatever the worth of these particular coins,
two of them were a gift of princely proportions, representing half
Sebastian's yearly stipend as a Matins chorister.   He had a meal,
continued his walk home and put the money by for other journeys.
He did not inquire who his benefactors were.   Perhaps for once
he was embarrassed and did not know how he could thank them.
He was, after all, only a boy of sixteen or so.   And he must have
felt and looked very disconsolate in that hour, since otherwise he
would not have attracted the sympathy of these well-to-do,
probably careless and casual passers along the road.   The story
crystallized into a domestic joke in Bach's family, owing to the
frequency with which he told it to visitors.   We can consequently imagine one of his children saying when herrings were
in the family dinner: 'Any ducats this time, father?'

Sebastian got to Celle likewise.   Now there is a mystery about
this particular matter.   Performance by the ducal band was given
in the ducal court before the ducal family and their guests: there
only, and before them only.   Sebastian could not be a guest.   He
could not get a friendly servant to let him slip in unobserved, to
hide behind an arras while the music was in making.   All that
would be too risky, for boy and servant alike.   He could hardly
get a member of the band to smuggle him in, as messenger or as
assistant, for neither messenger nor assistant could reasonably be
wanted.   If for special occasions the band had to be augmented,
and if the concert-master of the court asked for the additional
performers to be sent from Lüneburg, Sebastian's interested and
sympathetic friends there might have picked him for the work,
knowing how much the chance to hear novel French music

meant to him. This *accidentium* (as odd engagements were then called) might have led to a brief temporary appointment to the band, Sebastian replacing a member who had fallen ill or been called away. But nothing whatever is known except that Sebastian did hear this French music at Celle, not once, but several times. Perhaps the explanation of the mystery is the simple one that Sebastian heard the performances, not at the actual concert, but at the preliminary rehearsals. To these admission could easily be effected by the *Capellmeister*, in response to a request from a Lüneburg acquaintance that the privilege should be granted this exceptional young musician.

The 'Christ lag' arrangement (mentioned on page 20) is a masterly compression of the north German 'grand' chorale fantasia, which is a manner of treatment or arrangement that gives each line its own section and its own contrapuntal subjects. Its like does not exist among all the old chorale arrangements available for study, except the work on 'Ein' feste Burg' which Bach himself wrote at Mühlhausen. But it is clear that the youthful composer was acquainted with arrangements by Böhm of 'Auf meinen lieben Gott' and 'Vater unser.' The piece is actually a little magazine of north German forms, styles, themes and ways of treating a chorale melody. It owes nothing whatever to Pachelbel or other central Germans. The music is simple, but the touch is sure and certain; and when it is played with a properly informed understanding of it, it makes a vivid poetic impression, since its plan is the *dramatic* (in the way Schubert's *Erl King,* for example, is dramatic in plan), while its execution is the *lyrical*: dramatic, because each line has for intellectual subject the tangible idea that is expressed in the text of the line; lyrical, because the subject is dealt with emotionally, not realistically. (In works of this sectional kind it is apparently the first verse of the hymn that is interpreted: see the Weimar arrangement in four sections of 'Jesus Christus, unser Heiland'). The treatment of the melody of the first line of the tune, which is also the third line, proves this: the statement in the first line is that Christ lay in the bands of death (yielded to them for our sin); that in the third is that He is now arisen (and brings us the joy of salvation).

A model Sebastian might have had for such lyrical flights as these is the 'Allein zu dir, Herr Jesu Christ' by Daniel Erich, of which the second line is as follows:

III

It was held generally that Bach lived at Lüneburg three years, his return to Thuringia taking place early in 1703. Documents discovered since 1900 prove that he was back there in the last quarter of 1702.

In little more than two years he had taken all that north Germany held for him at this moment in his life, except what was to be gained from contact with the greatest musician of all, Buxtehude of Lübeck. The divine restlessness must therefore have seized him again.

This time it required for its assuagement that he should have an organ of his own. His need now was to perfect himself as a performer, which was a dual task, since in those days performers, whatever their instrument, wrote a good deal of what they played, and the public expected them to do so. Bach the organist must therefore be Bach the composer of organ music. He must set his executive ability task after task by his creative ability; and he must also reverse the process. Neither power must lag behind the other. Above all, material form and substance must be in harmony with spiritual. The idea and its realization and manifestation must be one. Nothing was to be attempted that could not be done. Nothing must be done that was not the solving of a problem. And all that had been observed and stored in memory from these broad days in the north must be made a part of his developing individuality, what was external being made internal and sent forth then as unique art.

Time and opportunity for all this could be established only in the conditions of an official appointment that would afford him at once a living and an instrument. No such appointment was in prospect in the north. If a vacancy occurred, a dozen men or experience, pupils of famous local masters, were on the spot to try for it. Sebastian therefore must go south again, to the land where he as a Bach was well known and where his youth and inexperience would not count much, if anything, against him.

He heard of a vacancy in the south in the autumn of 1702 and went to try for it.

We can believe that the call was urgent, and that he left the north suddenly and unexpectedly. Otherwise he would never have gone without visiting Lübeck and Buxtehude. And it would be precisely in this period of the year—late autumn and early winter—that he would have planned a visit to this farther northern town, because it was then that certain very famous performances of church music were given by Buxtehude in his church.

CHAPTER V

WEIMAR (1703)

THE post Sebastian applied for was at Sangerhausen, a town some fifty or sixty miles from Arnstadt and Eisenach. He secured it in open competition. Then the local ruler intervened with a man of his own choice. He ordered the church to appoint him. The church obeyed, and Sebastian was turned down. This town, by the by, comes into the story of Bach's life a second time: the occasion was more than thirty years later, and the circumstances were tragic, because they involved the disgrace and early death of one of his sons.

It was in November 1702 that Sebastian won and lost the Sangerhausen appointment. He was seventeen years and eight months old, and dependent upon himself for his livelihood. It is not known what he did or where he lived for the next few months; but at Easter 1703 he became a court musician at Weimar, the capital city of Saxe-Weimar-Eisenach. There were two ducal establishments here: that of the reigning duke and that of his brother. Each maintained an excellent musical organization. Some years later Sebastian was to be organist to the reigning duke. Now he was violinist in the court band of his brother, Duke Johann Ernst. He was not the first Bach to be in the town, for it was at Weimar that his grandfather had been lackey and musician some seventy years earlier.

Duke Johann Ernst was a lover of fine music, his taste inclining to the new Italian instrumental kind. His orchestra was his pride and joy, and his organist was a famous performer named Johann Effler. (Effler had followed a Bach as organist of a church at Erfurt, and preceded one as organist of a church at Gehren; but that was all many years ago, before Sebastian was born; and Effler was now an old man.) The duke's sons were also musical, with tastes likewise inclining to the Italian. The younger was, in this year of 1703, a boy of seven. He developed into a good amateur composer in the Italian manner; and Bach did a large amount of work with and for him when he was organist to the ruling duke; but he was doomed to die at nineteen.

Sebastian did not take this appointment because he wanted to be a *Hofmusicus*. If he had been content to be a fiddler in a band he could have got a post anywhere, under a duke or a town council, or in fact under both at once. It must be that he took it simply because he had to. No church appointment looked like coming his way yet awhile. In the meantime he must earn a living. But he was merely waiting. The moment something suitable turned up he would be after it, and if he was successful in his application he would go to it.

This suggests that there was a quite unusual condition in the terms of his engagement with the Duke Johann Ernst. In the ordinary way a musician did not necessarily undertake to serve a royal person for life. But once signed on, he could not end his contract without the consent of his employer. Sebastian would have starved rather than bind himself so. Fourteen years later, indeed, he went to prison rather than submit to a continuance of the bondage into which he had delivered himself. He must therefore have had an understanding with the duke from the start that when a church appointment opened itself for him he should be allowed to leave at once. This, then, betokens a friendly interest in the youth on the part of the duke, who was willing to help Sebastian, first as a wage-earner who must work for his living and secondly as a gifted student who would benefit from experience of the particular kind of music he favoured. Thus this brief Weimar appointment added to Sebastian's store of knowledge the Italian instrumental music of the day.

The desired church appointment materialized in a few months. The building of a new church organ at Arnstadt was finished in the summer. Sebastian was engaged, as an expert in organ construction, to test and prove the instrument, so that upon his recommendation the builder's account could be passed. He made his examination on 3rd July and, as was customary, gave a

recital afterwards. The church people were so profoundly im⸗
pressed by his playing that they offered him the post of organist:
fortunately for Sebastian their present organist was a man of
mediocre attainments, and they badly needed a change. He
accepted the offer. On 14th August he was formally appointed.
And so at the age of eighteen years and five months Johann
Sebastian Bach was established, in conditions that for him at the
moment were ideal. They became less satisfactory as time passed,
and when eventually he left he was very glad to go. Just now
however, he was thoroughly satisfied. And before long he was
to meet in the town the girl who was to become his wife.

CHAPTER VI

ARNSTADT (1703-7)

I

ARNSTADT, Erfurt and Eisenach are the towns chiefly associated with the Bach family. Johannes, the eldest of the three brothers who were born early in the seventeenth century, had been organist of a church at Erfurt and head of the town band: descendants of his were heads of the band until the middle of the eighteenth century, and for two or three generations there were always other Bachs among the members; the people of Erfurt got into the habit of referring to the bandsmen as 'the Bachs,' and the name persisted long after the Bachs had all disappeared from the town. Heinrich, the youngest of the three brothers, was organist of the churches at Arnstadt for fifty-one years. Eisenach became a Bach stronghold because Heinrich's gifted son, Johann Christoph, and Ambrosius, Sebastian's father, lived there. It was in one or other of these towns that the family had their annual reunions, when as many as could manage it gathered together to talk things over, make music, display their abilities, eat and drink in company, and foster generally the clan spirit of which they were so proud.

When Sebastian went to Arnstadt, Heinrich had been dead since 1692. Dead since 1693 was Johann Christoph, his father's brother, who had been court musician and town musician there. Living in the town was this Johann Christoph's widow, with her family, of which one was a girl named Barbara Catherina. Also living in the town, or due to come shortly, was the widow of another of Heinrich's sons: she had a daughter named Maria Barbara. Thus Sebastian had two girl cousins at Arnstadt, and he was to marry one of them.

There were two churches at Arnstadt when Heinrich went there in 1641. One, the chief, was called the Upper, or the

31

Franciscan. The other was called the *Liebfrauen*, or 'Our Lady's.'
Heinrich was organist of the two simultaneously: he could
manage the double post readily, because the *Liebfrauen* was used
for an early Sunday service only. A third church, called either
St. Boniface or 'the New,' was built in 1683; and it was of
this church that Sebastian became the organist.

His duties were light. The chief service was the one on Sunday
morning, from eight to ten o'clock At this mass was celebrated.
And before the sermon there would be a piece of figural music or,
on special occasions, a cantata. A service fell in the week on
Thursday, and another on Monday: at these only hymns were
sung. And that was all, except for a matter of semi-voluntary
work that the council of the church asked him to undertake.
This last, however, was the chief cause of the troubles that descended upon the Arnstadt organist and his superiors after the
first year of the appointment. It was to train the boys of the local
school who formed the choirs of his own church and the Upper.
Sebastian undertook it. But it was not expressly stipulated in
his agreement. And when eventually he got tired of it, and
indeed disgusted with it (for reasons not of a musical nature), and
deliberately dropped it, his answer to complaints was that it was
not in the bond.

His salary was made up of 50 florins and 30 thalers. The
florins were his pay proper, the thalers his board and lodging
money. Their English equivalent is a little over £8. Heinrich's
pay as organist of two churches was £5 6s. That of the organist
of the same two a generation later was £7 5s. Sebastian's salary
was thus exceptionally high, both absolutely and in relation to his
age and experience.

No speculation concerning this favour leads to anything. The
church itself was very poor. It could not build itself an organ
until now, and now only because a rich man bequeathed half the
cost of the instrument. It could, indeed, find only 25 florins for
Sebastian out of its funds. The other half had to be taken from
the beer-house taxes; and the 30 thalers were taken from the
funds of a municipal home for old people. Under these cir-

cumstances the salary for the organist was more likely to be low rather than high. It could not be that the church was intensely anxious to secure the brilliant young Bach, and that he, learning of this, took advantage of conditions and held out for a handsome price: he himself was too anxious to have such a post to haggle over terms, if the terms were in any degree reasonable. Nor could it be that the church recognized the coming greatness of his genius and wanted to help him to develop it swiftly and securely: churches have never acted so, in any age or land; and besides that, no one in Arnstadt then, or later, seems to have suspected that their organ player was potentially one of the exceptionally great musicians of the near future. Perhaps influence had something to do with the matter—the influence of men in lofty city places who had known, loved and respected their two Bachs of the preceding generation and wanted now to honour their memory by thus distinguishing a later member of their family: for at this time the Bachs were an institution in this part of central Germany. Towns seem to have been pleased to say 'We have a Bach here'; and the Arnstadtians might have liked to hear other folk say 'They have had Bachs in Arnstadt for over fifty years—and see what they pay the one they have now.'

The organist at the Upper Church was named Christoph Herthum. He had married Heinrich's daughter and so succeeded him in his organist's post. This means that in Frau Herthum Sebastian had another relative in the town, the lady being his father's first cousin. Another organist there was an Andreas Börner: he played as assistant at the Upper Church and at the *Liebfrauen*; and he was the Herthums' son-in-law. These men, especially the younger, were insignificant musicians. Between them they did whatever was wanted in the way of organ music at the ducal court. Bach had no official connection with them. His occasional employment at the court was as violinist or harpsichordist.

The count's director of music (*Capellmeister*) was an elderly man named Paul Gleitsmann. He played several instruments, and by his ability, knowledge and experience he would be a musician with whom Sebastian could associate himself pleasantly and profitably. The rector of the school, Johann Friedrich Treiber, was a lover of music. His son was the same: in addition, he was a composer and a writer on the theory of the art; and he was also a freethinker or atheist, and so got into trouble for his unorthodox beliefs. The Treibers are assumed to be the authors of one or more comic operettas that were performed by the local amateurs. Sebastian may have had something to do with the one that was produced during his stay at Arnstadt. But he would benefit little or nothing from the father and son, except out of discussions with the son on theoretical subjects.

Thus Arnstadt was a place without a distinctive musical life, and Sebastian was consequently altogether free to expand and develop himself in privacy and solitude.

II

It is calculated by Spitta, and his calculation is generally accepted, that Bach wrote two cantatas for the Easter of his first full year in the town (1704). These he fused together later, when he was at Leipzig, and the resultant work is known as 'Denn du wirst meine Seele nicht in der Hölle lassen' ('For thou wilt not leave my soul in hell'). He may have written similar works for the preceding Christmas and New Year. But after the Easter of 1704 he wrote no more. Nor did he produce any by other composers. And the reason was that he fell out finally and irrevocably with the boys and youths of his choir and refused to have anything further to do with them.

The fault was partly Sebastian's, partly the boys' and young men's. The head of the school was weak as a disciplinarian, and in consequence the scholars became a rough and unruly lot. Indeed, they became a disgrace to the town. More than that, they became an actual danger, wandering the streets at night, gangs of young ruffians. In the July or early August of 1705 Sebastian himself had a particularly unpleasant experience. He was walking home with one of his girl cousins when he was waylaid in the street by one of the gangs, at the head of which was a young man named Geyersbach who played bassoon in the local band. Geyersbach challenged Sebastian on a disparaging remark he had made concerning his abilities as a bassoonist and demanded a withdrawal and an apology. Sebastian refused, and Geyersbach set about him with the stick he was carrying. But Sebastian happened to be wearing a sword. He drew this and kept Geyersbach off with it. The others, seeing their leader's danger, intervened and dragged him away; and Sebastian and his cousin then resumed their journey. Whichever Barbara the girl was, she no doubt admired her escort for his courage and swordsmanlike qualities. And it is likely that the swordsman himself did not altogether regret the occasion that had enabled him to reveal himself in so conspicuous and exceptional a way.

On several occasions—6th and 29th August 1705 and in the February and November of 1706—he was summoned before the consistory to explain why he now refused to train the choir of boys appointed to his church and to produce concerted music with them. Each time he replied that he was not compelled to do this by the terms of his appointment, and that therefore he would not do it. But he said he would do his share if a proper director of the choir were provided, who would discipline the boys and be responsible for their actual musical instruction: his share being to supply the accompaniments and to see that every-thing was done to bring about a right artistic performance. The consistory told him that it was impossible for them to find and pay such a director. They told him it was his moral duty at least to do what he had promised to do when first established as organist of the church. Their appeal had no effect on Sebastian: he was innately stubborn, concerned to an extreme degree about his strict rights, and so a fighter. (He showed this later on at Weimar, and again at Leipzig.) The consistory were remarkably patient with him: they were certainly mild and gentle; but in the end they said he must conform, or they must get another organist who would. This did not frighten Sebastian. The consistory did not carry their threat into action. But the next year (1707), finding a suitable opportunity, Sebastian removed himself.

The young organist was to blame because he did not attempt to control his nature. He did not understand boys and men of his own age. He could not handle them the right way. When they displayed their bad qualities, he hated and despised them. They for their part found out how to drive him in a moment into a frenzy of anger. They guyed him. And when boys, especially the rough, illiterate and vulgar ones, start to guy a teacher or a superior, the position is hopeless and recovery is impossible. Sebastian would have been as great a disciplinary genius as he was potentially a musical one if he had succeeded in putting matters to right when they had once got to this pass. He was actually a bad disciplinarian. And his pride, in such a regard as this, was his master. It remained so to the end of his life. He always got into trouble with fools.

III

In the late autumn of 1705 Sebastian obtained a four weeks' leave of absence. He wanted to visit Lübeck, where Buxtehude lived. He had been at Arnstadt two years, spending nearly all his time on organ practice and organ composition, and making very rapid progress. The history of the art of this instrument during the next twenty-five years shows that already, at the age of twenty, he must have been the most brilliant performer in the country. Within a few years he was universally acknowledged to be that, and the fact would exist long before it was perceived. He was also in all probability the most brilliant composer, since with him capacity to perform and capacity to write for performance were always abreast. Thus his ability in both directions is recorded in his current compositions.

What those compositions are, however, is not known authoritatively. Bach rarely dated a work. A chronology for many of his works has been established by the help of his handwriting and of the music-paper he used in different periods of his life; but such help is not available in the case of his earlier organ music, because it survived only in later copies, and often only in copies made by other persons. Thus it is the works alone that pronounce their date. And on this subject they speak differently to different individuals. The student who has been able to learn the music of Bach's elder contemporaries receives one message, the student who has not had that advantage receives another. The latter tends to place many works forward into the Weimar period that began when Bach was twenty-three. The former tends to place them backward, not only into the Arnstadt period generally, but into the first two years of that period: that is, into the days before Sebastian's famous visit to Lübeck. He does this because twentieth-century editions of old German organ music have revealed to him the music young Bach knew, and because he knows of Bach's practice of working fully and exhaustively at particular models while they are immediately fresh for him. (It was not until 1927 that a complete knowledge of the works of Georg Böhm, for example, could be gained: in that year all his extant works were published by Breitkopf & Härtel; previously only four chorale arrangements and one clavier movement were available, and these only since 1904 and 1907.)

The cantata 'Gott ist mein König' is known to date from February 1708. The clavier capriccio, 'On the Departure of a Beloved Brother,' celebrates an event in the family the year of which was 1704. Thus we have a cantata that tells us of Bach's ability when he was nearly twenty-three, and a poetically connected series of clavier pieces that tells us something of the same when he was nineteen. If it is allowed that Bach was progressive in his development, it follows that things not so good as those were written before them.

The early organ music, however, is in a special category. It was produced during a period of almost exclusive application to the instrument, and in what was the composer's spring-time, when growth is most rapid and most forceful. Consequently he would write at nineteen a bigger and better fugue for the organ than the post-horn fugue for the clavier in the 'Departure' Capriccio. He would certainly not write one less good. It is possible, therefore, that he wrote before he was twenty such works as the Fugue in G major in 12–8 time (Breitkopf edition, No. 34) and the Prelude and Fugue in C major (No. 25). The gigue-rhythm of the G major piece was popular with the north German composers. The solo pedal subject of the C major Prelude is a copy of that in Böhm's Prelude and Fugue in C, and the fugue subject has lineaments that Böhm's subject has. The Prelude in G major (No. 29) resembles parts of the prelude of a Prelude and Fugue in G by Nikolaus Bruhns, a pupil of Buxtehude's (Peters edition, No. 4301): Bach could have written this before he was eighteen. The Fantasia and Fugue in A minor (No. 16) and the Prelude and Fugue in A minor (No. 24) he could have written when he was fifteen or sixteen, since in no place do they sound a note that is Bach's and they are technically just what a gifted and ambitious youth would produce from models lying before him. The Prelude and Fugue in C minor (No. 26) he could have written for his trial at Sangerhausen.

It is customary to say that Bach could not play (and therefore would not write) such works as these while he was but eighteen or nineteen, because his executive technique was insufficiently advanced. The works are not, however, harder to play than many written by north German composers. The pupils of those masters could play the works. Therefore Bach, the most gifted student of the time, could play them. And playing them, he would write them.

In chorale arrangements he was probably more advanced even than he was in preludes, fantasias and fugues on free themes. This kind of music has poetic subjects that inspire and direct the composer, as the poetry of a song does. The subject is a *locus adjumentorum*—an assisting topic, of which the substance is a defined and determined strain of feeling. The 'Departure' Capriccio, like the Kuhnau 'Bible Sonatas' which it imitates, is a series of such subjects, and it shows what Bach could do with them at nineteen. Therefore any chorale arrangement of Bach's in which there is no poetic emotion, but only a fine, simple *musical* feeling, could have been written during his first months at Arnstadt, but more likely before then. And chorale arrangements that do possess a poetic emotion, but are not obviously mature works of art, could have been written later, but before Bach was twenty. Examples of the former class are 'Der Tag, der ist so freudenreich' (No. 86), 'Gelobet seist du, Jesus Christ' (No. 94) and 'Gottes Sohn ist kommen' (No. 96). The first of these is, indeed, fixed as written when the composer was not more than eighteen, because it was copied into a manuscript book by Johann Christoph of Eisenach, and Johann Christoph died in the year Sebastian came to that age. Examples of the latter class are 'Erbarm dich mein, O Herre Gott' (No. 91), 'Ach Gott und Herr' (No. 63) and 'Das Jesulein soll doch mein Trost' (No. 85). The first of these is like the prayer in Kuhnau's Bible sonata *David and Goliath*, which is a setting of the chorale 'Aus tiefer Not schrei' ich zu dir.' The second, which is for manuals only, converts the chorale tune into a sensitive lyrical melody: another piece of the same type is a treatment of 'Wer nur den lieben Gott lässt walten' (No. 147), the original of which belongs to the Arnstadt period. The third contains in bars 13-16 a construction like that of the second number of the 'Departure' Capriccio, namely the exact repetition of a fugal passage a tone lower in the scale. Its contrapuntal style is advanced, though not more so than is that of the post-horn fugue in the Capriccio.

Whether or not Sebastian had reached the position outlined above, he had reached one where he needed fresh experience and the inspiration it always brought him. At fifteen he had exhausted the interest and the value that conditions at Ohrdruf had for him: he could write a work like the arrangement of 'Durch Adams Fall ist ganz verderbt' (No. 89), with its minim rhythm and its primitive, quasi-vocal style; he wanted to write a work like the partita on 'O Gott, du frommer Gott,' with its rhythms of quavers and semiquavers and instrumental figuration, and so he betook himself to Lüneburg. Now, at twenty, he had exhausted the virtue of what he had gathered at Lüneburg—or, at least, had exercised it as far as he wanted to. Again he must energize his mind anew, by direct personal contact with living things that had the power to affect him so. Therefore he went on this visit to Lübeck, which was the one place in Germany that contained what he needed; namely, the inspiration of a warm, romantic, glowing quality of art—the art that had developed during the years in the hands of such men as Franz Tunder, Daniel Erich, Johann Nikolaus Hanff, Matthias Weckmann, Nikolaus Bruhns and Dietrich Buxtehude. These men exercised that quality chiefly in their *Chorale Bearbeitung.* Led astray by Spitta, who inexplicably regarded the cool, unimaginative Pachelbel as the ideal composer of music on chorales (calling him, indeed, 'the virtual creator of the organ chorale'), writers on north German musicians uniformly refer to their chorale music as 'the weaker side' of their art. Their critical opinion was formed at a time when Bach's chorale music was little known and less understood. A different opinion may be formed when it is known thoroughly and the corresponding music of Bach's north German prede-cessors is regarded in the light of that knowledge. It is then realized that though the earlier men stand to Bach as Marlowe does to Shakespeare, they still possess, as Marlowe did, powers that make them great and satisfying in themselves. Young Bach certainly thought so. He received inspiration from them. Their forms and styles gave him instruction. Their feeling, both purely musical and poetic, directed him to the path that led him to his supreme achievement in the art of 'working up the chorale,' which is to express the sentiment of the hymn in the composed counterpoint accompanying the tune. For ten years at least, from the time he was twenty to the time he was thirty, not less than half his work as a composer for the organ was concerned with carrying to the heights of perfect achievement this kind of music. And at every point it can be seen that his achievement was the fulfilment of the ideas, ideals and efforts of the musicians of the Buxtehudean school. He was, indeed, the great son of that school, as he was the great son of the family of the Bachs. Those who created it bequeathed him a heritage; and when he went to Lübeck he entered into its possession.

It is said in the family records that Sebastian walked from

Arnstadt to Lübeck. The towns are 225 miles apart on the map. By road they are anything up to 300 apart. If the traveller averaged thirty miles a day, he would use up twenty days of his leave on the double journey. His leave being four weeks, this would leave him only eight or ten days to do what he wanted to do in the north.

IV

It is customary to say in books on Bach that 'he timed his departure from Arnstadt to permit of his hearing the famous *Abendmusiken* of Buxtehude. If he did, he acted dishonourably by his employers. For the *Abendmusik* started the third Sunday in November, and Sebastian was due back at Arnstadt by then. He left well before the middle of October. He did not return until shortly before the middle of February. He was away, not four weeks, but sixteen. And it seems, from what happened on his return, that he had no communication with his church during that long period. Of course, he had left a deputy there, who is assumed to be Johann Ernst Bach, the cousin who succeeded him at the New Church. On that point his conscience was clear. On any other point it did not trouble him, since the claim of his art was his sole moral guide.

The *Abendmusik* (evening music) was a sacred concert given in Buxtehude's church on the last two Sundays of November and the last three of December. It was an institution several genera-tions old. Under Buxtehude it had become famous throughout Germany. It consisted of cantatas and other concerted works with an orchestra sometimes of forty performers, of pieces of solo song with orchestral accompaniment, of psalms and chorales and of organ voluntaries by Buxtehude and, possibly, his advanced pupils. Admission was free. But expenses were met by con-tributions from the townsfolk, who were reminded tactfully of the opportunity to give to a good cause by the distribution at their houses of printed copies of the season's programmes. The concert lasted an hour.

On 2nd and 3rd December of this year there happened to be

two special performances in the church—one a memorial service to the Emperor Leopold I, who had died in the summer, the other a tribute to the new emperor. Sebastian was therefore exceptionally fortunate in the rich feast of music available for him: the five evening concerts, the high services on the Sundays and these two ceremonial functions. And there he was, at each and all, 'a curious boy, peering, absorbing, translating,' like that American boy generations later who listened to the feathered guests from Alabama and received from them impressions which, translated into thought, flowed forth in perfect and eternal art.

He was in the north some fourteen weeks. He could not sit about from service to service, waiting a week to hear the great man play. If Buxtehude grew interested in him and adopted him as a free pupil for a while, the spell of time is still much extended. And within a month he would get from the old man's art, even if heard only in the church services, all that it had for him except what was better gained from study of works in manuscript. Something additional must therefore have combined with his primary artistic need to go north, and kept him there. It was perhaps the idea, and the hope, that he might succeed Buxtehude.

Buxtehude was only sixty-six. But he was apparently an old man for his age. He certainly died at sixty-eight. But he did not want to die, nor yet to retire, until his successor was found and appointed, because he had a daughter who was unmarried and in her thirties. This is a matter that would not come into consideration in modern times. In Germany then it was crucial. If an organist's post was coming vacant, and if the organist, soon to be the late organist, had an unmarried daughter, it was a *sine qua non* that the new man must marry that daughter. Two years earlier Mattheson, aged twenty-two, and Handel, aged eighteen, had gone to Lübeck to look into things for themselves: Mattheson to take the post and the girl if he felt like it, Handel to think about it if his friend did not. Neither did. But the episode proves that the organist's post of St. Mary's, Lübeck, was in the market and waiting only for a suitable bidder. It was a famous position.

It carried a salary of £60 a year, with many exceptional advantages and perquisites. And the organ was a splendid instrument.

Sebastian Bach, aged twenty, can have been filled with one only ambition and one only determination: to master his art, to realize it to the full and to place himself where he could exercise it freely and completely. In the final issue he wore himself out at sixty-five. He taxed his eyes until they failed him. He always did, in the way of creation, more than he need have done. He always did better than was demanded. A great part of his work was voluntary and unprofitable, except that it was impelled by the power of his genius, which worked as the tides do, and except that it paid in the sense that it satisfied that genius. Only injustice, or what he considered injustice, deflected him a moment from his way. It is natural, then, to fancy that he contemplated offering himself as Buxtehude's successor, even at the cost of being his son-in-law. The marriage would be a marriage of convenience, a prostitution of a *man*. But it would not be the first. And it would be for a worthier cause than most.

If all this were so, his long stay is understandable. But he could not in the end suffer himself to fall as a man, even to rise swiftly as an artist. Perhaps he entered intimately into Buxtehude's family. Perhaps he discussed the situation with them earnestly and anxiously. If he did, Buxtehude would talk of his similar problem of thirty odd years ago, which was for him to take over Franz Tunder's daughter and be organist of St. Mary's, or refuse and miss the appointment. Whatever the worth of this fancy (and it is the sheerest fancy), Sebastian returned free to Arnstadt. Anna Margreta Buxtehude became a Frau Schiefferdecker (in English a Mrs. Slater), and Johann Christian Schiefferdecker became Buxtehude's successor at Lübeck. He was a man of about Sebastian's age, that is, twenty. He was already a widower. And he was to be a widower again in ten or twelve years. For Anna Margreta died then—one of passing millions, but abstracted from the mass and kept in knowledge by a solitary item in the early history of Johann Sebastian Bach.

V

It would be interesting to know how Sebastian financed his Lübeck expedition. Unless some well-to-do citizen gave him money for it, the means could come only of savings during the two years so far spent at Arnstadt. He was away four months. Each month away could cost little less than two months at home. Therefore he must have saved eight months' earnings out of the twenty-four. During the four months he earned nothing at Arnstadt, and there were no herring heads farced with silver ducats on this return journey. Consequently he must have started again with a low exchequer, if not an empty one. He did not resume work in the church until February was at least a week or ten days old. Yet at the end of the month his employers paid him a full month's salary. Their generous treatment of him, all along the line, is conspicuous: it suggests, indeed, that Sebastian had friends among them who were determined to give him every possible help.

On the 21st of the month Sebastian was summoned before the consistory (the clerical board) to say who gave him leave of absence and where he had been for so long a time. He replied that he had received permission from the superintendent (the head minister) and that he had been to Lübeck to study matters connected with his profession. The consistory then asked him to say why, having asked for and received permission to be away four weeks, he was away four months. To this he replied that he had taken it for granted his deputy would continue with the work, and that there could consequently be no complaints on this score. The terms of his answer show that Sebastian had no communication with Arnstadt during his absence. With it, however, the board let the matter drop. Again they were lenient with their young organist. Such leniency could not but weaken their authority. And it was probably that weakening which brought about such unruliness in the scholars and choristers.

At this meeting the vexed question of the training of the choir and the use of part-music in the service was raised again. Sebastian, as ever, merely said that there must be an official director of the choir if such music was to be sung. The board then spoke to him about the way he accompanied the chorales. They said that lately he had played in such a manner that he confused the congregation and put them off their singing, for he treated their melody of long, plain notes to variations and embellishments which in fact blotted it out. They then pronounced their order: 'If in future you want to introduce a *tonus peregrinus*, you must keep to it, and on no account fly off instantaneously into a *tonus contrarius.*' Bach, according to the minutes, made no comment whatever upon this complaint, and the consistory let the matter pass. The prefect of the choir then told the board that the organist used to prelude for too long a time before a chorale, and that when remonstrated with about this he had simply stopped preluding altogether. The board recorded the point in the minutes, but did not ask Bach to say anything about it. . . .

The prelude before the hymn was an important element of the service. It was, indeed, a vital one; and the ideal it served was such that a good deal of the rise and development of music in Germany during the seventeenth century is to be attributed to it. The prelude, or as it was frequently called, the preamble, was a piece of artistic music based on the melody of the hymn. In its best state it was charged with the spirit of the hymn, and was therefore expressive, poetic or characteristic. Thus it inspired the congregation. It lifted them up on wings of song. And when they began their long slow notes they sang with a particular spiritual fervour. Practical considerations made it necessary for the prelude to be kept reasonably short, except in the case of the chief seasonal hymn—the 'hymn of the day,' which was sung between the gospel and the epistle: the prelude for that hymn could be longer and more elaborate. Also the preludes to the hymns sung while the people were communicating could be lengthy when the number of communicants was large. Bach, transcendent artist, feeling and seeing much, having much to express, became absorbed and went on too long. He was then a nuisance. Requested not to exceed customary lengths, he flared with anger, sneered to himself 'Ah, pearls before swine!' and stopped preluding altogether. In this he was a nuisance again, selfish in another direction, and failing in his legal obligation to take a service in customary manner.

The accompaniment also was important, since it surrounded the congregational song with a kind of developed music. The people sang in unison, and when the choir did the same the organist could enrich the harmony. They sustained the last note of a line, and against it the organist played something in the way of an interlude. He was not bound to play the simple minims and semibreves of the tune, but could embellish them with runs and turns, so that the tune became a kind of lyric melody. At certain points in a verse the singing could be held up completely while the organist played a brief passage of composed music. Surviving among Bach's organ works are several accompaniments, of which the most elaborate and most mature is that to 'In dulci jubilo' (Breitkopf, No. 106). Another, less elaborate, but more formal, is to 'Wer nur den lieben Gott lässt walten' (Augener edition, No. 9980). This is assumed to belong to the Arnstadt period. It has a prelude, postlude and interludes, and it is a proper composition, the ninebar prelude being made use of in the interludes and postlude. The tune is decorated: Bach afterwards abstracted it in this condition and set it out as a little solo piece.

Now if this accompaniment is typical of what Sebastian did at Arnstadt, the consistory were justified in their complaint, because —as the terms of their complaint show—he did not keep to one and the same accompaniment throughout a hymn, but changed it at will, perhaps for every individual verse. (The expression *tonus peregrinus*—'strange, foreign, unrelated tone'—was the old name for the Aeolian mode, which was more modern then and thus foreign to the old church modes.)

Some of these perpetual troubles were discussed again at a board meeting on 11th November. Nothing was settled, and nothing came of the orders delivered to Sebastian. He had made up his mind a couple of years before that he would do nothing with a id for the choir. He had found that he could get out of a board meeting by saying he would write his answer within so many days. And he had found that if he did not so communicate with the board the matter was allowed to slide. But there was a fresh point to deal with on this particular occasion, which is recorded in the minutes as follows: 'To make protest on his having recently allowed the stranger maiden to show herself and to make music in the church.'

Sebastian replied that he had already spoken to the church minister about this matter. Now the minute is most tantalizingly worded. The expression 'die fremde Jungfer' signifies that the girl did not belong to the town, but was a visitor there. It is taken by writers on Bach that she was Maria Barbara Bach, the cousin Sebastian married. Her mother, originally a native of Arnstadt, had died two years before. She, made an orphan then, could well have come into Arnstadt to live with her mother's relatives. And she would remain literally not an Arnstadtian. The girl in question could not have been the other female cousin, Barbara Catherina Bach, because that Barbara was a lifelong resident in the town; but she could, of course, have been any unmarried girl on a visit there. Then the expression 'show herself' suggests that the maiden was in the church with Sebastian on public occasions: that is, at one or more services; not there with him privately, to hear his playing on the organ. The expression 'make music' means properly to perform on an instrument. If the young man and the girl were together privately, she might have been with him to play violin to his organ accompaniment. Here, however, it may mean to sing. Therefore if she 'showed herself' and sang, it would be in connection with a service. Yet women singers were not at this time allowed to sing in the choir of Lutheran churches. And with this the matter must rest, with the pleasant thought abiding that the incident was, after all, connected with Sebastian's courtship. One thing is certain: the consistory did not object to Sebastian and a girl making music in the church, whether publicly or privately, and they raised the point, not, as has been said, because 'of gossiping interest in his private relationships,' but as a matter of form—the position was unusual, and the consistory must have it on record as considered officially and passed.

At Easter the year following, Bach underwent his trial for the post of organist at the church of St. Blasius in Mühlhausen. He was accepted, and he was appointed to the post on 15th June. On 15th September his engagement began.

On 10th August, while he was still at Arnstadt awaiting the end of the official year (14th September), his maternal uncle Tobias Lämmerhirt died at Erfurt, leaving by will a legacy of 50 guilders (£4 11s.) to each of his dead sister's surviving children. The legacies were paid at once, and Sebastian had a sum of money in hand which he had not expected.

On 17th October he married Maria Barbara. The marriage took place at the village of Dornheim, a mile or so out of Arn-stadt: the pastor of Dornheim and Sebastian had been acquainted at Arnstadt, and the pastor and Maria Barbara's aunt were shortly to be married; hence there were lively personal reasons for the choice of minister to perform the ceremony. The marriage gave his late employers a final opportunity to demonstrate their kindli-ness, goodwill and generosity to the young man. By legal custom a marriage fee was due from him to the council, a party of the marriage belonging to the town. They remitted the fee.

CHAPTER VII

MÜHLHAUSEN (1707-8)

BACH, aged twenty-two, went into Mühlhausen with joy in his heart, full of high hopes and with the loftiest of lofty ambitions. Nine months later he petitioned for his dismissal and left the town with thankfulness.

His disappointment was due to a twofold cause. On the one hand Mühlhausen was a self-centred, self-satisfied place, and as such it was snobbish. On the other his pastor, Johann Adolph Frohne, was a pietist, and as a pietist he objected to and opposed music as an art in church. Thus Bach and his wife as social persons were made to feel uncomfortable by the generality of the townsfolk, and especially by the typical members of the congregation. And Bach in his capacity of organist and purveyor of music for the church was vexed by a religious atmosphere inimical to him. He was vexed also by the circumstance that the congregation was accustomed to, and wanted, a very different kind of music from that which he gave it.

Mühlhausen was a free imperial city. That is to say, it did not belong to any prince, duke or count, but managed its affairs by an elected council. (Church matters were controlled by a parochial *conventus* or assembly.) In times past Mühlhausen had been a thriving and important place. During the seventeenth century it had fallen from its high estate. Also, a hundred years before Bach it had owned an excellent musical reputation. That too it had lost during the previous generation or so. But the people kept their good opinion of themselves. Indeed, they increased it. With all the weakness of pride they believed that anything they did was better than anything any one else did, and that nothing any one else did was, or could be, of much account. Let one of their sons write a hymn tune, and a town chronicler

49

would record the fact years and years later; let a visiting musician do some fine work in the town, and that same chronicler would ignore it.[1] The inhabitants did not know the expression, of course, nor would they admit the fact, but they were afflicted with an inferiority complex; and this filled them with the mood and drove them to the position which one finds in families suffer, ing from the same defect. Sebastian and Maria Barbara were strangers. They had to endure the treatment such people mete out to strangers. This was particularly galling to a man of Bach's temperament. And before long he found it intolerable.

Description of the other matter that distressed him may be post, poned. His work at the church of St. Blasius was even easier as regards time than his work at Arnstadt, since he had no week, day duties. He took the one high service on Sunday and the special services on festivals and saints' days. His salary was what it had been at Arnstadt, with the addition of some corn, wood and fish. He was certainly given responsibilities that were usually undertaken by a cantor. That is, he had to select the music used in the services and, as it would seem, to train the choir. But this was exactly what he wanted. It was his supreme desire to lift the music of the church to the highest possible level. It was also the desire of the parochial assembly that he should so elevate it; for the members of the assembly were men of a more reasonable and broad, minded kind than the bulk of their fellow townsfolk. Bach, indeed, would almost have sacrificed a part of his salary to be thus privileged. In fact, he did sacrifice some of it, and in addition a large part of his time, in his labours to create fine music in St. Blasius's; for 'regardless of expense' (as he says in his petition for dismissal) he made a collection of compositions 'from near and far,' and copied them for practical use.

During the preceding two generations it had come about that the organist of St. Blasius was regarded as the chief musician of the town, though the church of St. Mary was the principal church, its pastor being archdeacon of the town. But this was chiefly because the two organists before Bach had been natives of Mühl,

[1] See Spitta, Book iii, Chapter I.

hausen: a circumstance that, of course, made them *ipso facto* superior to all others there who happened not to be natives. The parish, and with the parish the town, did not care to extend this recognition of pre-eminence to this young newcomer. They also disliked his newfangled notions. The two preceding organists —father and son, by name Ahle—had been good musicians of the old order. They had written pieces for performance in the service that were short, simple and mellifluous. Such pieces were called arias, and in their most advanced condition they were no more than elementary partsongs with instrumental prelude, postlude and interlude. In text they were like hymns. The congregation was startled and annoyed by the kind of music Bach produced: it was as if a congregation accustomed to Stainer's *Crucifixion* had imposed on them the Brahms *Requiem*. In his petition for dismissal Bach said that he thought 'the people might in time have come to approve.' But he said this after the event. And it is unlikely that he truly thought they would ever come round to his way of thinking and acting.

His pastor was a Christian of the saintly and living type. For him religion was a personal matter, a thing between the man and his God, inwardly experienced first, then outwardly manifested. Formulated creeds, even the Bible itself, the Word of God, were dead matter when not read and maintained with eye and mind spiritually enlightened: man must pray for that enlightenment, and he must know by subjective conviction (in other words, by *conversion*) that his prayer was answered. The pastor was thus of the religious persuasion to which belonged many English puritans and men like John Bunyan and John Wesley. Like them he was opposed to the established 'orthodox' church in so far as that church was a matter of forms, ceremonies and creeds rigidly subscribed to and carried on lifelessly. And like them he was attacked and persecuted by the orthodox: what he taught and preached was a reproach to the orthodox; it disturbed them, and if they were professionals in religion it weakened their official authority.

All this concerning the pietist is to the good. And if it is translated into terms of the artistic it becomes a description of Bach's attitude towards art—especially of his attitude towards art used for sacred purposes. It may be imagined therefore that Bach sympathized with Pastor Frohne. Actually, however, he was in the ranks of his opponents. He was there for two reasons. First, he was born and bred in orthodoxy, and he was satisfied with it, because it had never entered his head to question it, and because he himself lived so intense and complete an inner life as an artist, and strove so patiently, earnestly and faithfully for spiritual reality in his art, that he had simply never discovered what a dead thing his religion was among other people. Secondly, the pietist, like the average puritan and men like John Wesley, regarded art as a worldly thing—a thing attractive in itself and therefore bound to draw men from what must be their only concern, namely the purity and safety of their souls, which can be attended to only by constant and exclusive concentration upon the task of establishing direct communion with God. Wesley, for example, would have no contrapuntal music in the church, because in such music different words are uttered at one and the same time. 'And what,' he says, 'could be more shocking than that?' Thus where pietism was, music was not. And where music was not, Bach could not be. In his petition for dismissal he puts the matter in this way: 'My work has been done not without difficulty and opposition, and there is no apparent likelihood that things will be altered.' It followed, therefore, that he must go. The musician who in his art was essentially a pietist could not have a place where pietism prevailed practically in religious doctrine and procedure.

On 4th February 1708 came the one great opportunity of Bach's stay at Mühlhausen to reveal himself as a composer. The occasion was an annual festival service connected with the municipal council. The church in which it was held was St. Mary's, but custom from the time of the Ahle father and son had fixed it that the chief work at the festival should be one specially composed for the year by the organist of St. Blasius. A full orchestra was provided, complete with trumpet and drums. The choir was undoubtedly enlarged. The soloists would be the finest available. For these forces Bach wrote a cantata. It can be imagined with what eagerness he bent himself to the task. For the first time in his life he had an absolutely complete instrumental and vocal combination at command and a free hand in his choice of subject and in his treatment of it.

Moreover, it survives in a printed edition of the parts that the parochial or municipal authorities caused to be made soon after the festival. This distinction was apparently accorded now for the first and last time to an 'Inauguration of the Council' work. It shows that the authorities thought highly in the extreme of Bach's composition and were pleased and proud to have it. There is no evidence of what the general congregation at the festival thought of it, nor of what the other congregation of St. Blasius thought when it was performed again a few days later in Bach's own church. But it was probably the first time that a cantata in the new style had been heard in the town, and it is more than likely that they did not care for any portion of it—except perhaps the movement in which the ruling monarch is prayed for; and this they would approve of for extra-musical reasons.

A non-fugal chorus in 'Gott ist mein König' shows the capacity he had at this time to write expressive harmony for voices:

'Gott ist mein König' makes manifest Bach's swift development as a composer in the four years separating it from his Arnstadt Easter cantata 'Denn du wirst meine Seele nicht in der Hölle lassen.' It is critically assumed that his wedding cantata 'Der Herr denket an uns' ('The Lord hath been mindful of us') was written while he was at Mühlhausen. The occasion is taken to be the marriage of Pastor Stauber of Dornheim to Maria Barbara's aunt, which took place on 5th June. If the critical calculation is correct the composer and his wife would be back for a little while in the church where they themselves had been married. There, in a village named Langula, which is just outside Mühlhausen, Spitta discovered a fragmentary cantata of Bach's composition that must have been written during this year: it has never been published. While at St. Blasius's he drew up a plan for the reconstruction of the organ: the work was completed a couple of years later, and Bach was engaged to examine it and to give the customary opening recital; and critical calculation has decided that his chorale fantasia on 'Ein' feste Burg is unser Gott' ('A stronghold sure our God is He') was written for this occasion. Nothing else in the way of composition is directly attributable to the year.

At Mühlhausen Bach had a house of his own for the first time. He could therefore take in a resident pupil in the manner of the times. This he did, his pupil being one who was to stay with him for ten years, first as an organ student, then as assistant and copyist. The youth who has this distinction was named Johann Martin Schubart. He was five years younger than his master. When Bach left his next post Schubart succeeded him in this. But he died within four years, thirty-one years old.

It is interesting to note that the choir prefect of St. Blasius in 1708 was named Johann Sebastian Koch.

At Arnstadt Bach was succeeded by a cousin, Johann Ernst. Here at Mühlhausen he was succeeded by another cousin, though one in the relationship of twice removed: he was a son of Johann Christoph of Eisenach, and so a grandson of Heinrich of Arn-stadt; and his name was Johann Friedrich.

Leaving Mühlhausen

When Sebastian and Maria Barbara went from Arnstadt to Mühlhausen, the parochial *conventus* provided them with a wagon for the transport of their goods over the forty miles between the two towns. The journey now of about the same distance from Mühlhausen to Weimar does not seem to have been helped in any similar way.

CHAPTER VIII

WEIMAR (1708–17)

I

IN the genealogy that he wrote about 1735 Bach says that he went to Weimar in 1707 to serve the grand duke in two capacities—as organist and as chamber musician. In his request for dismissal from Mühlhausen he says something different, which is that the appointment offered him is that of chamber musician and member of the court band. He says nothing about going there as organist.

There is no doubt that he did go as organist. Why, then, did he not say so to the Mühlhausen council? The reason that suggests itself has an informative human quality that makes it worth while to outline it. The duke's organist for many years was the Johann Effler mentioned above as successor a generation earlier to Johannes Bach at Erfurt and predecessor of Johann Michael Bach at Gehren. He was now an old man, and ill, indeed dying, his death taking place this year. It is not known at what time in the year he died. But it seems that he was still alive while negotiations were in hand between Sebastian and the duke. As will be shown in a moment, the duke was a hard and masterful man in some respects, but he had this rare quality of excellence—he never dismissed a servant for age or infirmity. Therefore it would be against his nature to stamp finality upon Effler while Effler yet breathed, which would have been done by the announcement that his successor was already appointed. The duke needed to have the successor ready. Therefore he engaged Bach. But he brought him into his court in a kind of disguise, as violinist in his bands. Thus practical considerations were served, and an old and faithful servant was not pained.

The duke was a religious man, who made his devotions daily. He started being religious at as early an age as John Stuart Mill started to learn the classical languages, which was three; and he

prepared and preached a sermon at seven.   He was a book-lover
and a numismatist.   He liked to have church ministers about him
in their professional garb, and he seems to have known personally
each of the hundred or so there were in his dukedom.   He kept
track of everything that went on in Saxe-Weimar, controlled and
advised on everything and was a true philanthropist.   He made
it possible for every child to have a good education (as education
was understood in those days).   He went to bed at nine o'clock
in the summer and eight o'clock in the winter, and so did, by
order, every member of his household: only a mouse dared be
about in any of the two hundred odd rooms of his palace after
those hours.   He hated change.   He was married, but his wife
had left him after a year or two.   He was childless, with heirs
apparent and presumptive whom he hated.

The heirs were, first, his brother, Duke Johann Ernst, in whose
band Sebastian Bach had worked those few months in 1703, and
then his nephew, Johann Ernst's eldest son.   There were conditions in the control of the duchy that made relations between
any reigning duke and a next brother inevitably bad; but there
must have been a special animosity between the brothers of this
generation, since when the younger, Johann Ernst, was dying in
1707, the elder, Wilhelm Ernst, would not visit him.

The duke extended his hatred in a most lively manner to his
dead brother's successor, the eldest son, Ernst August.   During
the last years of Bach's employment in his court the quarrel became
so very bitter that he ordered his staff to have no intercourse whatever with the other family.   Bach apparently could not submit to
such an order.   From the time he went to Weimar in 1708 he had
taught Prince Johann Ernst, the younger son of Duke Johann
Ernst.   He had helped him with his composition and transposed
for clavier and organ a considerable number of the violin concertos the youth wrote.   And when the prince died, aged nineteen, in 1715, the friendly feeling his widowed mother and his
brother had for Bach persisted.   It was altogether against Bach's
nature to break such a connection in obedience to an arbitrary
command.   His employer therefore was vexed with him.   He

displayed his vexation in ways that need not be described yet. But it was largely because of this development of unpleasant conditions that Bach left Weimar—left, that is, after the duke had found that not even imprisonment could force the stubborn musician to give way.

The duke reigned from 1683 to 1728, when he died at the age of sixty-five. He left his little territory a model of what such minor sovereignties could be in the way of comfort, contentment and well-being. But it is impossible to believe he died a happy man, or that he had lived one.

II

There was, of course, no intimacy between Duke Wilhelm Ernst and his organist. But the two were in harmony. Each was an orthodox Lutheran, yet neither was rigidly so. Each thought that everything in the world was good if, treated faith-fully and earnestly, it could be accounted to the glory of God and manifested a gracious gift from Him. Nobleman and musician therefore worked together to elevate the music of the private chapel, the one commanding, the other obeying. This was good for Bach, since it was his expressed desire in this period of his life to improve, purify and extend church music. Until external affairs intervened, he must have been very content with life and work at Weimar.

He started with an annual salary of £14 12s. 6d. This stood for three years. Then began a remarkable series of increases, and all in successive years: to £19 14s. in 1712, to £20 in 1713, to £21 15s. in 1714 and to £24 11s. 6d. in 1715. There was no advance in 1716 or 1717. When Bach went to Cöthen it was to a salary of £43 12s. 6d.

The court had two bands. The larger contained sixteen or more members, the smaller four. The large band played in the church, accompanying cantatas, and on ceremonial occasions. When a state function was toward, the men were dressed as hey-ducks: 'heyduck' was the name originally of the Hungarian foot-soldier, then of Polish liveried servants and finally of the servants who were similarly garbed in German courts. Carlyle, writing of the court of Frederick the Great, speaks of 'shining particoloured creatures, heyducks so called'; and since Bach often played with this band he must have suffered temporary change into a shining particoloured creature.

The small band consisted of string players who performed privately to the duke. It was his *Kammermusik* (chamber music). A member of it was a *Hofmusikus* (court musician), but in this connection he was also a *Kammermusikus* (chamber musician). He was not always, however, exclusively a member of the establishment. Indeed, in the case of Duke Wilhelm Ernst's private band one of the performers lived at Jena and came to Weimar when he was wanted.

The band proper was the court *Capelle*: in English 'chapel.' The term was applied originally to the chapel choir, which was called the chapel. The new kind of church music that arose in the seventeenth century (of which mention is made above in connection with Bach's life at Lüneburg) was for instruments as well as voices, and *Capelle* became the name of the full combination of forces. In time the instruments became an independent organization, and the name remained with them, even though the employment of the band was secular within the court.

The *Capellmeister* ('master, or director, of the band') was the chief musician of a nobleman's establishment—or of a theatre where opera was performed. This official at Weimar was Johann Samuel Drese, who had held the post since 1683, the year when his master succeeded to the dukedom. Drese was getting on in years when Bach went to Weimar, having been born in 1644. He had been ill, however, since 1688, when he was only forty-four. The duke, true to his nature, did not dismiss him. Instead, he appointed an assistant *Capellmeister*, at a salary of £18 15s. The assistant from 1705 was a son of Drese's. He was a musician of very low ability indeed. One of the duties of his office was the composition and performance of cantatas. He managed by one means or another to fulfil this responsibility until about 1714. And then the task was transferred to Bach.

The result was some of the loveliest, most moving and most immediately attractive of Bach's many cantatas. The text for them was provided mostly by Salomo Franck, the castle librarian, a man of true poetic gifts and the second master of the new cantata form (the first being the clergyman-poet who established it, Erdmann Neumeister, of Hamburg).

In 1715 Bach's official status in connection with the small private band was dignified by the title of *Concertmeister* ('concert-master'). This does not mean that he was given the task of arranging 'concerts' for the duke. In those days a *concert* was a band of performers, whether vocal or instrumental. (In England the word was 'consort,' as in the term 'a consort of viols.') Bach had from the start played violin or viola in this little band, and now he was made its master or director. He still had to play, but was distinguished henceforth as the chief member of the quartet. The title had no real significance. It coincided with his new additional duty now to produce a cantata a month for the chapel and with the final increase in his salary; and it was perhaps given him to elevate him in rank in the musical establishment, and so to justify his position as its church composer.

III

As organist he did not have to write organ pieces for the service. In addition to accompanying all the vocal music, he had to play voluntaries, interludes and preludes to the hymns. His solo items in all numbered about six in a service. All this work he could do by improvisation. But it was at Weimar that he wrote the greater part of his organ music. He was a master of the instrument when he went there at the age of twenty-three. There was no finer performer in Germany, and so none in the world. There was, indeed, no finer performer in all the generations before him. Now he was to make himself the finest composer of organ music the world was to know. Already, in pieces written at Arnstadt and Mühlhausen, he had imposed his will on this most intractable and self-assertive of instruments. He had made it express what he wanted to express. At his command it received and rendered back a kind of music that in the hearing makes the listener forget the instrument that is sounding and makes him conscious only of the art which the performer is re-creating: that is, when the performer plays the music properly. Now, between twenty-three and thirty-two, Bach was to fulfil his destiny in this respect. He was to bring to ultimate flower and fruit all that had been implanted in him during earlier years, and in the years of his ancestry. He was to make a garden of poetic music with his chorale arrangements, of which about a hundred survive from this period. With his other works, those on free and independent subjects, he was to make a forest and a vast spreading landscape of pure music. On the one hand he was to write pieces like the three arrangements of the Advent hymn, 'Nun komm, der Heiden Heiland,' the arrangement of 'An Wasserflüssen Babylon' and that of 'Schmücke dich, o liebe Seele.' On the other hand he was to write preludes, fugues, toccatas and fantasias like the famous works in D minor, D major, C major, E minor, A minor, A major and G major. For twenty years after leaving Weimar he wrote little music for the organ. Among what he did write in these years the G minor Fantasia and Fugue stands prominent, as the rock of Gibraltar does at the approach to the Mediterranean. In his later years he returned to his first love. Then he wrote great things on chorales, and things almost greater on free themes: for example, the transcendent, almost unattainable, arrangement of 'Vater unser' and the Prelude and Fugue in B minor. These are loftier works in some respects than those produced at Weimar, because they are the creation of a mind that expanded and grew to the last. But they do not advance the art of organ performance. Nor do they carry farther the kind of music that results from thinking in *terms* of the organ. All that—the art of performance and the art of right and exclusive composition—was done in these nine years at Weimar. And Bach did it, not as an official in the employment of a duke, but as an artist whose duty to God and man it was to act so.

His organ at Weimar was a typical one, of two manuals and

pedals. That is, it had two lines or masses of manual tone that were well balanced and well contrasted, and one of pedal tone that was equally full and individual. The three elements of the instrument were of the proper proportionate size: nine stops on the one manual, eight on the other and seven on the pedals. Pedals were not known in England in Bach's time, nor for a hundred years after. When they were introduced, it was thought sufficient to supply one pedal stop to manuals totalling from twenty to forty stops. Not until the twentieth century was it realized that the pedals are in themselves an organ, as a manual is, and must be equally complete. And not even then was it realized in England that the art of the organ in Germany, in the seventeenth and eighteenth centuries, was based on the practice of using the pedals as a solo instrument, on which the organist played a bass melody, a tenor or a high treble, the while the hands were engaged with the rest of the music. The bad effect of Bach's music as performed in modern times is due largely to this circumstance. Even when a work is written on manual staves only, it is often intended that certain inner parts shall be taken by the feet.[1]

IV

An organist and composer of great contemporary fame lived at Weimar. He was employed at the parish church, and his name was Johann Gottfried Walther (1684–1748). The two men were some kind of cousins, because their mothers were members of the same Lämmerhirt family of Erfurt. Walther was an admirable composer. His music is clear, cool and altogether natural. It is also fascinatingly ingenious, though the ingenuity is something that delights the performer, who can see it written,

---

[1] Georg Böhm had at Lüneburg a three-manual organ with the following stops: (1) twelve, (2) ten, (3) eleven (one of these a vox humana) and (4, the pedals) fourteen. The pedal organ contained two mixtures, three four-foot stops and two two-foot.

What would Milton not have said about the organ (in *Paradise Lost*) if he could have known one with such a pedal!

more than the listener, who can only hear the sounds. Critics of the time set him above Bach as a composer, as they did dozens of others. Bach, after his genial habit, himself thought a good deal of him. Walther thought less of Bach, if the evidence of his manuscript volumes of music is significant, for in these volumes (and he was an enthusiastic and systematic collector) there is little of his cousin's music.

Also at Weimar were two educationists who entered into Bach's life to his pleasure and profit. One, the rector or warden of the local gymnasium, was the Johann Christoph Kiesewetter who had been in office at Ohrdruf when Sebastian lived there with his brother. The other, corrector or sub-warden, was later rector of the school at Leipzig. He was one of the leading scholars of his age, and in one of his translations from ancient authors he incorporates a eulogy of Bach that is like a beam of light across the generations.

At some time during his last year or two at Weimar, Bach had with him Georg Erdmann. This friend and companion of the Lüneburg years had not followed the musical profession. He had studied law, gone to Russia and become the legal representative of a military establishment. Now he was back in Germany, settled in Danzig as agent of the Russian government. Bach and he corresponded in later years. In 1730, when in distress about his life and work at Leipzig, Bach wrote to Erdmann to ask him if he knew of any post he could recommend him to try for: the letter is one of the few intimate things connected with him that have survived.

Another connection with the past was effected in 1717, when one of his Ohrdruf nephews entered his house as a pupil. This son of his elder brother was named Bernhard. He is remembered in the story of Sebastian Bach for his assumed share in the writing of a large volume of musical compositions. The volume survives from the library of a younger brother of his. But it is held that he began it, and filled many of its pages, when he was at Weimar. (All Bach's pupils had to make such manuscript copies of works they were to study and to use in later life.) This particular volume contains a good many of Bach's compositions, and so it fixes the latest dates for their creation.

V

Of some importance to Bach as a continually advancing student was the work he did with young Prince Johann Ernst from the time he went to Weimar until the youth's death in 1715. Walther taught Johann Ernst clavier playing and composition. Bach gave him some help with his violin playing. As a composer the prince adopted the Italian style, as did so many musicians of the time. He wrote in all about twenty instrumental works, of which Telemann published six violin concertos some three years after his death. Bach entertained and instructed himself during these Weimar years by adapting for clavier or organ a number of instrumental works by Italian composers, or by German composers who followed the Italian manner. His treatment of the works is not simply that of transcription. Nor is it that of simply fitting violin music to the keyboard. It is actually that of thinking along the lines of the music in hand by his own processes of musical thought. He adds and subtracts, enlarges and condenses, all as seems to him advisable to the end of producing satisfactory music.

His work in this direction survives in sixteen clavier concertos, a Concerto for four claviers, and four organ concertos. The Italian composer chiefly represented is his contemporary Vivaldi. Two of the clavier concertos are by Johann Ernst. Another is believed to be by him, and Bach so liked this one that he adapted it also for the organ. The organ arrangement is the first of the four concertos as published. Playing it to-day, we observe what this young nobleman did more than two centuries ago, and what pleased Bach particularly among his productions: since if this concerto is not actually by Johann Ernst, it is still from the mill in which he laboured.

Bach was drawn to this task of adaptation by the element of pure *form* that obtains in the music. His studies hitherto, and his chief concern as a creator, had been with music rather of *ideas*.

Something to say, and the saying of it, had mostly occupied him; as it had previously occupied the masters of north Germany. Now he observed architecture in music, not poetry. He wanted a quality of creative technique that should clarify and purify the expression of his ideas. He found that quality in this so often insignificant music of the Italians. And his ultimate fusion of the two is apparent in many of his subsequent compositions: above all in the Prelude of the B minor Prelude and Fugue for organ that he wrote at Leipzig.

VI

His powers of extemporization and sight-reading are frequently spoken of in eighteenth-century writings. Extemporization was then largely practised by organists, both for convenience in the church service and for purely artistic purposes: in a recital the performer was expected to incorporate at least one example of music spontaneously conceived and performed. Since Bach was known among his contemporaries as supreme in this direction, his powers must indeed have been marvellous. It is said that he could, and often did, continue working on a musical subject for two hours. After a preliminary flourish of the toccata type he played a prelude and fugue: this was probably of a light and fanciful kind. Then he played a free piece in the lyrical vein: this employed the pleasant solo stops; and if the tremulant of the instrument 'worked smoothly' (as he required that it should) he would no doubt make use of that generally discredited, yet actually most precious mechanical device for discovering the soul of such music. He proceeded next to a chorale arrangement: to the tune of a hymn that was familiar to the audience and to himself he added a contrapuntal accompaniment of which the main subject was the theme upon which he was working; and since the *Bearbeitung* (working-up) of a chorale offered almost illimitable scope for the exercise of the imagination, this portion of Bach's extemporizing would run to half an hour—which was the space of time the north German composers liked to fill with a 'grand' chorale fantasia. Finally he played a grand and solid fugue of the *pro organo pleno* order—such a thing, perhaps, as that triptych in E flat major which is known in England as the 'St. Anne Fugue.' Thus in a two hours' extemporization he displayed many aspects of the art of music, and all on one theme (as in *The Art of Fugue* he wrote at the end of his life, and in *The Musical Offering* he wrote in the same period on the theme given him by Frederick the Great). And he displayed also every virtue of the instrument on which he was performing.

As a sight-reader he liked to play from the separate parts of a piece of concerted music. This is indeed a wonderful thing. On the desk above the keyboard of the clavier stand the two, three or four sheets of paper, each with its single lines of notes. The performer cannot see them all at once. He must glance serially from one to the other. He must remember what the glance gives him of each, and assemble the parts into unity. Especially must he remember where he is in each sheet; and that is not the same place in each, for when he is at line 3, bar 5 of one, he may be at line 6, bar 3 of another, and so on throughout the set. His fingers have to execute what eye and mind have taken in at the running glance. And while they are doing this, eye and mind must be engaged in taking in what comes next in the music. The performer in these conditions does not, of course, proceed beat by beat or bar by bar. He proceeds by phrases. The phrase may be four bars in length, of eight or of sixteen; and all that the phrase contains must be seen in one sweeping glance, memorized and played in its last moments while fresh material is being assimilated. Bach's powers in this direction were akin to those of the chess player who can carry on a host of games simultaneously, to the powers of the mathematical genius who can solve a problem almost before its terms have been fully outlined to him, or to those of strange memory who can repeat a poem or a chapter of a book after it has been read to them once.

Bach liked also to combine his powers of extemporization and sight-reading. He would set the parts of a string trio on the desk, read the music, and add to it as he read a rich and full clavier accompaniment in which was nothing of what was written on the pages.

There is a story, beyond question authentic, of a failure on his part to play some music on sight. He was trapped into the failure, certainly; but he did fail. The incident occurred at Weimar. If the trap was set by a local musician, that musician could only have been Walther. The story is as follows—it being accepted for convenience that the other individual concerned actually was the clever organist of the town church. Bach had often said that he could now never find music which he could not play right away. Walther determined to show him that, on the contrary, it *was* possible to have music that beat him in this direction. He therefore wrote such a piece. Then he invited Bach to breakfast one day. He put the manuscript on his clavier, and when his guest arrived went into the kitchen to get breakfast ready. The guest went to the clavier, saw the piece of new music and began to play it. All went swimmingly for a while. Then came first a faltering, then a halt. The performer retraced his steps, began again and again broke down. He heard his host laughing in the kitchen, got up from the clavier and said: 'I see it is, after all, possible to have music that can't be played at first sight.'

Now speculation is baffled as to what Walther could possibly have written, since it was something Bach could not get through even at the second attempt. This could not be a matter of harmony, of key or of modulation. It could not be a flood of chromatic chords. It could not be such a technical matter as an assembly of wide skips in a number of contrapuntal parts, because such a ganglion of activity is in any case impossible of execution on an organ, clavier or piano: if it had been that, Bach would simply have said 'This isn't clavier music.' All that remains for speculation to ponder on is a maze of semiquaver figuration. North German composers of the seventeenth century, and all German composers of the eighteenth, liked to have passages where several parts move polyphonically in semiquavers. These are readily playable when each part pursues the direction it starts with. They are exceedingly troublesome when even one of the parts suddenly doubles like a hare and goes off in a new direction. Elementary examples of this lively, brilliant style of writing are in Bach's early organ Fugue in C minor and his 1708 piece on 'Ein' feste Burg.' There is a very slight touch of it in the last bars of one of Böhm's arrangements of 'Christe, der du bist Tag und Licht.' Quite elaborate examples are at the end of Tunder's work on 'Komm, heiliger Geist' and in the *primus versus* of Buxtehude's long organ work on the Te Deum. Bach could sail serenely through all such passages as these. If he encountered something equivalent to bars 75–7 of his own great organ Fugue in G minor, he would have to do nothing more than yield it a little time (in the *tempo rubato* of his day, which provided for a slight slackening of pace when writing became exceptionally full and intricate). Walther could conceivably have written such a passage as this last in music of four or five parts. He could have blended it with some curious and involved harmonies. He could have extended the passage until performance became something of a strain. Then, at the point when the strain threatened to become too much, he could have introduced (without actually leaving proper clavier idiom) a perfectly outrageous flight of fiery and independent particles that arrested mind and fingers and compelled a stop. Bach would not mind his breakdown. He would admire Walther's cleverness. He would enjoy the joke. And he would tell people about it, since he had no false pride.

VII

When the duke visited other courts he took some of his household, including his musicians, with him. One such occasion was a journey to Saxe-Weissenfels, in February 1716. The meeting between the two noblemen was marked by a hunting festival, and after one of the evening banquets a secular cantata of Bach's, written at the duke's command, was performed. It was his first secular cantata, and its opening words are 'Was mir behagt ist nur die muntre Jagd' ('What pleases me is this—the merry chase').[1]

In addition to such ceremonial excursions as these were journeys Bach himself made as a musician. He used to have leave of absence in the late autumn, and he went away to give organ recitals, to hear the music performed by other people in other places and to make the acquaintance of notable artists. He was at Cassel in the autumn of 1714—a town about eighty miles from Weimar. There he played to Prince Friedrich in his royal chapel; and his performance so pleased the prince that, in the manner of such personages at all times and in all places, he drew a ring from his finger and presented it to him.

In the September of 1717 he was in Dresden, which is more than a hundred miles from Weimar. Visiting the court there at that time was Louis Marchand, the most famous of living French players of organ and clavier. Two opposed camps arose in the place, one favouring Marchand, one Bach. It was arranged that there should be a contest between the two great men, so that a jury of capable musicians and music-lovers might determine which was the better. It is not clear what was the form of the contest—whether it was to be extemporization, sight-reading, organ playing, clavier playing or any or all of those activities. In any event, Bach went to the contest, but Marchand did not. He had heard Bach at work after the meeting had been arranged. What he heard broke his pluck; and on the chosen day he slipped secretly out of the town at dawn.

This victory for German music was blazed throughout the land. As a result Bach's fame was extended to every quarter. But it was as performer, not as composer. He never was to be recognized in his lifetime as a master creator, but only as a performer and, in the writing of music, as a skilled contrapuntist. His spirit, and his views of the essential nature and purpose of art, were alien to those of his contemporaries.

In 1713 Bach was at Halle, a journey of some sixty miles from

---

[1] It is this work which contains the lovely and justly popular aria 'Schafe können sicher weiden' ('Sheep may safely graze' or 'Sheep in pastures safe abiding'), for soprano with two flutes *obbligato*.

Weimar. The post of organist to the chief church was vacant:
it had been held previously by Friedrich Wilhelm Zachau, known
in history chiefly as Handel's early instructor in music. It
seemed to Bach to be a good post. Moreover, a new organ was
about to be built, at the cost of £590—an instrument that in
modern times would cost several thousand pounds. He offered
himself for the post. His offer was accepted, and he was asked
to submit to his 'trial' at once, so that the matter could be settled.
A trial included the composition and production of a cantata.
Bach wrote a cantata there and then at Halle, produced it at the
church, and returned to Weimar after a stay in the town of from
fourteen to twenty-one days. The church people considered the
matter as settled and in December sent Bach their 'vocation' or
call to the church, in which they specified his duties and how he
was to carry them out. Bach was not pleased with the terms and
the conditions. He had to play on Sundays and at the vespers
service on Saturdays, on all festivals and at the evening service on
the day before a festival, also at all weddings performed publicly
in the church. He also had to be at the organ when sermons on
the catechism were given in connection with candidates for con-
firmation. He had to write a cantata once a month for the ordinary
services, another for each festival and shorter works for the two
days following a festival. He must accompany the chorales in a
particular way: namely, on the diapason with two or three other
stops of soft quality, changing the stops for each verse, but never
using the reeds or mixtures. (This to Bach!) The great organ,
the small organ and all other instruments in the church were to be
used exclusively for church services: if a secular concert was given
in the building the performers must not on any account use them.
The organist must consider himself strictly bound to the church,
and do no teaching and accept no outside engagements if these
interfered with the fulfilment of his church duties. He must look
after all the church instruments, and he would be held responsible
for any damage that might befall them. His salary was 164
thalers (£17 17s. 6d.), with an additional thaler for each public
wedding and another for each cantata.

Bach wrote back to say he would have to consider the matter afresh. He and the council must discuss some of the terms and conditions, which he found unsatisfactory. Especially must the salary be discussed. If agreement on these points could be arrived at, and if he could get his dismissal from the duke, he would confirm his application for the post and accept the appointment.

Agreement was not reached. Bach thereupon withdrew. The church then charged him with having put in for the appointment solely to the end that he might use it as a lever to get an increase of salary from his present employer. Bach replied that this was not so. He pointed out that he was already in receipt of a larger salary than that offered by Halle (£20 against £17 17s. 6d.), and this for fewer duties. He said that there was no need for him to descend to underhand means to persuade his duke to increase his salary, since the duke was generous and made increases whenever they were justified. He said he had offered himself as a candidate so that he would be justified in inquiring closely into the revenue the appointment might afford. The inquiry had made him see that work at Halle was not likely to bring him in enough for his needs. No one could be expected, he said, to give up a salary for a smaller one, or even for one of equal proportions. And that was why, with profound respect and appreciation of the honour shown him in offering him the post, he had to decline it.

The hard feelings engendered by this business did not last. Three years later, in April 1716, Bach was one of the three experts engaged to approve of the new organ, which was just then completed. His fee for the examination and the report was 6 thalers (13s.), the Halle church recognition, by the way, of the worth of six cantatas. The business took six days. On the last day a banquet was provided to honour the occasion, at which Bach and the others ate stewed beef, spiced and larded; fish with sauce; roast veal and roast mutton; smoked ham; peas and potatoes and other vegetables; fried cakes; a salad of lettuce, radishes and asparagus; and candied peel and preserved cherries. Perhaps Zachau's ghost hovered about the gathering, wondering why he had been removed from such delightful things before he was fifty.

VII

The next year Bach left Weimar. He was probably getting restless again, in the way of his genius. His vast work with the art of the organ was finished. Once more had he exhausted the particular inspirations that descended upon him. He needed now different contacts and associations, so that his nature might extend itself further. And, as ever, the opportunity came exactly when it was essential for his artistic well-being that it should come.

It came because of his intercourse with the family of the dead younger brother of the duke. That family had consisted, since 1715, when the gifted Prince Johann Ernst had died at the age of nineteen, of the widowed mother and her elder son, Ernst August. In January 1716 Ernst August married a sister of Prince Leopold of Anhalt-Cöthen. This brought Prince Leopold to Weimar, where he discovered Bach. Discovering him, he coveted him; for he was a music-lover who was himself greatly attached to the violin: it is said that he used to start practising and playing as soon as he was up in the morning and before he dressed for the day. The next year he offered Bach a post in his musical establishment, and Bach accepted the offer in August.

He had a pointed reason for being dissatisfied with Weimar this year. Drese, the old *Capellmeister*, died after thirty years of invalidism. Bach, who had for a long while done many of the chapel-master duties (though he seems to have refused to write cantatas after the late autumn of 1716), expected to be promoted to the post, which would have meant a larger salary and a more elevated position. But the duke passed him over and put Drese's son, the incompetent assistant *Capellmeister*, into his dead father's place. The duke's action is regarded as inexplicable. He certainly knew a good musician from a poor one, and he liked to have the best he could get of the men available for any post. But it can be taken that he was gravely displeased with Bach over his refusal to obey orders that no member of the establishment should have anything to do with the other family. He did not want to get rid of Bach. But he would not advance him in office.

It was in this atmosphere that Bach asked for his dismissal. At once the duke would be doubly angry. Not only did Bach want to leave him—and he hated change—but he wanted to leave him for a close connection of that other family, the brother of his hated nephew's wife. He suspected an intrigue to annoy him by tempting away a member of his staff, and he said no, firmly and, as he fancied, finally.

Bach, however, was made of stuff equally stern. He renewed his petition time and again. At last he presented it in terms that the duke considered insolent. He therefore summoned Bach before him in his hall of justice, and when Bach refused to withdraw his petition he ordered him to be held under arrest until he should come to his senses: that is, until he should yield.

The imprisonment does not mean that Bach was put into a dungeon dark and damp. It would be no more than house arrest, with suspension of duties in church and castle. Bach would therefore live in comfort, able to occupy himself with composition, but unable to go out of doors.

The sentence was passed on 6th November. On 2nd December the duke gave way. He realized that the position was rather ridiculous. As it became known among the nobles and musicians of Germany it would raise a contemptuous laugh against him. He therefore repealed the sentence, gave Bach his dismissal, and Bach went to Cöthen.

He was not again at Weimar until after the duke's death, which took place in 1728. He then visited the town to honour the new duke (who was the nephew Ernst August) with the performance of a cantata: but the cantata was the 'Was mir behagt' he had produced at Weissenfels in 1716, with the name 'Christian' changed wherever it occurred to 'Ernst August.' Bach did not believe in wasting good material or in working unnecessarily.

CHAPTER IX

CÖTHEN (1717–23)

I

THE nobleman to whom Bach now engaged himself was twenty-three years old. Duke Wilhelm Ernst of Weimar was then fifty-four. Bach was thirty-two. The difference in age between duke and prince was as nothing in comparison with that between their characters and conditions. Prince Leopold of Anhalt-Cöthen had a free and lively mind. He was gay and spontaneous, and interested in all alert and pleasant things. His portrait suggests that he was the kind in whose expression is always the spirit of a smile (which is not the same as saying one who has a smile always on his face). His interest in music was genuine and un-trammelled. His desire, indeed, was for music of the purest and truest kind, which is music for instruments only; which is why he reached out and secured Bach as soon as he could, it having been borne in upon him that he could give him what he wanted, and himself wanted to give it. A personal affection grew up between the two. In the letter he wrote to Georg Erdmann in 1730 Bach says: 'My gracious prince loved and understood music, and I expected to end my days there at Cöthen.' The friendship re-mained after Bach left him for Leipzig. Several times the prince invited him and his wife back to his court on a visit, giving him money for the cost of the journey. He bestowed upon him, when he left, the title of Honorary Capellmeister to Prince Leopold or Anhalt-Cöthen, and Bach acknowledged the gracious favour by writing several complimentary odes to him and his wife, which he travelled to Cöthen to produce. And when the prince died, at the age of thirty-four, he honoured his memory by writing and producing a *Mourning Ode* at the memorial service given at Cöthen the following year.

Cöthen was a place where the 'reformed' or Calvinistic religion obtained. Consequently there was no art music in the churches of the town. There were, indeed, no choruses or choral singers there. In cantatas or serenades Bach wrote for the court he could employ only solo singers; and when in a work written at Leipzig for Cöthen he needed a chorus, he had to take one from Leipzig. The prince liked solo song. He was himself an excellent bass singer. But his heart was in instruments, on three of which he was a reasonably good performer—the violin, the viola da gamba and the clavier.

The town had no organ of importance. The court had only a small one; yet this was unusual in the respect that its pedal extended to the high F sharp, and it is held that certain organ works by Bach that use pedal notes higher than E date from this period of his life.

The *Capelle*, that is, the band, numbered eighteen. Of these, eight were called 'chamber musicians'; three others were called 'musicians'; there were two trumpeters, a drummer and another man who in the court records is simply a member: Bach, the director, and two copyists made up the total. The salaries of the band as a whole amounted to about £215 a year. This was a large sum for the prince, because his state was small and his revenue consequently moderate: it seems, in fact, to have been less than £1,000 a year. Moreover, Prince Leopold's eager interest in music led him to give casual engagements to many touring performers, both vocal and instrumental, and both male and female.

The band rehearsed in Bach's house. There for the first time were heard the Brandenburg Concertos and the many other things which, written at Cöthen, give a shining and a glory to its name. The *Capellmeister* was paid £1 6s. a year for this use of his rooms.

The band is referred to officially as the *Collegium Musicum*: the Musical College. The term incorporates the word 'college' in its primary signification of 'union' or 'company': we speak of the College of Surgeons, the Heralds' College, and so forth. As a rule, a *Collegium Musicum* was a union of singers and instrumentalists who made music under a conductor, in the first

place for their own pleasure and in the second for the entertainment of the public. There were several *Collegia Musica* in Leipzig, for example, which gave concerts, in the modern sense;
and they had good audiences. No evidence exists, however, that
Bach and his band were anything other than a private band for
Prince Leopold, or that they played anywhere else than at his
court. It is not known how often the prince gave himself concerts. It was probably very frequently—once a week, or at still
closer intervals. And being himself a performer, he no doubt
fiddled with them regularly, as Frederick the Great did with his
Potsdam band; though in Frederick's case the royal instrument
was a flute.

II

The prince had so living a joy and delight in fine instrumental
music that when he went to Carlsbad, to take the waters, Bach
and a selected number of his bandsmen went with him.

It was on the return from the Carlsbad visit of 1720 that Bach
suffered the most shattering blow of his existence. He entered his
home to greet his wife and children; he found that there was no
longer a wife. Maria Barbara, *die fremde Jungfer* (as we let ourselves believe), who in Arnstadt days had made music with
Sebastian in the church, had died of a sudden illness a few days
before, and was already buried.

Wilhelm Friedemann was then in his tenth year, Carl Philipp
Emanuel in his seventh. Philipp Emanuel was thus a very
young child at the time of the tragedy, but the impression it made
on him remained vivid throughout his life, as can be seen from
the record of it which he wrote for Mizler's necrology, after his
father's death. It was a family tradition that while father and
elder son were in closest affinity, it was mother and younger that
stood so. This may perhaps explain the dislike Philipp Emanuel
seems to have had for his father's second wife. He would feel
that she was an intruder, a supplanter of a loved one. But it
does not excuse his mean and cruel treatment of her in the years

of her widowhood, when she lived on official charity and lapsed into a pauper's grave.

Prince Leopold, like Duke Wilhelm Ernst, gave Bach permission to take various engagements in other places. His only reservation seems to have been that these must not clash with any ceremonial at home, such as a birthday anniversary.

Two such engagements brought Bach into Leipzig. One fell in the third week of December 1717, when he was engaged to report on the splendid new organ in the university church of St. Paul. He would meet Johann Kuhnau again, the cantor of the Thomas School, and the two men would recall the banquet they had shared at Halle. The other Leipzig visit fell in a year that cannot be determined. Its period covered Advent Sunday, which is the first Sunday in December, and Bach was in the town to fulfil an engagement to accompany the morning service at St. Thomas's Church and to produce a cantata. The cantata was his 'Nun komm, der Heiden Heiland' (No. 61), which he wrote at Weimar in 1714. On the score of the cantata he jotted down an outline of the service, as organists in strange places have done ever since the dawn of the accompanied church service. (He noted one item wrongly and had to cross it out.)

It would be interesting to know what brought him to Leipzig for this particular duty. The occasion could have arisen only while he belonged to Cöthen. At Weimar he was wanted for every Advent Sunday, for the special music then performed there. It could not have arisen when he was cantor at Leipzig, because by the time Advent Sunday came round in his cantorship he knew all about the order of the service in his church; and, moreover, he was not the organist of the church, and was therefore unlikely to play through a service. Nor could it well have been in this December of 1717: the visit to examine the new organ centred round 17th December; and since it was at the beginning of that December that he began work at Cöthen, he could hardly have asked for a couple of leaves of absence in the first two or three weeks. The point is not materially significant, of course; but it shows two things—one that Prince Leopold allowed his

Capellmeister a good deal of freedom, the other that Bach liked
very much to take a service in a place strange to him, to learn of the
organ and the vocal forces there and to produce one of his cantatas.

The most famous of these journeys from Cöthen is the one to
Hamburg in 1720. There he met Reinken again. At least
seventeen years had gone by since the youth Sebastian had met
him before, walking the long stretch between Lüneburg and
Hamburg, and aided on one of the journeys by the silver-mouthed
herring heads. Now the unknown youth was a performer famous
throughout Germany, and the veteran of seventy-eight was an
almost mythological figure of nearly a hundred—yet in harness still
and functioning well.

Bach played to Reinken, who sat in the church with some civic
dignitaries who had come to honour the occasion. He gave them
one of his two-hour performances. And in it he paid homage
to the art of north German organ music, which he loved and
respected so deeply, and from which he had learnt so much.
There is no documentary evidence, but it cannot reasonably be
disputed that the homage consisted in one instance of the G minor
Fantasia and Fugue. The Fantasia is the ultimate manifestation
of that art in its rhapsodical aspects. It is the high final set upon
the mighty construction that the men of the north had created
during their century. It lights that art like the lantern of Jupiter's
temple. The piece must have set the blood streaming more
quickly through Reinken's ancient veins; and it must have drawn
to a point for him all the generations he had lived through, he
himself and his fellows—the latter all dead now. And the
Fugue, which is the most sheerly brilliant of all the brilliant organ
fugues in existence, must have shown him that there was a fugal
construction, and with that a fugal performance, of which neither
he nor his companions had ever dreamed.

More intimate still, by reason of a personal circumstance, was
the homage Bach paid in an improvisation on a chorale. In the
years of his prime Reinken had 'worked' into what is called the
north German grand fantasia the chorale 'An Wasserflüssen
Babylon.' His piece is of typical length, namely, something

between 300 and 400 bars of a broad and leisured time. It is motet-like of form: each line is abstracted and treated individually, first in a fantasia on a subject constructed on the melody of the line, and then, after this organic prelude, in clear and elevated solo. Such works were the organ symphonies of the day. Bach followed his model. His Grand Chorale Fantasia lasted a full half-hour. It was an improvisation, though no doubt thought out previously. If it had been written down, either before or after, we should—given survival of the manuscript—have had what we have not, that being an example from Bach of what these vast rambling pieces of musical architecture, in which corridor succeeds corridor, and hall hall, could come to in his culminating hands. When it was over, Reinken went to Bach and took his hand, and said: 'I thought this art was long dead, but I see it lives in you.'

There is a further matter that is to be regarded as connected with Bach's last meeting with Reinken. Among his organ works are three arrangements of a setting of the chorale 'By the waters of Babylon.' The earliest was written during the first years at Weimar. The second contains a double pedal part. The third reverts to the first, and it is marked by some expansions that show how poetic or dramatic thought sometimes influenced Bach when he was working afresh over an old composition. Writing for the pedals in two parts was exclusively a practice of the north Germans. Bach himself employed it very rarely indeed. Therefore it is certain enough that he made the second of these arrangements for Reinken, to show him how very natural and beautiful this further element of his art could become.

One of the leading churches at Hamburg wanted an organist at this time. Bach put in for the post, and he would have been particularly glad to have it, because the pastor of the church was Erdmann Neumeister, the poet and creator of the new cantata form. He could not stay for the testing of the candidates, however. Moreover, there was an implicit condition of the appointment which he himself could not fulfil; this being that the successful candidate for an organist's post in this church should make a present to the church funds. The sum the successful person on this occasion paid in was £267, which represents the salary for five or six years. But that did not matter for the new organist, since his father was a rich merchant citizen of the town.

A year before the expedition to Hamburg Bach and Handel were within an hour or two of meeting. Handel was over from England on business connected with his London enterprises; and at this moment he was at Halle, visiting his mother. Bach went to the town, and found Handel had left earlier in the day. He probably wanted to arrange some kind of contest, since he was an inveterate challenger and found it getting harder and harder to find a worthy opponent. It does not seem, however, that he had previously tried to get into touch with Handel, for all that Handel had been in Germany for the whole of the preceding twelve months. Handel would know of Bach merely as a brilliant organist and clavierist, and would consequently have little if any interest in him.

Ten years later, in June 1729, he was again at Halle. Bach was then ill and unable to travel. He therefore sent a message to Handel, asking him to come and see him at Leipzig. If the message arrived safely, Handel paid no attention to it. Thus the two men, alone pre-eminent in their day, never met.

III

The year after the Hamburg visit Bach had a second legacy from the Lämmerhirt estate. The death of Tobias, his mother's brother, in 1707, and the consequent first legacy, had helped him in his marriage with Maria Barbara and his setting up home in Mühlhausen. The death of Tobias Lämmerhirt's widow was to help him in his marriage with Anna Magdalena. The sum he received was about £55. But the matter was tinctured with a projected legal process that is interesting in itself and in the light it throws on certain persons and conditions.

Sebastian's co-beneficiaries were two groups of individuals. One group was himself and other direct nephews and nieces of

Tobias. The other was the nephews and nieces of Tobias's wife. Tobias left the residue of his estate to his wife, but with the proviso that the capital was to be kept intact, the widow living on the income from it. At her death the estate was to be divided. One half was to be distributed in equal shares among the one group of beneficiaries, the other half similarly among the other group. The widow, making her will, mistook the situation. She made in the first place a number of private and personal bequests to other persons, and only then did she proceed to directions for the dividing of the estate.

The members of Sebastian's group as named in the will were himself, his brother Johann Christoph of Ohrdruf, his brother Johann Jakob in Sweden, his married sister Maria Salome Wiegand of Erfurt and the married daughter of a brother of Tobias, whose name was Agnes Christine Zimmermann. The two ladies were annoyed with the dead Frau Tobias. They considered that she had worked a sharp deal behind their backs. They therefore put their heads together and engaged a lawyer to draw up an appeal contesting her will. They said nothing to Sebastian about this, or to Johann Jakob, or to Johann Christoph. They could not, indeed, very well have communicated with Johann Christoph, because he had been dead a year. Nor could they conveniently have communicated with Johann Jakob, because for many years he had been lost sight of: it was not known whether he was alive or dead, and only by official inquiry in Sweden could the matter be determined. They also said nothing to Johann Sebastian, either because they did not know where he was or because they thought it best to keep quiet about their proceeding until it was a *fait accompli*. To guard against any awkwardness in this last direction they entered Johann Jakob as authority for Johann Sebastian's share in the action. It is clear that the ancient clan spirit of the Bachs, their unity and consistent intercourse, was no longer vital in this anxious seeker after the main chance, Sebastian's sister Maria Salome.

News of the matter came to Johann Sebastian by chance, through a third party. He at once wrote to the authorities concerned repudiating any share on his part in the project, or on Johann Jakob's. (He does not mention Johann Christoph in his letter, which is curious). He said he was fully content with things as they were. And that ended the matter. Maria Salome and Agnes Christine would withdraw in anger. They would talk about the affair to the end of their lives. And Maria Salome would never forgive Johann Sebastian.

Bach married again on 3rd December 1721. He had been a widower for nearly eighteen months. He was thirty-six, his wife twenty. She was a daughter of a court trumpeter at Weissen-fels named Wilcken. She sang well and was, indeed, a pro-fessional singer: she had been engaged at a neighbouring court and at this court of Anhalt-Cöthen since the preceding year. Her salary was about £21 16s. a year, which was just half her husband's salary; and her engagement continued, with the salary, after her marriage. This woman is the one whose name seems like a flower or a star in the story of Johann Sebastian Bach's remaining twenty-nine years, so faithful was she, so unwearying, so simply useful and so courageous, with the courage that only women have or by natural decree need to have.

Anna Magdalena took, with Johann Sebastian, four step-children: Catherina Dorothea, aged thirteen; Wilhelm Friede-mann, aged eleven; Philipp Emanuel, aged seven; and Johann Gottfried Bernhard, aged six. Three other children of the former marriage had died in infancy. She was herself in childbed twelve times in the fifteen years from 1723 to 1737. The years free of a nine months' pregnancy were 1729, 1734 and 1736; whether they were absolutely free in this respect cannot, of course, be said. Eight of the twelve children perished, at ages varying from an hour or two to five years. One of the remaining four was an idiot son, who died at thirty-nine. Thus but three of these spells of pain, labour, anxiety, expense, discomfort and distraction came to any-thing of possible human or economic value. In 1742 Anna Magdalena had her thirteenth and last child, after an interval (so far as recorded births and baptisms show) of five years. She was then forty-one.

In the same month of December 1721 Prince Leopold married. This was the beginning of the end for Bach at Cöthen, and it was the same for the prince as an unfettered lover of good music. The new princess was a light and gay person. As Bach says in his letter to Georg Erdmann, she was an *amusa*, by which he meant one opposed to the muses (i.e. the arts), just as an atheist is opposed to God. She was nineteen. The prince himself was but twenty-seven. She demanded all from him. He, fascinated by her and by the charming novelty of a married life, gave her all. Music became more and more neglected. Bach felt more and more that he was living in a void so far as active, practical music-making was concerned. He was also realizing that a finish was near to the phase of creative work that marks this period of his life. He was thus growing restless again for a change. The opportunity for the change came a little over a year later, and he went to Leipzig. The princess died in April 1723, a few weeks before he actually left Cöthen. But her death could not alter the situation. Nor is it likely that the prince could have picked up his former life again even if it could have been altered.

IV

The Bachs began to teach their sons to play the clavichord when they were nine or ten. Therefore when Wilhelm Friedemann entered into his tenth year his father took him to that instrument. He prepared a volume of music manuscript, wrote on it 'Little Clavier-Book for Wilhelm Friedemann Bach: begun at Cöthen 22nd January *anno* 1720,' and put down on the first pages what the child was to start with. The pieces are little preludes, dance tunes and chorales. One of the chorales is the melody-part of that accompaniment for 'Wer nur den lieben Gott lässt walten' which Bach wrote out, probably at Arnstadt: the melody is decorated in much the same way, and the two-part accompaniment remains for the left hand; the piece is only the third in the book, and it would be incredible that a beginner should get so far in so short a space, if we did not know that Bach kept pupils at hand and finger exercises for many weeks. Gradually the pieces advance to a number of sketches that were soon to be worked out in full in the '48.' And eventually they become the famous sets of two-part and three-part *Inventions*. The music of all the pieces, however small their form, is purely and exclusively Bachian; and most of them have been published in modern times for the use of teachers.

Two years later Bach began to teach his wife clavier playing, and for her also he prepared a manuscript volume of pieces. These are not nearly so difficult as those for Wilhelm Friedemann, nor do they advance in difficulty in the same way. It would seem that Anna Magdalena wanted to do little more at first than tinkle out pleasant bits of elementary music on the keyboard. On the inside front cover Sebastian wrote: '"Against Calvinism" and "School for Christians": *Item*, "Against Melancholy": by Dr. Pfeiffer.' These are titles of books which were then, and were to the end of his life, in his library. Why did Bach catalogue them in this place? It could not be to remind Anna Magdalena that she was to read these particular works, so as to guard herself against the baleful religious atmosphere of this Calvinistic town. Such a direction would not need to be written. It can only be that the titles were set there, at the beginning of the collection that was gradually to appear, with a symbolical significance. Music, says the husband in effect, and certainly *my* music, is opposed to the dry, barren, soul-killing tenets of Calvinism; it is music for true Christians; it is opposed to fear, despair and melancholy. Just so did he write 'In the name of Jesus' over the *Application* (that is, 'Assiduous Effort') which forms Wilhelm Friedemann's first exercise. And just so did he write such an inscription on all paper when setting out to compose a new work.

When they had been in Leipzig two years, Sebastian made Anna Magdalena the present of another manuscript volume—this time no humble little thing like the first, but one larger and handsome in gold and brown silk. In this book are copied a number of vocal pieces. One is the famous song 'Schlummert ein, ihr matten Augen' ('Fall asleep, eyes faint and feeble').

Another is a minuet melody for a poem of five verses, of which the first is a comparison of the singer's life to a tobacco pipe, soon smoked out, swiftly broken! Another song is of one loved one speaking to another:

> Be thou by me, and I with gladness
> Go to my death and to my rest.

A third is a wedding song:

> Your servant, dearest maiden bride!
> Good hap for this day's gladness!

Such things as these did Anna Magdalena sing in her home, while her husband, the great Johann Sebastian Bach, who gave her the music for them, sat and listened.

V

Cöthen was a stage in Bach's work, the measured portion of a journey. It began at a point, being led into by the stage preceding it. It ended at a point, being itself the lead to the stage following it. The earlier stage is to be summed up in the word *organ*, the later in the term *church music*. This present Cöthen stage is to be expressed by the term *instrumental music*, used with the signification we of later times convey by the words 'orchestral,' 'chamber' and 'solo.' The forms employed in the three stages are respectively (1) prelude, fugue and fantasia, (2) suite, sonata and concerto, and (3) cantata, Passion-oratorio, mass and motet.

The organ was finished with at the end of the Weimar period. There are shades of feeling that this instrument cannot express, even by the most sensitive of its solo reed stops, or by the fullest, purest and richest of its chorus stops, which last are the diapasons and flutes. There are also alternations of feeling—contrasts, and ramifications of variety—that the organ cannot express. Its utmost in these directions is rendered in one direction, and briefly, in the toccata of the popular Toccata and Fugue in D minor, and in another direction, at greater length and more finely, in the fantasia of the great Fantasia and Fugue in G minor. And it must be recognized that each of these pieces is actually a *tour de force*—something done, and done to perfection, but in defiance of probability and not to be repeated. There are, furthermore, flights of fancy that the organ cannot take and render in art—moods and experiences wherein things drift along as if to be perpetuated so, like large white clouds in a blue sky, or a bird planing on motionless wings. Once in a while Bach made the attempt to win such themes for the instrument. He did not altogether fail, as is evidenced by the opening and closing movements of the early three-movement Fantasia in G major. But how far these are from perfection is seen when they are compared with the C major prelude of the first book of the 'Forty-eight,' or with the sixty-five-bar cadenza for the clavier at the end of the first movement of the fifth Brandenburg Concerto.

For all such spiritual materials of the art of music as the foregoing, instruments are wanted that the performer can affect by pressing, as he affects his own organs of speech. They are wanted in combination. And they are wanted in forms of the rarest freedom and individuality. Bach had the instruments and forms at his personal disposal when at Cöthen. His duties let him exercise and employ them as he would; and it is likely that nowhere else in the whole of Germany could he have had such an advantage.

Thus when he finished at Weimar, his need was to think outwardly from the organ into pure instrumental music, released from the restriction of lifeless pipes and one man's feet and fingers. The instrument and its forms had served him well, as he had them. Just so, three generations later, was the piano and the piano sonata to serve Beethoven. And as Beethoven was to pass, phase by phase, from the piano to the orchestra and to the string quartet, and to express, in those more complete forces for pure music, what he had discovered and realized at his solo instrument, so Bach passed now from the organ to the orchestra and to combinations of solo instruments, with their contrasts of *concertante* and *ripieno* (or in more familiar language, solo and tutti).

Thence, after five years, he passed to the combinations of chorus, solo singer and orchestra that were his forces at Leipzig; for the next stage was ready and waiting for him. With this stage he left that of pure instrumental music, as Beethoven was to do when he ascended to the finale of the ninth Symphony. He left it, of course, for the same reason, which is, that with him music had now come to the point where in its journey it must again traverse a poetic path. It must have its moods settled and determined. It must have them designated and declared. They must be named; and the name may be a simple exclamation like 'Halle-lujah' or 'Sanctus,' or an entire text of mass, Passion or cantata. Wordsworth said: 'In Nature everything is distinct, yet nothing defined into absolute independent significance.' Let Pure Music be read here for Nature, and a description of pure instrumental music is arrived at; and at the same time information is implied as to the character of the art to which Bach went on leaving Cöthen —art in which, as Spitta says (in his own average, typical manner of perfect understanding and wise, temperate and lofty expression), 'The solemn, calm and rapt solitude of the organ blossoms out into blooming beauty and the living speech of man.' Then finally, after this essential phase of creation at Leipzig, Bach reached his ultimate goal in the sphere of pure instrumental music. There he produced the 'Prussian Fugue' of *The Musical Offering*, certain works for the clavier and *The Art of Fugue* (until recently regarded as impracticable and inexplicable). And in such vocal movements as the trio of what may be his last-composed cantata —'Du Friedefürst, Herr Jesu Christ' ('Thou Prince of Peace, Lord Jesus Christ')—he took the 'living speech of man' into that abstract world of the ideal. Thus was his artistic journey ended.

The foregoing remarks are generalizations. At Weimar Bach wrote a dozen sacred cantatas, among them some of his loveliest and most moving. At Cöthen he wrote two at least. At Cöthen he wrote also a number of secular cantatas, as his office required of him. At Leipzig he wrote organ music, some on free themes, some on chorales. He perhaps wrote there one or two orchestral suites. He certainly wrote (or brought to a definitive condition) a good deal of clavier music: the second book of the 'Forty-eight,' the Goldberg Variations, the Italian Concerto, suites and partitas, the Chromatic Fantasia and Fugue and some concertos for clavier and orchestra. But our remarks are still faithful to fact. They pronounce Bach's fundamental purpose during the three portions of his life that they touch upon. And the mental picture they evoke makes simple the task of apprehending the range and depth of the man's nature and his development of his nature—a conscious development, since Bach was of the type that sees from the start what it wants to do and to be, and how it must set about things in order to win success.

When at his death Bach's manuscripts were divided between his two eldest sons, some of the Cöthen manuscripts went to Wilhelm Friedemann. These are lost. The others, which went to Philipp Emanuel, survived, and they can be taken as representing roughly half the instrumental works written at Cöthen. Among them are three violin concertos, perhaps some of the orchestral suites, about twenty sonatas and suites for solo instruments and clavier (violin, flute, etc.), six sonatas or suites for unaccompanied violin and six for unaccompanied cello, a quantity of clavier music (the Toccatas in C minor and F sharp minor, the first book of the 'Forty-eight,' the French Suites, etc.), and the Brandenburg Concertos.

The instrumental compositions of the Cöthen period are therefore numerous and varied. They are, however, all of the same order, and they have one purpose. The *Inventions*, and the preludes and fugues of *The Well-tempered Clavier*, differ in no spiritual respect from the concertos, suites and sonatas. A piece may be difficult to understand. It may be hard to receive into the soul. Such a piece is the Chaconne for unaccompanied violin. On the other hand, a piece may flow with the milk and honey of obvious beauty and everyday feeling. Such a piece is the C major Prelude of *The Well-tempered Clavier* (which a Gounod could translate into, or explain by, a typical romantic *Ave Maria* of the nineteenth century), or the aria from one of the orchestral suites in D major (if this suite is from Cöthen), known under the title *Aria on the G string*.[1] Whatever a number may be, it will have some quality or other of grace, humour, tenderness, vivacity, tranquillity, high spirits, solemnity or *Aufschwung*—flight upward and away, yet true to the kindred points of heaven and home. And each and every quality will be one of pure music.

Whether or not the quality will be realized in actual performance is another matter. Fate has intervened in some cases by altering circumstances, so that what cannot be readily played on the modern violin could be done on that of Bach's time, which had a flatter bridge, while the bow-hair was kept comparatively slack, so that chords could be played with greater ease.

In other cases Bach is to blame. He wrote at extreme length, which wearies the attention. Or he wrote in terms of extreme technical difficulty, which may set all but a few performers problems that prevent the realization of the spiritual intent of the music.

VI

Bach's first large work at Cöthen was the Brandenburg Concertos; his last was the St. John Passion. Shortly after starting office under Prince Leopold he came in passing to the knowledge of Prince Christian Ludwig, margrave of the Prussian province of Brandenburg. This prince had a good *Capelle*, and he gave Bach a kind of commission to write him some works for it. Bach went at the task leisurely enough. He had, indeed, something to do which was not quite so easy and straightforward as writing a number of pieces of music. He had to evolve a technique and an art of writing for instruments in the combination of *concertante* and *ripieno*. That technique and art did not really exist anywhere at this time. Less than a hundred years had passed since composers began to try to write music of an instrumental character. Such a work as Gabrieli's Sonata for brass

[1] This was due to Wilhelmj, who arranged the slow movement for accompanied solo violin, transposed into a lower key. Performances on one string were an invention of Paganini's, and unknown in Bach's time.

89

instruments, which dates from the end of the sixteenth century, shows that within a century before Sebastian Bach was born a musician who wanted to write for instruments could think only in terms of the vocal music of the day. Much had been done in the intervening generations. Certain composers, German, French and English, could write charmingly and effectively for combinations of instruments. But nothing had been arrived at comparable to the art and technique of the organ which north German composers had evolved, and which had given Bach so splendid a start. Certainly nothing had been arrived at that was wholly suitable for the particular kind of music he wanted to write. He therefore had to experiment and to try out his experiments practically before finally passing his ideas. Haydn was to do the same a couple of generations later. And Bach, like Haydn, had at his command a well-trained band, and one, moreover, that had the essential benefit of constant training under himself. The result of all this was the six orchestral concertos, in which a kind of instrumental art is carried to the point of perfection; and all within the years from 1718 to 1721, when Bach sent the works to the wealthy Prussian prince.

There is no record of any acknowledgment by the prince, or of any payment by him. The manuscripts survive, and their state suggests that the prince never even had them played. When he died, his musical library was sold. Works by certain Italian composers were listed and priced individually. Other works to the number of seventy-seven, by various composers, were lumped together in one lot; and still others, to the number of a hundred, in another. The smaller bundle was priced 28*s.*, the larger 35*s.* Bach's set of concertos was in one of them. Yet this was not an insult. It is what any librarian or auctioneer's clerk would have done at the time of Bach's death, and for a generation or two after it. Bach as a composer pleased some of the few who were near him. Prince Leopold was no doubt thrilled when he heard the Brandenburg Concertos in his hall. He probably demanded them time after time, as Count von Kayserling did his precious Goldberg Variations. But for the world at large Bach counted for nothing as a composer beyond the degree in which every capable professional band- or choir-master counted, and was expected to count. A few men rose above the level. Over them all towered Telemann. These few struck lucky. They caught the ear and the fancy of the public. Bach happened not to, and it was natural therefore that these present scores of his should be stringed with a hundred others *sine nomine*.

The third Concerto, in G major, in two movements only, is popular among Bach's orchestral works much as the C minor and B minor Symphonies are among Beethoven's and Schubert's. But the set as a whole is well known, because it has a convenient nickname and can be readily referred to.

Bach himself gave the title to the works, and by his action took away from the word 'Brandenburg' its significance as the name of a tract of land and gave it an entirely new one. It was accident that allowed him to do this—the accident of a Prussian noble-man's telling him casually to write him some music—and probably forgetting all about the matter a moment later. By similar acci-dents other works have living nicknames; for example, the 'Waldstein' and 'Kreutzer' Sonatas of Beethoven, which were dedicated to a count and a violinist respectively. There is no consistency in the process. Beethoven's fourth Symphony is not called the 'Oppersdorf,' as it could be by the circumstance that named the 'Waldstein' and the 'Kreutzer.' Bach's 'Schübler' chorales have their name merely because their publisher was named Schübler. His 'Goldberg' Variations ought properly to be called the 'Kayserling,' because it was a Count von Kayserling who commissioned Bach to write them: Goldberg was only the clavierist of the count's *entourage* who played them to him. Not always does a given name take root and live. Bach wrote a great fugue on a theme given him by Frederick, the king of Prussia. He called the fugue the 'Prussian' Fugue. We have to call it the fugue in *The Musical Offering*. The name 'Brandenburg' did take root and live. It lives with an exquisite vitality. But it brings to us no thought whatever of the man whom Bach thanks in his dedication for his 'gracious and condescending interest in the insignificant musical talents' he may possess, and whom he begs, in French, not to estimate the works by his own 'pure and refined taste,' but to regard them solely as a humble and respectful expression of the musician's obedience to the great person's wishes and commands.

VII

Bach's last compositions at Cöthen, the St. John Passion and two or three church cantatas, were written for Leipzig. The Passion was a commissioned work, not an official one. The order for it was given in December, when it was not known who was to be the new cantor of St. Thomas's School, or when the appointment would be determined. Bach eventually secured it, but only after it had been rejected by two other musicians of superior position and (as the authorities considered) superior capabilities.

One of the two was Telemann, who at that time filled the heavens of German church music and to-day is but a telescopic star. He was appointed *Capellmeister* in August. His church at Hamburg thereupon raised his salary; and Leipzig having served his turn he threw it over.

The council had therefore to consider another batch of appli-cants. Among these was Bach. Opposed to him was Chris-toph Graupner, court *Capellmeister* of Darmstadt. The position Graupner held was one of a metropolitan magnificence and wealth; and he was, moreover, a composer well-known and eminent. By comparison with Darmstadt, Cöthen was an obscure provin-cial quarter; and Bach, though himself famous, was famous only as an organist and clavierist and gifted contrapuntist. Graupner underwent his trial in January, Bach his in February. (The cantata he wrote for the occasion was 'Jesus nahm zu sich die Zwölfe'—'Jesus called to him the Twelve.') Graupner won the majority of the votes and was appointed. His employer, the landgrave Ernst Ludwig, thereupon raised his salary, undertook to pension his wife if he left her a widow, promised in that eventuality to launch his children in life, and gave him a cash present of something like £300.

Thus Leipzig had now served Graupner's turn also, and he duly threw it over. Bach being next in the running, the council offered him the cantorship. He got his dismissal from his prince in April and signed on as cantor in May.

It was the custom in those days to have some newly composed music for one of the services of a festival or other important season. It was the cantor's duty to provide it, though the organist might have the task allotted to him: this had been the case at Weimar. St. Thomas's at the moment had no cantor. The organist of the church was not competent. The council could not see in December when this business of a successor to Johann Kuhnau would be settled. They therefore commissioned Graupner to write a Latin Magnificat for Christmas vespers, and Bach to write this Passion for Good Friday vespers.

Bach had about ten weeks for the writing of his Passion. Such a period is short or long according to the nature of the composer and the character of the music he produces. It was long for a Telemann, who could write a chorus in an hour and a cantata in a day, and who actually produced in all forty-four settings of the story of the Passion. Bach wrote at the most five Passions only, and he was not as a rule a lightning-swift creator. Ten weeks was not an over-short time for him to do this present piece of work. But it was short enough to give him a sense of urgency and to compel him to work at high pressure. And this circumstance profoundly and exquisitely affected his St. John Passion, making it different in many respects from the St. Matthew Passion he wrote under more leisured circumstances some five or six years later.

The sense of urgency, the working at high pressure, caused Bach inevitably to yield to the emotional qualities of his nature and, indeed, to summon them to his aid. He was caught up into his subject. For a lifetime he had contemplated it, and it was all real for him. It was real not simply in a doctrinal manner, as something to be believed in because taught by the church. Reality of that kind could be dealt with musically by any *Capellmeister*;

all that it required was an accompaniment of solemn and re-
strained sound—such sound as is called devotional. The theme
was real for Bach in a human way. It was drama. As drama, it
was something of which he was a part. It was indeed something
that was a part of him. It was his symbol—he had enacted it,
either positively or potentially, and the third person singular of
the language that narrated it had become for him the first. He
was Jesus, as Shakespeare was Hamlet, Lear, Othello and Macbeth. Expression of his theme was therefore expression of himself, sublimated, transfigured and glorified, yet still himself.
Emotion consequently dominated him. He was rapt in a flood
of feeling as a boat is in a strong incoming tide that bears it irresistibly to land. He was an artist and could therefore maintain
control; but he was a man, and he must therefore yield to powers
that lie beyond art. Thus in this piece of work he had to abandon
himself more than he usually did to the elemental qualities of his
nature, and the peculiar spiritual power of his St. John Passion is
due to this circumstance. For the work has a freshness and an
immediacy of appeal to what is human in us that is wellnigh
unique. It consequently finds a way to the hearts of men and
women, and especially to the hearts of those for whom the particular phase of religion the story appertains to is but one of many
phases; and such men and women hold that this Passion will
remain, equally vital and equally moving, when that phase has
given way to another—one with the *Divine Comedy, Paradise
Lost* and the creations in art that express the soul of ancient
myths.

The emotional quality of the work entered into German church
music generations before him. It rose with the rise of chorale
music; with hymns sung with divine unction by millions of
worshippers over a century, and with poetic compositions expressive of the hymns written by hundreds of musicians. It is
fully apparent in organ works of the first half of the seventeenth
century: for example, in the fantasia on 'Ich ruf zu dir, Herr Jesu
Christ' ('I call to thee, Lord Jesus Christ') by Samuel Scheidt,
the first master of chorale working-up. It is the spiritual keynote

of all the romantic music of the composers of north Germany. It was a part of Bach's heritage directly, since it is present richly in the music of those ancestors of his who were creative, as the sons of Heinrich, his father's cousins—Johann Christoph of Eisenach and Johann Michael of Gehren. It was there before him, as a dramatic art was before Shakespeare. But, as with that art, so with this: Johann Sebastian was required to bring it thus to final fulfilment.

There is a further consideration that explains the character of the St. John Passion. For the first time in five or six years Bach reverts to the kind of music that is his chief joy and need. And he reverts to it with the supremest and most direct theme of all, in which there is nothing doctrinal or disputatious, but only actuality. He goes from the chamber to the church, from instruments which, however fine, are still instruments, to 'the living speech of man.' Thus the occasion was one of release for him. It brought him home and filled him with an ardour like that of a loving comradeship.

All this is apparent in the recitatives of the work—that element of music which Bach made his own, helped in the beginning by the ideal recitative verse created by Erdmann Neumeister in such texts as that of the cantata 'Ich weiss, dass mein Erlöser lebt' ('I know that my Redeemer liveth'). It is apparent in the chorales, which do not suspend the dramatic music any more than does an actor's silent gesture or a poetic turn of speech in the mouth of Hamlet or Macbeth. It is apparent in the emergence from the narrative of an aria, the melody first in the instruments, then in the voice. It is, of course, supremely apparent in the dramatic choruses, in which one can forget music and conceive only spectacle and character. Criticism points to the composer's 'inexperience' as a librettist; for Bach was his own librettist here. It points to inexplicable repetitions of musical passages to differing texts. But any defects that might be proved are all swallowed up in the victory of total achievement.

Thus Bach ended his Cöthen period in glory. He went as on wings into Leipzig. He was to find there much in his daily life to drag him down. At times his official duties were to compel him to little more than a dull routine of composition. As he grew older, romance, which is the novel emotional perception of beauty, poetry, which is vision, reality, which is drama, and passion, which is the fresh stirring of the soul, were to change for him and to become fused again into a pure and comprehensive ideal. But this fulfilment of the twenty years of his life from eighteen to thirtyeight must ever have remained for him what it was while he was effecting it: a miracle of the musical expression of truth, before which one repeats with Browning 'Thou mad'st moonbeams marble!'

CHAPTER X

I

At Leipzig Bach was officially a member of the teaching staff of a school. His subjects were singing, elementary Latin and the Latin form of the Lutheran catechism. The school was a public school, having day scholars. Having endowments, or 'foundations,' for the boarding and educating of children, it was also a residential school. The head was the rector or warden. Next below him was the conrector or sub-warden. Next in the grading was the cantor.

A school cantorship ranked lower in the scale, professionally and socially, than a court *Capellmeister's* post. Bach was sensitive to this. He was therefore grateful that his friend and former employer, Prince Leopold, appointed him honorary *Capell-meister* of his court when he left Cöthen for Leipzig. But he consistently refused to consider himself a cantor only. By reason of certain things connected with the cantorship of St. Thomas's School, he could name himself Director of Music in the University Church—and, indeed, Director of Music to the entire town of Leipzig, so far as its church music was concerned. He did so name himself. And since other interested persons opposed his claim, he was frequently involved in disputes and battles.

His great intention was to establish a fine body of choralists of university students and his foundationers in the school, to unite all the church musicians of the town and to create, for the greater glory of God, a noble art of church (and eventually other) music in Leipzig. The town council, which was in direct official control of the school, did not help him. Instead, it hindered him for a while by every means in its power. The church musicians were not willing to be united. On the contrary, some of them fought against him.

97

As one of the head members of the staff, Bach lived in the establishment. His rooms had been occupied by Johann Kuhnau for more than twenty years, and nothing had been done to them all through that long period. Thus they had to be gone over in preparation for Kuhnau's successor. When Anna Magdalena set up house, she found a new oven in the kitchen. She also found that walls and ceilings had been whitewashed. Finally, she found that the place had been cleaned through by a char-woman. The woman's name survives in official documents: it was Eva Klemm.

The school was an old building, long neglected and falling into decay. It was unhealthy and was called 'a hotbed of disease.' What with this, and what with the wild, unruly and often immoral life they led, many of the boys and youths of the foundation were constantly ill. Ernesti, the rector, a man nearly seventy, was a good scholar but a bad disciplinarian. He could control neither pupils nor teachers. The latter quarrelled among themselves and neglected their duties. The townsfolk had no respect for the school. They held it in suspicion and long before Bach's time had begun to send their children for ordinary education to other Leipzig schools. Membership consequently declined, and with it revenue. Thus the Thomas School was a poor, dilapidated, unhealthy, uncontrolled, unambitious institution, with no hope of change for the better until there should be a radical alteration in the management. The vocal art of the foundation scholars, their interest in music and their attitude towards church music were all on a level with the rest of the school.

The musical foundation existed to provide choirs for local churches. It consisted of sums of money bequeathed by the pious of past generations for that purpose. Boys were elected to it after examination. They had to show general intelligence, musical ability and promise of vocal powers. The school educated them, fed them, boarded them, trained them in music and singing and made them perform music in the churches and wherever else in the town a choir like theirs was wanted.

A foundation scholar was the foster-child or *alumnus* of his school. The choir of which he was a part was its *alumneum*. He was nine or ten when admitted. He had to undertake to stay for at least five or six years. And in certain cases he could stay until he was twenty or twenty-one, or even older; and it was these senior scholars who provided the tenors and basses of the choir. The boys of the Thomas School foundation numbered fifty-five. During Bach's twenty-seven years there he admitted about 250 fresh scholars in all. Thus the average school life of his choristers was between four and five years—a period that is most distressingly brief for a choirmaster.

II

The *alumneum* provided choristers for four churches. Full choral services, with cantatas, Passions, masses and contrapuntal motets, were sung at the churches of St. Thomas and St. Nicholas. At the church of St. Peter and the church that was called the 'New' the music was congregational: that is, it consisted of chorales; these two churches required no more than a choir of from four to eight boys, and the boys selected for them were naturally those with the weakest voices and the lowest musical ability. (The university church was not connected, in this matter of choristers, with the Thomas School.)

The choirs for St. Nicholas and St. Thomas were named the First and the Second. They each sang at two services every Sunday. The morning service was that of holy communion, the afternoon that of vespers. The morning service had a cantata immediately before the sermon. This was sung on ordinary Sundays by the first choir only, one week at St. Thomas's, the next at St. Nicholas's. The second choir made the reverse alternation, and it sang in a chorale where otherwise the cantata would have been sung.

For certain festivals there was a cantata at each of the two services of the day, and in both the churches. The second choir had then to learn and perform a cantata. But the business was so managed that only two cantatas in all were wanted: the first choir sang its cantata at St. Nicholas's in the morning and at St. Thomas's in the afternoon; the second choir did the same with its own cantata, again reversing the alternation of the churches. The special services of the great festivals of Christmas, Easter and Whitsuntide, however, extended over the Monday and Tuesday, and cantatas were sung on those two days as well as on the Sunday. It was so arranged that only four cantatas in all were needed, yet preparation of them immediately before the occasion must have been a taxing matter.

Settings of the Magnificat were sung at vespers during the chief festivals. Similar settings of the Passion were sung at vespers on Good Friday; but this was only biennially in each individual church—one year at St. Nicholas's, the next at St. Thomas's. On great occasions settings of the mass were sung: the 'mass,' musically considered, was the Kyrie and the Gloria; this is conveniently, though incorrectly, called the 'short mass.' Bach wrote several such settings, and his work in B minor was originally regarded by him as finished when it consisted of only those two portions of the office. But the Sanctus also was sometimes sung to elaborate music.

The cantata was a kind of sacred concert, of which the English representative is the anthem. It contained choruses, chorales, solo arias, duets, trios and quartets, recitatives and sometimes orchestral numbers, all at the will of the composer and in accordance with the requirement of his text. Authorities of a church were generally anxious that its music should not be theatrical, that is, operatic, in style. It was found as a rule, however, that when the music was thus theatrical the singers were pleased and the congregation contented: Telemann understood this well enough, and much of his great contemporary popularity was due to that fact. The cantata lasted about twenty minutes. Sometimes it was in two parts, each from fifteen to twenty minutes long, and the second part was then sung after the sermon. The sermon, by the by, lasted an hour by the hourglass: in winter, when the church was cold, the boys were taken back to the school while it was being delivered; they did not, however, miss a sermon, for one was read aloud to them while they waited to be taken back to the church for the rest of the service.

The learning of the cantata was the chief task of the week. The full rehearsal took place on Saturday afternoon, in the school practice room, when the instrumentalists joined with the boys. Cantatas were not sung during Lent, nor on the last three Sundays of Advent. But fifty-nine in all were wanted in the course of the ecclesiastical year.

Funerals kept the scholars busy throughout the year. In a year when people died normally they averaged one a day. Revenue from this source was then satisfactory. In a year when the air happened to be good, and people died in smaller numbers, the revenue was of course diminished. Then the Thomas School, staff and scholars alike, all of whom shared in the fees, got anxious: Bach makes this clear in his letter to Erdmann. Moreover, not a few families had their funerals without music: this particularly disgusted the Thomas School, because it was an infringement of what the school considered one of its essential rights. Fees varied according to the attendance ordered from the school, which might be the entire establishment or only a few boys. The cantor's share was at the best about 3s. 6d., at the worst less than 1d. At a funeral with music the choir sang a motet outside the house of mourning, and accompanied the procession to the grave, singing chorales on the way. This was bad for the boys' voices at all times, but especially in wet, foggy or dusty weather.

Weddings also kept the foundation boys busy. For these the choir sang in the house from which the wedding proceeded. With them likewise the school had cause of complaint, many persons doing without music or even slipping out of town to be married in some nearby country parish, where their meanness would not be noticed so much. The cantor's share of the fee for a wedding was, in the best instances, about 4s. 6d. Occasionally he was commissioned to write special music for a wedding or a funeral: Bach's great funeral motets were thus brought into existence. He of course received payment for this music. And as a rule he himself attended a wedding or a funeral only when such a special work was to be performed: on other occasions a prefect was in control.

Income was added to by the money collected by the choir on their street perambulations. These were not unlike the organized Christmas carol singing which was carried on in England by parish choirs during the nineteenth century, except that they took place periodically all through the year. The boys paraded the streets, halted at appropriate houses, sang, collected what was offered them and then hurried off to another place. A very substantial sum was thus gathered during the twelve months. It was shared out in mathematical proportions to the entire school, all, from the rector down to the newest foundation child, receiving something. But the work was evil upon the voices.

Another source of income was a matter of small donations made weekly by various citizens of the town. These were collected by a number of the boys, who for this particular occupation were called 'runners.' Bach had his nicely calculated share of 'runners' money.'

His official salary, as teacher of Latin, master of the foundation scholars, operative cantor of the churches of St. Thomas and St. Nicholas, supervisor of the music in the New Church and the church of St. Peter, instrumental instructor of selected boys for the instrumental part of church compositions and composer of cantatas, Passions, Magnificats, masses and so forth was £10 10s. a year. This was paid him by the town council, and it was fixed and safe. Another 25s. was fixed and safe, since it derived from three or four of the endowments. The rest of his income was from *accidentia*—weddings, funerals and special engagements— from commissioned works, from engagements to report upon new organs, from his share of the street collections and 'runners' money' and from private teaching. In the letter to Erdmann he says that his total income is about 700 thalers a year, which is between £75 and £80. (He remarks to his friend that living in Leipzig is so expensive that he could do better in Thuringia on 400 thalers.) His earnings were about the same as those of a moderately successful shopkeeper or a foreman joiner, mason or metal worker. But he had no rent to pay. His estate at death was valued at 1,158 thalers (£126). It is unlikely that any Bach in the musical profession left so much. His widow, however, was soon in receipt of official charity. And, it is worth repeating, she was buried in a pauper's grave.

III

When we look at a piece of Bach's church music in a finely printed modern complete edition, we see it in an ideal artistic condition. It is all there before us at once—the living harmonies, the almost incredible counterpoint, the daring fancies, the profound and sweeping exercise of the imagination. When in the same way we recall performances experienced by ourselves, it is perhaps of something ideally proper and complete. The chorus was of anything from 50 to 300 voices, well trained, adequately rehearsed. The soloists were gifted and experienced musicians. The orchestra was a band of safe professional performers, the conductor a famous man. The audience was an intelligent gathering, come together as lovers of the best in music. The occasion was felt by all to be good and worthy, significant in itself immediately and precious as offering something of a lasting value for the future. And we think that matters were always so, and that Bach's personal experience was akin to ours.

We think wrongly. The reality was a different matter altogether. The original choir was at best a band of twelve or fifteen boys and youths from a kind of charity school, aided perhaps on very special occasions by two or three moderately musical students from the University and a couple or so of local amateurs. The boys have nothing of particular beauty and power in their voices. Most of them are poor specimens of humanity, with none of the bright, seemly and cherubic qualities of the finer type of boys in modern cathedrals and churches. They have no artistic pride. They have no desire even to be good in their work to the end that they may profit by it financially. They have colds and coughs, and are hoarse with the hoarseness of overtaxed and abused vocal organs.   And they are soloists as well as choralists.   The band is an assembly of mostly second⁄ and third⁄grade players from the town band, companioned by a few young professional students of music who are learning instruments.   The occasion is a routine church service, in a building that is never radiant, that is very chilly in winter and that is lit by a few candles: for the performance takes place very early in the morning.   The audience is a congre⁄ gation assembled not for art, but for conventional religious observance, and is therefore not a gathering between which and the performers flow electric rays of pleasure and appreciation, so that each body is mutually inspired.   There is no applause, de⁄ monstrative or murmured.   The conductor, if a prefect, is un⁄ inspired and uninspiring, since he is himself little more than a senior choirboy; and if he is the cantor, he is certainly alert to all practical and material details of the performance, but for the rest— for the elements of artistic loveliness, sustained power, graded and contrasted effects and spiritual expression—he is content to look within, experiencing again subjectively what he experienced in the original act of creation.   The music exists on pieces of manu⁄ script, perhaps written very hurriedly.

The singing must have been very bad indeed, because apart from poor voices and lack of interest, Germany had no grand vocal traditions and no finely tested methods of training and pro⁄ duction.   Yet it is certain that an adequate technique of execution existed and that musically gifted boys could acquire this fairly readily.   Otherwise they could not have performed such music. When in the middle of the nineteenth century Sterndale Bennett set about introducing Bach's vocal works into England, it took him several years to train a body of singers: the task was found so difficult that it was several times nearly given up in despair.   Even in the twentieth century, when a Bach technique has been de⁄ veloped, a choir needs several hours of rehearsal before it can sing a cantata chorus or a motet.   And such a choir is helped by the circumstance that it has many voices, which makes the work of the individual member easier.   The singing classes in the Thomas

School met for some hours a week.   Half the time may have been given over to preparation for the coming Sunday services.   Yet even that amount of time would be inadequate to-day for the learning of a motet, a *missa*, a cantata and perhaps a Magnificat. The whole of Lent could be devoted to preparing a Passion, because concerted music was not sung during Lent.   But at certain high festivals four cantatas were used in two days; the task of preparation must then have been severe, and only the possession of a peculiar technique could have made it possible.

This technique consisted, first and foremost, in the ability to keep a strict, immaculate time.   Nothing must interfere with that.   Time must be mathematically exact, however long the sustained notes, however brilliant the divisions, however awkward the intervals or extreme the modulations.   In performance there was, certainly, a flexibility of time, which was employed at the will of the conductor, and when the writing was of a particular kind.   It was a relaxing and modifying of the length of the beat that was not unlike what in modern days is called *tempo rubato* (a term that was known in Bach's days, but was used to describe an expressive treatment of notes that could not be stated in the written page).   Such local freedom, however, demanded an even finer sense of time, since it was licence in the application of rule. The next element of the technique was accuracy of ear.   By its aid the singer could pitch every note dead in its centre, in other words sing properly in tune.   Next, the tone produced must be a true singing tone, with nothing cramped or contracted, as when singing is attempted with a method that is right only for the speaking voice.   Beyond these qualities, the technique demanded nothing   If the voice was naturally lovely (as Sebastian's was when he was a boy), so much the better.   But a lovely voice was an accident, nature's gift, and not to be thought about if nature happened not to be in the giving mood when the boy's vocal organs were fashioned.

For Bach, then, a trained and 'serviceable' chorister or soloist was a little musical instrument.   It took a year or two to make him.   All the work was done in class, and the classes amounted to only some seven or eight hours a week. Bach gave much of his time to training boys privately and individually in the business of playing the violin, so that they might provide the accompaniments in cantatas. He could give no such time to training boys in the business of singing, though he had to take them apart to teach them solo numbers. He expected no impassioned rendering, such as an artist in opera gives, or a woman, or a *tenore robusto*. All he strove for in this respect was appropriate tone and style, light and gay when the subject was joyful praise, calm when it was a devotional theme and solemn when it was a grave one, such as death.

Even so, Bach set his singers a very difficult task indeed. Not only was his vocal style hard to overcome, but his subject, musical and poetic, was often hard to apprehend. Thus the how, the why and to-what-end alike offered serious problems. These could not be solved by boys and young men whose musical gifts, general intelligence and interest in immaterial things were never high, but for the most part low. Bach's vocal music is the hardest of all written before Beethoven's Mass in D and choral Symphony. Compared with Handel's, it is unnatural (which is one reason why Sterndale Bennett's amateurs, cast in Handelian mould, had to labour so anxiously to master it). Its spirit, its poetic *raison d'être* is rarely on the surface. Often it is remote, dwelling at a second or third remove from the immediate idea of a subject. It is not too much to say that quite frequently Bach's art is, in comparison with Handel's, as Browning's is to Tennyson's. This is because it is himself, as his organ music is. His organ music could be played properly only by himself, or by those who were trained by him or were like-minded with him. His vocal music could similarly be sung properly only by persons who were so constituted that they could receive inspiration from him.

He went into Leipzig with a high ideal: how high the St. John Passion with which he really introduced himself to the town shows. It was to develop a taste for fine art music in the church, among his pupils at the school and in his congregations. To this end he produced for many years many examples of such art. Always he did his best. Only when conditions were adverse, as when time was unexpectedly and hopelessly short, did he fall below his normal standard. But he miscalculated. Few of his boys were potentially fine artists. Few members of the congregations could enjoy music like his, or profit by it spiritually. There is no evidence whatever that the works of their cantor pleased them. There is ample evidence that as soon as he was dead those works were dropped, except for the funeral motets, which did have occasional performances during the second half of the century. One of Bach's pupils, by name Gerber, tells the following story. An 'elderly lady of noble birth' was in the congregation at a performance by Bach of one of his Passions. She was scandalized by the music, and said to the town officials who were attending her: 'What does all this mean? God help us, if it is not for certain an opera-comedy!'

Until about 1735 Bach maintained this fight with apathy and low desires, clearly delighting in the exercise of his creative powers in such a pure and noble purpose. Then flagged in him something of vigour, enthusiasm, impulse and the eager search for newness and individuality. This was natural in a way, because he was then fifty. But it went beyond what age alone accounts for. It took him, in his church works, into a sphere that was more abstract. He produced there his chorale cantatas, which are things precious for the Bachian, but for him only. And it seems that during this last period of his life his boys were even less competent to perform his music than they had been in his great middle period, or in the days when he first took office as cantor.

IV

At the outset Bach had counted on regular help from musically minded students of the University. Kuhnau had enjoyed a measure of this in his earlier days. During his last years he had lost it, for reasons that will appear in due course. Bach hoped to restore it. That is why, two years after coming to Leipzig, he fought a battle with the university authorities on a 'right' of the cantorship. He fought the battle ostensibly on a matter of principle, but actually for a practical issue, which was this of being in a position to attract to him, as cantor of the two churches, some of the students. The first story to tell, however, is that of his trouble with the town council, because this gave rise to a report on conditions that provides a unique picture of the world in which he (and many another church musician of the time) had to carry on his work.

The town council disliked Bach from the moment they realized his character. They were sorry they had appointed him cantor. When the old rector, Ernesti, died, and they had to set about finding a successor to him, they said: 'Let us hope we are more fortunate with the rector than with the cantor.' When Bach died, they said: 'We must not forget that we want a schoolmaster, not a musician.' The trouble was partly Bach's independence. They were his direct employers, who paid him his official salary of ten guineas a year. They had a right to control his movements and actions, in so far as these affected his work. They were an *Obrigkeit*—an authority, a magistracy. As such, they represented sovereign royalty, as that represented God. They were, in fact, divinely appointed, as were all who were above others. The church taught so, and custom maintained the church. Therefore Bach should be submissive to them, and subservient. But he was not, and thus hurt them on their most sensitive spot.

Now it must be admitted that Bach was a bad schoolmaster and a failure as choirmaster of boys and youths. He had shown this at Arnstadt, when his age was nineteen or twenty; and years had confirmed his nature in this respect. He had no patience with careless, unruly, uninterested boys, though with earnest, gifted pupils he was the wisest, calmest, kindliest of teachers. They, for their part, had no respect for him, for, like the young people in the Arnstadt choir, they found they could easily make him angry; and that was fun. It must be admitted also that Bach did leave more and more the drudgery of class teaching to his assistants, and that when he absented himself from town for another engagement he stayed away as long as the occasion required: he was still the person who obtained a month's leave of absence from his Arnstadt employers and without explanation expanded it to four months. And he was still the person who, admonished concerning various actions while at work in that town, got out of the situation by saying he would write an explanation and then by failing to write. Never would he use words to explain or justify anything he had done of a personal character.

Things came to a head with the Leipzig town council in 1730, when Bach had been there seven years. The preceding year they had overridden him on a point of great importance, and their action could have been dictated only by a determination to show him that they were the superior authority. A number of vacancies had occurred in the foundation. Bach had examined the mass of candidates who entered for them and put in a report recommending some boys and rejecting others. Those he recommended were musical and would eventually be useful in the choir. Those he rejected were unmusical and therefore no good for the purpose for which this portion of the school existed. The council had filled half the vacancies with boys whom Bach had rejected, or whom he had not even examined. This was foolish. But it was done, and the doing reveals the intelligence of the men who disliked and opposed Bach.

At the council meeting on 8th June 1730 it was recorded that in the opinion of a member named Job the cantor was insensitive to warnings and admonitions and that he was so stubborn as to be past all hope of amendment. Another member said that the cantor did nothing. When he began office Bach was allowed to delegate to another teacher in the school his duty of teaching Latin, he himself paying his substitute a salary. The council did not propose to alter this arrangement, except to the extent of now changing the substitute for another teacher on the staff; but it was proposed that the cantor should be ordered to do some general teaching in one of the lower classes. This, however, was too flagrant an infringement of the terms of Bach's appointment, and the proposal was defeated. It was then proposed that certain emoluments of his office should be stopped; and the proposal was carried by seven votes to four. (The post of rector had been vacant for some months, owing to Ernesti's death; the salary of the post had accumulated during those months; such accumulations of money became a 'benefit' to be shared out among the 'superior' members of the staff, of whom Bach was one; the council allocated it so, but with Bach left out of the reckoning.) Finally, the meeting condemned the shortcomings of the choirs and declared that the bad state of affairs was entirely Bach's fault.

Bach paid attention only to this last expression of opinion. He sent the council a statement of what should be available for use in the church music and what was in actuality. The following presents the substance of his remarks.

A cantata choir should have four soloists and eight choralists. This gives the chorus two singers for each part. There are, however, exceptional conditions where the soloists ought to number five, six, seven and even eight. These conditions obtain when the soloists sing *per choros*. (Bach's Latin expression is ambiguous, and English writers on Bach seem to have given it up as untranslatable: it may mean 'through the chorus,' as when the soloists and the chorus sing together, but in two individual bodies, each with its own contrapuntal parts. A grand combination like this would be, in effect, a double choir; and it can be understood that in such conditions the soloists should equal the choristers in number.) Thus the number of singers in a cantata choir ought to be sixteen.

Actually, however, sixteen is not enough. Choristers are often unable to perform, because of illness—especially at this time of the year, says Bach, the time being the hot, dry summer. Therefore, to be on the safe side, there should be three singers for each choral part, making a chorus of twelve.

This consideration applies also to a motet choir (for example the second choir of the Thomas School boys, which on ordinary

Sundays has to sing only *a cappella* part-music). With a choir of twelve, there is a fair certainty that the motet will be sung with at least two voices to a part.

Motets are sung in the churches of St. Thomas, St. Nicholas and the 'New.' Consequently for these three churches thirty-six *choralists* are wanted, and four (or more up to eight) *soloists*—that is, in all forty (or forty-four). Some boys are wanted, further-more, for St. Peter's.

The total *coetus*, or assembly, of foundation scholars is fifty-five. If each member was a serviceable vocalist, conditions would be good. But in the nature of things this cannot be so. Some are beginners, others have their voices broken, others are musically incapable. As matters are at present in the school, seventeen scholars are serviceable, twenty are in process of training and are not yet serviceable, and seventeen are useless. Thus there are seventeen boys available for a minimum requirement of forty. But not even the seventeen are in reality available for vocal work. Some of them have to function as instrumentalists in the per-formance of cantatas.

A cantata requires in the lowest computation 2 first violins, 2 second violins, 2 first violas, 2 second violas, 2 cellos and a double bass: 11 string players in all. In the wind department it requires 2 oboes, 1 bassoon, 3 trumpets: 6 performers in all. A drummer being also needed, the grand total is 18. It is, however, better to have three players for each of the violin parts. Moreover, a third oboe and a second bassoon are sometimes wanted. Finally, flutes are frequently used. Thus the band should number twenty at the least, to balance the chorus of twelve (or sixteen), and it should number more if full satisfaction and complete equipment is desired.

The town council provides officially seven players only—2 violins, 2 trumpets, 2 oboes and 1 bassoon. Lacking are violas, cellos, double bass, drums, flutes, third trumpet and third oboe; and the violin parts are restricted to a single player for each. The seven instrumentalists are the employees of the town council. They form the town band. Several are old men, who should be retired. The others are not 'in good practice'; that is, they have not been able to keep up their technique.

Here Bach makes some general remarks:

German performers of instrumental music are expected to play without preparation, and at first sight, any music, whether Italian, French, German or Polish. They are expected to play it as if they were the native virtuoso performers who have studied it well beforehand, and, indeed, know it almost by heart. These virtuosi, moreover, are paid high salaries, and their diligence and care are therefore well rewarded. Not being filled with concern for their livelihood, they can cultivate their art and become agreeable performers. It is so with the musicians employed at the royal court at Dresden. Our German players are left to take care of themselves; they have to work for their bread and have therefore little leisure to develop their technique, still less to become virtuosi. They are filled constantly with anxiety.

Bach returns to his particular theme. In Kuhnau's time a few university students who played instruments used to help in the cantata performances, taking second violin, viola, cello and double bass. They did this willingly, because it gave them pleasure and because certain little sums of money were paid them for their services. That payment has been discontinued. The students as a result have gradually withdrawn, for no one will work altogether for nothing. The instrumental places vacated by the students have to be filled with scholars from the school. The boys have to be taught their instruments. But since these boys, naturally among the more gifted musically, are turned into instrumentalists, they are lost to the chorus, thus with serious addition to the vocal problem.

In the case of the festivals the position is worse. Cantatas have then to be performed at St. Thomas's and St. Nicholas's at the same time. The boys who are instrumentalists on ordinary Sundays have to become singers again; and the instrumental performers are in consequence still more deficient. Kuhnau and his predecessor enjoyed an advantage in their cantorship that no longer exists. In their time there was a certain member of the council who out of his own pocket found fees for university students who could come in at festival times and sing alto, tenor and bass. This gentleman also paid for additional instrumentalists, in particular for second violins.

Coincident with all this is a radical change in the public taste for music in churches. The kind of music wanted now is that for which competent performers are absolutely essential. They must be instructed in the new and special technique it requires, and only such persons should be selected and appointed as can benefit by the instruction and so please the congregation; to say nothing of pleasing the composer by a good rendering of his work.

Thus Bach, in one of the most informative and authoritative documents that survive from his time. It will be noted that only once, and that in the last abstracted phrase, does Bach let it be seen that he is himself directly affected by conditions. He is, without doubt, making a case. He presents every possible point. The picture is the blackest that could be drawn. But when all that is allowed for, one is still left wondering how cantatas could possibly be performed, and what kind of performance they could possibly have had.

The council received Bach's statement, filed it (because it was sent to them officially) and ignored it.

Fifteen years later—when Bach had been in office twenty-two years, had composed for the churches about 270 cantatas and had directed cantata performances to a number somewhere between 1,000 and 1,500—his first or 'cantata' choir was constructed as follows: 5 sopranos, 2 altos, 3 tenors and 7 basses. Bach's ideal was three voices to a part. Here his basses outnumber his altos by more than three to one, and his sopranos are nearly twice as strong as his tenors. The bad balance can be due to one condition only, namely, that he had these 'serviceable' singers in the school and no others, and had to put them into the choir. Thus it is clear that to the end his available forces were always wrong, and that he never heard his music in the 'good rendering that is pleasing to the composer.'

V

Two other conditions existed to make a good rendering im-possible: one the phrasing of the music, the other the preparatory rehearsals.

The manuscript scores—both autographs and copies made by other persons—have in the majority of cases no marks of phrasing. This led in the nineteenth century to the belief that Bach's music did not want phrasing in performance: it was simply to be reeled and rattled off, thumpity-thump. The position thus established was like that which might be established for an author of literary works if the belief was held that he was to be read without punc-tuation; or, if the author was a poet, without the form of his verse being created in the rendering. A considerable number of scores exist, however, in which the music is phrased. They prove that Bach phrased music when playing it himself, and that he wanted it phrased by other people. He omitted phrasing in most written copies for two main reasons: first, most performances were under his direct control, whether of a cantata by soloists, chorus and orchestra, or of a piece by an organ or clavier student, and he could explain and show what he wanted; secondly, there existed a general practice of phrasing, and indeed a science, which all musicians understood, or were supposed to understand, and which would be applied naturally to the performance of his works. The scores he does phrase vary from works like the Brandenburg Concertos to cantatas. These reveal a system that is frequently different from the system, or systems, of nineteenth-century composers. Some of the details appear arbitrary and casual to the modern student, because like groupings of notes are often treated to unlike phrasing. Often, indeed, the system seems unnatural, because it is so different from what the student expects whose ideas have been formed by the later systems of Schumann, Chopin, Brahms and other nineteenth-century masters. Perhaps for this reason editors of the great collective editions of Bach pub-lished during the nineteenth century ignored Bach's phrasings and printed the music naked of any of his signs. This can be seen in the Breitkopf & Härtel vocal scores of the cantatas, as published then. It can be seen, in startling and surprising manner, in the original Peters edition of the organ pieces on chorales: for example, in the arrangement of 'Kommst du nun, Jesu, vom Himmel herunter.' This is a transcription, made by Bach himself, from a cantata number (cantata 137). In Bach's manuscript of the cantata the music is phrased—for touch and for the grouping of notes—with a refinement equal to Schumann's. In the Peters edition the markings are left out.

Now it is often as difficult a task in the performance of Bach to give effect to his phrasing as it is to strike his notes. His instrumentalists could not possibly do it. The men of the town band were either old and weary or 'in bad practice.' The boys of the Thomas School were never more than moderately advanced executants. Therefore, since the phrasing in Bach is as essential as are the notes, no cantata, mass or Passion performance given in the conditions outlined above could have been artistically good, and Bach could never have heard with his physical ear what his inner ear had conceived.

Rehearsals for a cantata performance were restricted to one. It can be taken that some preliminary work was done. The vocal soloist would learn his piece during the week. The youth who was to play a violin obbligato to an aria would learn his part, and he and his vocal companion would practise together. The choir would learn their sections in the class. Thus for an ordinary Sunday performance, of a work got ready well beforehand, the one rehearsal would put matters into as good a shape as general conditions allowed. But it not infrequently happened that a new work was not finished until just before the performance. This was the case with the *TrauerOde* of 1727. The poet began his work on 3rd October and probably sent the first part of the text to Bach as soon as it was ready. Bach began composing at once. He did not, however, finish until the 15th. The performance was on the 17th. And between the 15th and 16th, which was rehearsal day, the parts had to be made of the number or numbers written last. However much preliminary practising may have been done as the ode was written, movement by movement, some of the music, in some of its parts, must have been quite strange to the performers at the full rehearsal. Thus the work as a whole could not have been well rehearsed, because it is lengthy, with three choruses, two arias and several recitatives, all with obbligato instrumental parts. The performance therefore could not by any possibility have been artistic or even uniformly safe and sound. Moreover, on this occasion some of the players and singers were university students, who were not accustomed to perform with the Thomas School forces; and the total must therefore have been something of a scratch team, defective as are all such promiscuously assembled groups. (The secular cantata 'Tönet, ihr Pauken' is noted on the score 'Finished 7th December 1733,' and the performance was on the 8th.)

One wonders what Bach found available on the Good Friday of 1723, when he went to Leipzig with the St. John Passion he had written during the winter with such concentration, sublimity of ideal and sustained inspiration. Things had got bad during Kuhnau's last years. For months there had been no cantor. There is no record of any special engagement of instrumentalists, either from neighbouring towns or from Leipzig itself, where there was an abundant supply. Women could not have helped, because women were not then allowed to take part in church services. It is not likely that university students or members of the local musical unions helped, for reasons that will appear in a moment; or if some of these did help, it could be in only a minor degree. The Passion would be sent to Leipzig portion by portion through the preceding months, and some local musician—probably the organist of one of the churches—would teach the music to the singers. But nothing could have been settled finally until Bach himself went to the town for his week of preparation and rehearsal. And whatever the force of his teaching and conducting, he could not bring about a rendering of the great work that would not distress a modern listener.

VI

Some twenty years before Bach went to Leipzig a brilliant young musician had shown that if a church organist or cantor wanted to make the music of his church popular and safe it was a good thing to be well in with the university students. The young musician was Telemann. He was a leading student of the University. He wrote poetry, played the organ, composed attractive music and understood how to produce opera. In 1704, when he was twenty-one years old, he was appointed organist of one of the churches that were under the control musically of the cantor of the Thomas School: at that time Kuhnau. It was the New Church, and so was not one of the important places of the four. But within a few weeks Telemann had made it the most attractive church in Leipzig. He had the goodwill of his fellow students, and many of them at once joined his choir as instrumentalists and as singers.

Then he founded a *Collegium Musicum*, or musical union, the members of which were mostly university students. The union met weekly for practice, in the summer in a garden, in the winter in a coffee-house. At certain times in the year it gave public concerts, when secular cantatas were sung and orchestral suites and concertos played. The union became exceedingly popular with members and with the public alike, and out of it Telemann gathered further strength for his choir at the New Church. Furthermore, he took control of an operatic organization that had been established at Leipzig about ten years earlier. For this he wrote operas, which delighted the students in a new direction. And once again Telemann deflected some of the enthusiasm he had aroused to the benefit of his church.

Kuhnau worried about all this. He hated opera. In particular he hated the use in church of music that had a theatrical tone: which was the tone of Telemann's church compositions and of his performances. Worse still, the opera, as enlivened by Telemann, attracted to itself senior members of the Thomas School. These young people found it profitable to work in the opera productions, for there was money to pay them fees; and if they made good, there were influences there that helped them to professional engagements in opera in other towns. Thus Telemann's successes hastened the decline, already serious, of the Thomas School and made it harder for the cantor to carry on with his work in the other three churches. He appealed to the town council, asking them to hold Telemann back and to compel him to recognize Kuhnau as his superior in the music of the New Church. The council, however, refused to do anything, and Kuhnau had to put up with discomfort, distress and misery.

Telemann left Leipzig after only a year at the New Church. His successors carried on his work. For some years, indeed, they increased its brilliance. Then certain conditions and circumstances changed. The New Church reverted to its former status among the four that were served by the Thomas School. The Musical Union continued to flourish. The opera gradually decayed.

As said above, Bach came into Leipzig with a plan of campaign. The victory he aimed at was a gathering together of the various forces in the town and their employment in the churches as a mighty and glorious instrument to the greater glory of God. He could give them the music to sing. He could lead them to the triumph. But first he must build his army.

The most important element of that projected army was the musically minded students of the University, of whom the new cantor wanted to win to himself a score or so of amateur singers and a score or so of amateur fiddlers and pipers. That he did not win them is shown in his 1730 statement to the town council about the musical condition of the school and the churches. Thus he failed in the prime essential element of his plan. And he failed first because the university authorities did not like him personally, and hated any enforced official connection between University and school, and secondly because a poor, arrogant, self-assertive, stubborn musician in their employ regarded himself as Bach's equal and from the vantage-ground of his position in the University fought to keep him out.

The cantor of the Thomas School had the right to call himself Director of Music (*director musices*) of the University. That is what Bach called himself from the start. Even when addressing the town council on a matter directly and exclusively concerned with the school he often signed himself, not cantor, but *director musices*; and every time he did this he poured oil on fire. He used the superior designation because it was superior and because he knew that the higher a man's title, the more ordinary people respected the man. The right to this title came about by reason of certain ancient services that were held in the university church, the musical direction of which was vested in the cantor of the Thomas School. They numbered eight a year. Three were the high festivals of Christmas, Easter and Whitsuntide. Another was the festival of the Reformation. The other four were the services that marked the degree-giving days: these were held quarterly. The director was paid for his work. His salary was 12 florins a year, which is roughly £1 2s. 6d. and works out at 2s. 9d. a time. There were, however, certain perquisites attached to the office that brought in further money: one was an honorarium (additional to the salary) for each of the eight meetings; another was the right to receive the commission to compose works for exceptional services—memorial services, for example, for the death of a royal person or services celebrating the accession of a ruler to his throne.

During Kuhnau's period of office the university authorities established a regular Sunday service. This was kept separate and distinct from the above eight, and to distinguish them the Sunday services were called 'the New' and the others 'the Old.' The University proposed to appoint an organist and a cantor for the exclusive official control of the New. This alarmed Kuhnau. He saw in it something that would weaken his position as Director of Music and perhaps destroy it. He therefore offered to take charge of the forty or fifty services of the New free of salary, without any financial return whatever. The university accepted his offer. Kuhnau did not, of course, attend the services in person. He could not, because until the cantata was finished he had to be at either St. Thomas's or St. Nicholas's. But he selected the music, supervised the practising of it and over⁄looked the work of organist and choirmaster.

When Kuhnau died, and the interval began between his death and the appointment of a new cantor at the school, the University put the direction and control of the Old Service and the New into the hands of a local musician. The man was Johann Gottlieb Görner, the organist of St. Nicholas's. Görner did not have to attend the Sunday services. Indeed, he could not, be⁄cause as organist he had to stay in his church until the last hymn was sung and the outgoing voluntary played. The University so adjusted the payments which Kuhnau had received as to make the 12 florins appear as a salary for the work done in connection with the New Service. The honorarium associated with the Old remained in its original position. Görner received both sums. He blossomed forth as Director of Music to the University. And the university authorities were happy in the thought that they had broken the former association between University and Thomas School—an association that was irksome to them, first because it shackled their independence to have a Director of Music who was an official in another institution, and secondly because there was a measure of bad feeling between them and the town council.

Bach appeared. He found that he was ousted from his right⁄ful position—rightful because established 'from time immemorial' —as Director of Music for the Old Service of the University. This could not be allowed. It defeated him at the first step of his campaign, as he had planned the campaign. And the defeat was one that made future victory impossible. He therefore attacked the University in the very heart of its citadel. With the help of the legal faculty of the University he proved that the University's action in cutting Thomas School cantor and Old Service director apart was illegal. The University thereupon admitted Bach to the directorship of the Old Service. They refused to let him have anything to do with the New. This, they said, was a recent institution, free of tradition and custom, and consequently for them to deal with as they would. Bach acquiesced, perforce. But though the University returned the direction of the Old Service to the cantor of the Thomas School, they did not return the salary—the £1 2s. 6d. per annum for the eight meetings. They returned only the honorarium. This for Kuhnau had been a matter of 6 thalers 18 groschen (14s. 9d.) a year. For Bach it was doubled, becoming 13 thalers 10 groschen (29s. 6d.). The University, however, repented of its arrangement with Bach and in respect of the honorarium paid him only what it had paid Kuhnau.

For two years and three-quarters Bach did his work in connection with the Old Service, arguing constantly with the authorities about financial conditions, but getting no satisfaction. At last he appealed to the king-elector in his high court at Dresden. The monarch ordered the University to make a report on the matter. They did this. Bach replied to it in an analytical statement a solicitor preparing a brief could not improve upon. (He had a fine talent for such work.) He proved that the University had fabricated untruths and were guilty of inconsistencies in their argument. The king-elector thereupon delivered his ruling, which was that Bach was legally Director of Music of the Old Service, that he was to receive the £1 2s. 6d. salary and the agreed honorarium of 29s. 6d., and that all arrears, calculated on these bases, were to be paid. In respect of the New Service, the ruling was that the University could legally appoint whom they would to be in charge.

Thus Bach won what he was fighting for immediately. He was, legally and incontestably, Director of Music of the University of Leipzig. But he did not win what he was fighting for ultimately: he was not able to bring university students to the help of the services in the churches of St. Thomas and St. Nicholas. His 1736 statement to the town council proves this beyond doubt.

Nor did he win in an associated matter that was of great importance, for his dignity and for his profit alike. Kuhnau, the musician in sole charge of the university services, both the Old and the New, had naturally been commissioned to write any work wanted for a special occasion. These *accidentia*, as they were called, were not dealt with from Dresden. Their allocation, therefore, remained open. Bach claimed them, by right of custom that dated from Kuhnau. Görner claimed them, by right of his favoured position with the University. The University hated having Bach thrust upon them, even though legally he should be where he was. His victory over them made them bitter. Moreover, they could see no difference between Bach and Görner as composers. They therefore backed Görner in this matter. And in 1727 they combined with him to offer Bach the greatest insult he received during his lifetime; or rather, they tried to insult him, since the insult rolled from him like water off the duck's back.

This Görner, by the by, was a trouble to Bach to the end. He was by twelve years his junior, the year of his birth being 1697. His highest positions were the organist's post of St. Nicholas's and, from 1730, that of St. Thomas's. He was so poor a player that, according to tradition, he could not accompany safely in the cantata, making so many mistakes that at one rehearsal Bach in anger snatched off his wig and either dashed it on the ground or flung it at the accompanist. He could not write music correctly, or even effectively. He certainly founded a second Musical Union in the town and conducted it with some success, and that was all he did, or could do. Yet he set himself up against Bach. He thrust himself forward as his worthy rival. And people took him largely at his own valuation. (There must have been good qualities in the man, however: when Bach died, he helped Anna Magdalena to round up and realize the estate, all out of sympathy; and what is infinitely more significant, he burdened himself with the guardianship of the four younger children—and this was a very great responsibility, since soon after her husband died Anna Magdalena was 'on the parish.')

The insult offered to Bach was that he should sign a document admitting that he had no right to call himself Director of Music, and that he would never accept a commission to compose music for any function connected with the University, unless the University had, upon his humble request, first said that he could.

The document was prepared by Görner. It was sent to Bach by an agent of the University.

The occasion was a memorial service for the dead queen of the king-elector. The time was October 1727. A young man named von Kirchbach had received permission, from Dresden and from the University, to give this memorial service, at which should be performed a mourning ode. He was to pay all expenses. He commissioned a local poet to write the text and Bach to write the music. He paid them in advance, and Bach got to work at once on the great cantata-like composition that is the *Trauer-Ode* mentioned above. When Görner heard of the matter, he was enraged and said: 'It is for *me* to do such work as this. I am Director of Music of the University, and fees of this kind are *mine.*' The authorities agreed with him and told Kirchbach to cancel his arrangements with Bach and to make fresh arrangements with Görner. Kirchbach refused. Görner and the University then said that Bach could write the ode, seeing that he had it in hand, but that the performance must be by Görner and his Musical Union. Kirchbach, irritated and disgusted, then threatened to abandon the business altogether. This frightened the authorities, and it was finally arranged that Görner should be paid (by Kirchbach) a special consolatory fee of twelve thalers. Kirchbach agreed. And then Görner and the University prepared their document. They sent it to Bach's house. It was taken in to him. But he simply declined to see the messenger in person, and after the latter had waited an hour, he went back and reported the complete failure of his mission. It was in these mean, shameful and degrading conditions that the *Trauer-Ode* was created. The story is a wretched one, but of great value in that it shows how external matters had no power to affect the workings of Bach's creative soul and the operation of his musical powers.

For the future the University seems to have put most of its musical commissions into Görner's hand. The students themselves had functions at which they produced cantatas and odes, and they for their part seem to have preferred Bach. They could tell the difference between the two men, and they had no reason to dislike him. Thus in the December of 1726 they ordered from Bach a *Congratulation Cantata* for a meeting where they welcomed a newly appointed professor. And in May next year they ordered from him a *Birthday Cantata* for evening performance outside the house where the king-elector was lodging: he being on a visit to Leipzig. On the morning of that day there was a ceremony in the university church that was connected with the royal visit: it included a Latin ode with music, and the composer here was Görner.

VII

Throughout his life at Leipzig Bach strengthened his position with the public and among other musicians and officials by his honorary appointments to the courts of rulers. These were desirable things and were much sought after. They were the musical counterpart in Bach's time of the modern institution of Royal Letters Patent, by which a piano manufacturer may advertise himself as Maker of Musical Instruments to Her Majesty . . ., or a butcher as Purveyor of Meat to His Royal Highness . . . The duties were, first to supply a composition for any court function at command, and secondly to attend at court if ordered.

Bach had a fortunate run of such distinctions. He went to Leipzig as honorary *Capellmeister* to his friend and late employer, Prince Leopold of Cöthen. The appointment lapsed when Leopold died in 1728. Apparently in this year, though it might have been earlier, he became—in the language of the period—'outdoor' (*von Haus aus*) *Capellmeister* to the Duke of Weissenfels, the friend and hunting companion of Duke Wilhelm Ernst of Weimar. This lapsed in its turn when the Weissenfels ruler died in 1736. And in that same year Bach received the most coveted distinction of all, namely that of Court Composer to the king-elector of Saxony. He had first begged the royal favour in 1733. The work he had sent with the petition was the Kyrie and Gloria of the Mass in B minor, composed specially to prove his justifiable claims to be thus distinguished. And now, at exactly the right moment for him, his petition was granted.

Yet 1736 was the year of the start of a quarrel at Leipzig that lasted two years and involved everybody it could involve.

VIII

Bach was very jealous of infringement of rights or rules of office. Even suspicion that such a thing was contemplated brought him out like a mother-cat fearful of danger to her kittens.

A preacher of the vespers service once took it upon himself to select the hymns which were to be sung in connection with his sermons. This seems a reasonable thing. But it was the cantor's duty and his right to determine all hymns for all services. Therefore Bach opposed the preacher. The latter received the support of the chief minister of the diocese, Superintendent Deyling, and the support also of the ruling assembly of the churches. Bach appealed to the town council, who had a strong say in all matters affecting the churches. He did this astutely, because of the bad blood between consistory and council, and reckoned on that to win him the council's help in the dispute.

Once again the council forbade Bach to proceed with preparations for the performance of a Passion, first because he had not submitted the text to them for their approval, and secondly because he had started rehearsal without receiving it. The council were legally right in their action. But they had not exercised their right previously, and the law of it had become a dead letter. Moreover, this particular Passion had already been performed three or four times. The council acted as they did now merely from a spiteful desire to trip Bach up by any means in their power. Bach did not argue with them. He notified the consistory that the council had stopped his work on the Passion and that, as matters stood, there would be no Passion on Good Friday that year. He then retired to the background to observe the two bodies fighting the case out between themselves.

But though he was, to an extreme degree, thus punctilious in protecting his rights and privileges from the encroachments of other persons, and especially of his superiors, he was not the same in respect of his own actions. Indeed, he regarded himself as above the law. Thus there was a clause in his agreement that he would not, as cantor, send choir-boys to sing at weddings and funerals in the country without official sanction. The clause was necessary, because without such a restriction a cantor could make a profitable business out of such employment of his boys, and music in the churches would suffer. Bach had solemnly pledged himself to the clause. But on one occasion at least the council had to reprimand him for dishonouring his pledge. He was also under contract not to absent himself from town without permission. This was an important point, since at any moment he might be wanted to discuss a matter with the council or to attend personally to some sudden emergency, and the council must at least know where their cantor was. Bach, however, went from town when he wanted to, without asking permission, and without notifying the council. This was inconsiderate at best, and dishonest at worst. Genius does not excuse it, because it is not connected with genius. When remonstrated with, and asked not to act so again, he refused to respond, and he would make no promise. And this was insolent, for he was the paid servant of the council. It really is no wonder that these men, proud of their dignity as Bach was of his, and insulted in its very heart and centre, should have disliked him.

The great quarrel mentioned above fell in the years 1736–8. It was with the new rector of the school, whose name was Ernesti (as was that of the old rector), and it concerned the appointment of prefects for the church choirs. Bach claimed that this was a matter for the cantor; and it certainly was that in any practical regard, seeing that a prefect was conductor of parts of the church music—the hymns and the motet—and that he was deputy cantor when the cantor was absent, having then to direct the performance of the cantata. A prefect therefore had to be a sound musician, and only the cantor could determine a scholar's ability. The rector of the school, however, had certain overriding powers. These powers Ernesti exaggerated. He was a scholar and teacher of the modern type (he was twenty-two years younger than Bach). He hated music and despised musicians. It was his intention to reduce the musical work of the school to a minimum, so as to make possible fuller and better instruction in general subjects. He therefore sought out means to belittle Bach and to weaken his authority. And he found it now in the opportunity to force Bach to take as prefect of the cantata choir a young man of twenty-three who was dissolute in his life and of poor musical abilities.

What developed was a public scandal. Bach found Krause, the foundation pupil in question, in charge at a service. He ordered him out and set another pupil in charge. Ernesti climbed to the choir gallery and ordered him back, and told the boys that if they obeyed any one but Krause he would punish them by denying them the sums of money accumulated for them in the school funds. Bach went to the head of the diocese, the super-intendent of the churches. The superintendent took the rector's part, and a friendship was broken that had existed between him and Bach since Bach went to Leipzig. The disturbance in the choir gallery was repeated Sunday after Sunday, to the annoyance and distress of the congregation (and hardly to that greater glory of God Bach found so precious). Bach appealed to the council, writing them letter after letter: in August 1736 he wrote such letters on the 12th, 13th, 15th and 20th. Ernesti likewise wrote letter after letter, and he was sharp, vindictive and not fully truth-ful; also he descended to personalities.

At last, in October 1737, Bach approached his 'most noble, most mighty King and Prince, most gracious sovereign.' (The council seem to have fought shy of the matter.) He begged the king to order the council to uphold his prerogative to appoint prefects, to direct the consistory to demand from the rector an apology for the indignity he had put upon him and to charge the superintendent to pronounce to the entire school that all must show him, Johann Sebastian Bach, the cantor, due and customary respect and obedience.

The king-elector responded, though not with undue haste.

He wrote an order to the consistory in December: they must take the matter up with the council and Superintendent Deyling, get a report from them, consider this and do what was right by the cantor. The consistory received the order in February. They sent it to the council and demanded the report within a fortnight. And at this point silence descends. The archives of council and consistory contain nothing further, which means that the matter was dropped officially by the parties concerned. The irresistible force had met the immovable object. Rock and sea had agreed to be rock and sea. Council, consistory, rector and the school supporters of the rector must have suddenly realized that this man was something more than a Thomas School staff-member, since he was the honoured of king-elector August, and that by belittling him they were risking trouble for themselves in the highest quarters of their land. The man himself must have recognized that morally he was not defeated. It can be assumed that some one set high in the world intervened privately, saying 'Let it all drop,' and that his advice was followed.

Ernesti continued to hate and despise Bach. Council and consistory left him more or less alone. As for Bach himself, he seems to have taken advantage of the situation to withdraw farther and farther from direct personal attention to the practical duties of his office, leaving the day-by-day exercise of them to his prefects and other assistants. He had the power to do this now. It was what he wanted to do, because once again he had exhausted position and opportunity and his genius imperatively demanded a change.

The change demanded was not one that necessitated removal to another material situation. It required only privacy, where the soul of his art could dwell and exercise itself as it would. He was now well into his fifties. He was becoming the old Bach of portraits and of conventional reference. And the way he must now follow was that which led to the vast revision of his earlier organ works, which was a task for a man in retirement, and to the creation of such a thing as *The Art of Fugue*, which was a task for a man fixed upon the heights of subjective isolation from the world and gazing upon the universal and the eternal.

IX

It may be told here that on the start of this last stage of his mighty journey Bach was attacked critically by a member of the new school of musicians. The date was May 1737, and the attacker was Johann Adolph Scheibe, a man aged twenty-nine. Scheibe was a native of Leipzig, had lived there as a teacher of music until 1735, and had then removed to Hamburg, where he had established a musical periodical. In 1729 he had tried for the organist's post of St. Thomas's and had been turned down by Bach and the other judges in favour of Görner. (Since Görner was not a good accompanist, Scheibe must have been a really bad one.) His failure rankled. He put it down to a fancy that Bach disliked him and had allowed his dislike to influence him as a judge. To revenge himself, he began to stir up a party against Bach, as a composer, in Leipzig. He was successful in this, especially among the group of university students who felt towards music as he did. This annoyed the other students, in particular those who formed the personnel of the Musical Union then conducted by Bach. They were therefore highly delighted when Bach composed for them his secular cantata of *Phoebus and Pan*, in which it is clear enough that the contemporary musician who is ridiculed in the character of Midas is this Scheibe. For the Scheibe type of musician Bach's music was 'pompous, vain and tedious.' Scheibe said as much in his 1737 article, and his critical charge aroused a good deal of attention. Those who thought differently of Bach's music argued against it. Chief among these was Johann Abraham Birnbaum, professor of rhetoric and poetry in the University of Leipzig, who wrote a pamphlet contradicting Scheibe. Scheibe responded, stating now that Bach could not possibly be a 'natural' composer because he was an ignorant and uneducated man. A musician, he said, must study natural philosophy; how could he have good taste if he had not first mastered by study the forces of nature and reason, and learnt the rules of oratory and poetry? Birnbaum had no difficulty in vanquishing Scheibe on such points as these.

Some years later Scheibe admitted in his periodical that he had been largely influenced in his attitude towards Bach by jealousy of his eminence and by excessive belief in his own virtues and powers as a musician. But this did not protect him from further ridicule. And so notorious was the matter that more than forty years later writers on musical subjects referred to it in scorn and derision.

But Scheibe was, none the less, an authentic voice of his genera⁄ tion. For that rising generation Bach's music was thick, confused and altogether unattractive. And it remained that for the next two generations. Indeed, it remains that for a majority of music⁄ lovers even in the twentieth century.

CHAPTER XI

I

BACH's creative life at Leipzig followed the courses it had followed previously. On the one hand he fulfilled, faithfully and generously, his official duty, which was to produce music for the churches—cantatas, Passions and the like. On the other hand he fulfilled, equally faithfully and generously, his duty to himself as artist. This was to feed and exercise his soul with pure art—art that need not be, except that without it the man would die: such art as a fugue for the clavier, which none might ever play but the composer, and of which the material existence might never be more than the original manuscript.

Subordinately, Bach welcomed (though always calmly and with due dignity) opportunities for 'occasional' works that brought him into contact with a section of the outside world; he published some compositions, and — especially in his last ten years — he collected and revised earlier instrumental works.

He began publication in 1726, when in his forty-second year, with a clavier Suite (or 'Partita,' as he called it). This was the first of his music to be engraved, apart from that cantata, 'Gott ist mein König,' of the distant Mühlhausen days; and it is believed that Bach prepared the plates himself. He published a second Suite in 1727, a third in 1728 and continued thus until 1731, when the six works were issued under one cover. The set is called the Partitas. Attempts were made in the latter half of the century to call it the 'German Suites,' after the earlier sets that are called the 'French' and the 'English'; but they happened to fail. Copies were sold by Bach at Leipzig (who required cash with order), and by his two eldest sons in the towns where they worked. In 1760 Breitkopf, the Leipzig publisher, acquired right of publication and sale. Forkel, writing in 1802, said that the partitas made 'a great noise' in the world of their day and that every musician who was anything of a clavier player was compelled by their fame to have at least one of them in his repertory.

The collected partitas appeared under the general title of *Clavierübung*, which means 'keyboard exercise.' Bach got the title from Kuhnau, who had used it a generation earlier. Later composers adopted it from Bach. The term 'clavier'—keyboard or set of keys—applies properly only to instruments that are played by hand; and, moreover, only to instruments with strings. In the case of the organ the claviers are called the manuals, to distinguish them from the pedals, which are played by the feet. But, as will be seen in a moment, Bach extended the expression 'Clavierübung' to cover organ music; and if he had been challenged to justify his action, he would probably have said that the organ pedals were, after all, a set of keys.

II

In 1735 he published Part II of his *Clavierübung*. The works forming this were the *Italian Concerto* and the *French Overture* in B minor, both for solo clavier. The Concerto is to-day one of Bach's most popular compositions. It is certainly as well known as the *Chromatic Fantasia and Fugue*. The *French Overture* (an overture in the French style, followed by a suite) is not well known, but it is all delightful music. Bach still sold copies of Part II from his house, though he had put the business of publication in the hands of a Nuremberg publisher named Christoph Weigel.

Part III came out in 1739: it contained organ music (the Catechism Hymns) that will be spoken of in the next chapter. In 1742 the 'Goldberg' clavier Variations were published as *Clavierübung*, and the book is regarded as Part IV of the series. Bach wrote it for Count von Kayserling, Russian ambassador to the court at Dresden, whose harpsichordist, Johann Gottlieb Goldberg, used to play it to him in the long watches of the night when his disease of insomnia descended upon him. The count gave Bach 100 louis d'or, less as payment for the music than as an expression of gratitude for something that never failed to soothe and strengthen him. Now in Bach's time a gold louis was worth 20 thalers of German money, and in these present pages the thaler has been taken as worth about 2s. 2d. of English money. Therefore this recognition of the count's was cash to the value of more than £200. Not for 100 cantatas in his official position did Bach receive so much, or for all the rest of his clavier music put together. But the count was a very wealthy man. He was also a friend of Bach's and a most warm-hearted admirer of him, both as man and as musical genius. He was, in addition, generous by nature. Consequently there is no need to doubt the story.

III

Six or seven years after the appearance of the Catechism Hymns, Bach took six chorale numbers from his cantatas, arranged them for the organ and published them through a music-dealer named Schübler. In connection with this set the power that decrees names for things went to the extreme of inconsequence and illogicality, since it ordained that it should be called the Schübler Chorales. One of the pieces is the splendid setting of the second verse of the chorale 'Wachet auf, ruft uns die Stimme' from the 'Wachet auf' cantata. Another is from the 'Bleib' bei uns, denn es will Abend werden' cantata ('Bide with us, for eventide approacheth'): this, 'Ach, bleib' bei uns, Herr Jesu Christ,' is naturally a nocturne; played correctly, it makes sensitive listeners say, even when they are ignorant of the title, 'That is like a walk on a quiet country road in the twilight.' The other pieces are 'Wer nur den lieben Gott lässt walten' (one of Bach's lifelong favourites among the German hymns), 'Meine Seele erhebt den Herrn' (from a versified form of the Magnificat), 'Kommst du nun, Jesu' and 'Wo soll ich fliehen hin.' There is some evidence, slight and indirect, that a second printing of the set was called for within two years.

IV

The next publication fell in 1747.   It is the *Musicalisches Opfer.*
The German word *Opfer* means, literally and generally, offering,
or gift presented for a purpose.   In the religious sphere it means,
as its counterpart does in English, an oblation, a sacrifice or the
victim of the sacrifice.   When the Peters edition of this work was
provided with an English title, the applied meaning of the word
was taken, and the title was *Musical Sacrifice*!

The work came into existence as follows: In May 1747 Bach
was in Berlin, where Carl Philipp Emanuel then lived.   Hearing
that he was there, the king, Frederick the Great, invited him to
Potsdam.   Bach went to the palace, tried the king's Silbermann
pianos and played a good deal to him.   The king gave him a
fugal subject and asked him to extemporize a six-part fugue on it.
Bach begged to be excused, since the subject was not suitable for
such immediate treatment.   He, however, extemporized a three-
part fugue on the royal theme, and a six-part one on another theme
of his own choosing.   Then he told the king that when he got
home he would write a six-part fugue on his subject and present
it to him with his dutiful respects.   But he did not do this on the
instant.   The task was a big one, and not to be hurried if it was
to be successfully carried out.   On the other hand, if his approach
to the king was delayed, the king might forget all about the matter.
Bach therefore made a kind of preliminary *Opfer*.   He invented
some puzzle canons on the subject, composed on it an extended
canon above a free bass, and wrote out his extemporized three-
part fugue.   He had this music engraved, printed on fine paper
and bound in tooled leather, and sent the book off to the king.
(The three-part fugue is particularly interesting, because it shows
that when extemporizing fugues Bach allowed himself ease and
relaxation in the way of interludes and episodes of a somewhat
old-fashioned character.)   He then composed the six-part work.
In addition, he wrote some more puzzle canons on the king's
subject, a perpetual canon for two solo instruments with clavier
accompaniment and a four-movement sonata for flute, violin and

clavier (Frederick was a flautist), all on the subject. These pieces were printed, and a copy was sent to Potsdam. Frederick certainly remembered Bach's visit and spoke about it thirty years later. But he was no Count von Kayserling: he made no monetary or other gift to the composer. The story of the meeting between king and musician, however, got abroad, and Bach's reputation in Germany was widened and deepened enormously. He was proud of his 'Prussian Fugue,' as he called it. He had a hundred copies printed, most of which he gave away in directions where he wanted this tangible record of the event kept green in the memory. And then he had more copies printed, which he sold at a thaler a copy.

The great fugue, like *The Art of Fugue*, remained until the 1930s among Bach's abstract works—things written not for practical performance, but to demonstrate some aspect or power of musical science and ingenuity. It was then brought forward into the concert world as music for stringed instruments and recorded for the gramophone; and the discovery was made that it is living music—pure and tender of spirit, easy and natural of style, so that it sings a perpetual song, and of an emotion transcendently serene. The same discovery was made at the same time in the matter of *The Art of Fugue*, which also was recorded for the gramophone.[1]

V

In 1747 Bach consented to become a member of the Mizler Society at Leipzig. The society, of which the founder was a local musician named Mizler, existed chiefly to encourage the art in its scientific aspects; but it was of very little significance, and for the eight years of its existence before 1747 Bach had not troubled to accept the standing invitation for him to join it. Members had to present their portrait in oils to the society: this Bach did, and

[1] There is an orchestral version of *The Art of Fugue* by Wolfgang Gräser. The original was published in open score by the Oxford University Press, with a conjectural completion of the final fugue by Sir Donald Tovey.

we owe to the circumstance the portrait we have of him in his sixties. They also had to present the other members of the society with a musical composition in which skill and science should be well displayed. The work Bach presented was a set of canonic variations on the Christmas hymn 'Vom Himmel hoch da komm ich her.' He had it engraved and printed; and with it he ended the line of creative labour he had started nearly a half-century before with the chorale partitas written at Lüneburg. Those partitas record the youth, whose art was a thing of grace and fancy. These variations record the master, old, wise and experienced almost beyond belief, whose art was Miltonic in majesty, ease and certainty, and uniquely inexhaustible.

VI

In the last year or two of his life an intense desire came upon him to bring the art of fugal composition to a point beyond which none should ever take it. He therefore planned a series of fugues on one and the same subject, that went from the simple and normal to the complex and unusual—unusual, indeed, to a degree so extreme that domains were entered which had previously been contemplated only theoretically. He all but finished the work, had it engraved, but died before the printing was done. Carl Philipp Emanuel published it in 1751. Several years passed, and only a half-dozen copies had been sold; and he therefore disposed of the plates as old metal.

When he had nearly completed *The Art of Fugue*, Bach began upon a fugue on three subjects, of which the third spelled, in the German names of its notes, his own name: B (which is B flat), A, C, H (which is B natural). He reached the point in the composition where the third subject was to enter,[1] and then had time for nothing else—except to dictate in his last hours of consciousness one final chorale arrangement to his son-in-law, Altnikol.

[1] Which should have been, or at any rate could have been, the main theme of *The Art of Fugue,* as Tovey has shown.

CHAPTER XII

THE 'CATECHISM' PRELUDES

THE organ music in Part III of the *Clavierübung* is a collection of pieces set out to represent a kind of ideal church service. We have to imagine as the centre of the service a sermon on the catechism. The sermon expounds the five chief elements of the catechism, which in the Lutheran order are the commandments, the creed, the Lord's Prayer, baptism and communion. The service is, of course, the High Service or Celebration of Holy Communion. In this comes the general confession ('We acknowledge and bewail our manifold sins and wickedness'). The confession is not dealt with in the catechism, but it is inseparable from communion, and its place in the service is, of course, before the partaking of the elements, since it purifies the believer to receive them. Bach therefore brings this further subject into his scheme.

Each subject is represented by a hymn, and the hymns are the following: (1) *Commandments*, 'Dies sind die heil'gen zehn Gebot'' ('These are the holy ten commands'); (2) *Creed*, 'Wir glauben all an einen Gott, Schöpfer' ('We all believe in but one God, Maker'); (3) *Lord's Prayer*, 'Vater unser' ('Our Father'); (4) *Baptism*, 'Christ unser Herr zum Jordan kam' ('Christ, our Lord, to Jordan came'); (5) *Confession*, 'Aus tiefer Not schrei' ich zu dir' ('In deepest need I cry to thee'); (6) *Communion*, 'Jesus Christus, unser Heiland, der von uns . . .' ('Lord Christ Jesus, our Redeemer, who from us . . .').

Each hymn is worked twice. The first piece is a chorale fantasia in the cases of Nos. 1, 3, 4 and 6. The tune is present in full, and the accompaniment or counterpoint is a fantasia on characteristic themes. In the case of No. 5 the first piece is cast in the form of fugal preparations—each line is preluded, or 'prepared,' by a short fugal working of a subject created from the melody of the line. It is composition in which the poetical subject changes as well as the musical. The poetical course, which is from the gravity of a sense of sin to the radiant joy of a sense of redemption, is the course of thought in the hymn itself, and it gives the piece in brief the total form and character of a cantata or Passion. Buxtehude among the northerners wrote well in this manner, a fact illustrated by his arrangements of 'Christ unser Herr zum Jordan kam' and 'Durch Adams Fall.'

The first piece of No. 2 is a chorale fugue. The subject is formed from the opening line of the tune, and it proceeds until towards the end (bar 89) the melody of the line appears in full. The fugue is for the manuals only. The pedals have an independent subject, which strikes in freely from time to time; though in one passage it yields its first notes for treatment by the manuals. This piece was nicknamed by certain English organists in the nineteenth century the 'Giant's Fugue,' because, as they said, the pedal subject suggested a giant climbing the stairs and then tumbling down from the top to the bottom. The idea is typical of most realistic or pictorial interpretations of Bach, since it embodies, first a disregard of the positive subject of the piece, which is defined by the hymn, and secondly a metaphorizing of music that leads to very ambiguous issues indeed: thus the giant figures the believer, and if his experience is a 'here we go up and here we go down,' the moral is that the believer simply cannot remain believing.

The second pieces in the set are chorale fugues in the case of Nos. 1, 2 and 4. These pieces are short and in the strongest possible contrast one with another. The piece is a chorale fugue in the case also of No. 6; but this time it is lengthy: it has strettos in the *per arsin et thesin* syncopation; it is very rich in harmony; and (like the long first piece of No. 2) it opens out at the end to the clear presentation of the full melody of the line. In the case of No. 3 the second piece is a presentation of the entire melody of the chorale, to a counterpoint of flowing semiquavers. And in the case of No. 5 it is another working of the whole melody with changing fugal preparations. Here is fine and intricate science, for the fugue subjects are worked in direct and inverted condition, as in the opening chorus of the cantata 'Wär Gott nicht mit uns dieser Zeit.' The music is lofty and unique in concentrated spiritual power among the larger Bach organ chorales.

The high service on ordinary Sundays included the metrical versions of the Kyrie and the Gloria of the mass. Bach therefore brings these two hymns into his present scheme of an ideal service. He writes three chorale fantasias on the three forms of the melody of the Kyrie hymn: 'Kyrie, Gott Vater in Ewigkeit,' 'Christe, aller Welt Trost' and 'Kyrie, Gott heiliger Geist.' The latter is perhaps Bach's grandest piece of chorale music for the organ. He also writes three short chorale fugues to follow the long pieces, exactly as he writes such for three of the catechism hymns. For the Gloria hymn, 'Allein Gott in der Höh' sei Ehr,' he writes two complete chorale fantasias, respectively in G (Breitkopf, No. 71) and F major (No. 66), and a chorale fugue in A major (No. 73). The latter is a little double fugue, the subjects from the first and second lines of the tune.

The high service opened and closed with organ voluntaries. Bach therefore set a prelude at the beginning of his ideal service and a fugue at the end. The prelude is a majestic thing that seems to express a conception of celestial movement and song like that which inspires the relevant passages in *Paradise Lost*. The leading subject is in the dotted-note rhythm. Contrasted with it is a large fugal section on a toccata-like theme, the music of which seems to traverse passages and corridors. Linking the two sections in which the leading subject is worked is an episode that first—by a spacious echo effect—appeals to the imagination as question and response, and then—by a kind of lyrical cadenza—takes the soul of the listener into the world into which so many of Bach's arioso recitatives take it. All in all, this prelude functions in respect of the chorale pieces that follow it much as the *Mastersingers* and *Tristan* preludes function in respect of their operas. The fugue is a triptych. Its subject is the melody of the first line of the hymn 'Was mein Gott will, das g'scheh allzeit' ('What my God wills, be 't always done'), with the first two notes reversed—the G and

B♮ of the tune becoming B♭ and G in the fugue subject. Modified thus, the melody is note for note that of the opening line
of the English tune 'St. Anne,' to which is sung the hymn 'O
God, our help in ages past.' The prelude and fugue are in E flat
major, and are published in all editions of Bach's organ works as
what indeed they are, companion pieces. The prelude is generally
played in quick time; this gives it a jaunty, even flippant air, which
in the end makes it tedious.

At the high service the people communicated after a hymn or
the second part of the cantata had been sung. This, of course,
was after the sermon. Their partaking of the elements took a long
time when their numbers were many, and organ, band and choir
filled the time with music. The music consisted of hymns,
chorale arrangements on the organ and instrumental pieces of the
nature of concerto movements. (It is Forkel, Bach's first biographer, who gives the information that orchestral music was put
to this *sub communione* use, and he had it from Bach's sons: it may
therefore be accepted as true.) In his ideal service Bach represents
the communion music by four duets. These are regarded as
clavier pieces and are published as such (Peters, No. 208). Their
style does not, however, differ essentially from that of many
authentic organ pieces—for example, the 'Herr Gott, nun schleuss
den Himmel auf' of the *Little Organ-Book*, the chorale fugue on
'Dies sind die heil'gen zehn Gebot'' of the present work and
various passages in two parts in the great organ fugues. Moreover, there was at this time a recognized form of organ music
exclusively in two parts, to which the name *bicinium* was given. In
any case, the music of the duets is in keeping with that of the
chorale arrangements here, especially in spirit. And that Bach
regarded them as an integral part of his plan is proved by the
simple fact that they are in the work, since it is impossible that they
got there by accident.

The work is not known as an entity. None of its numbers is
in the regular repertory of organists, except the Prelude and Fugue
in E flat and the first piece on 'Wir glauben all.' The latter is
known in England chiefly from the circumstance that it was

published in an English edition in the second half of the nineteenth century as a piece of free organ music and with that nickname of the 'Giant's Fugue.' The first setting of 'Aus tiefer
Not' is regarded as impracticable, because of its double pedal-
part. The first setting of 'Vater unser,' which follows a symphonic course, is regarded as unintelligible.

The work lacks a name. It cannot be called Part III of the
Clavierübung, on the analogy of Part II of *The Well-tempered
Clavier*, because 'Clavierübung' has itself no life. It could be
called only the Catechism Hymns, even though the arrangements
of the catechism hymns form but the smaller part of the book:
they number twelve, whereas the pieces on other subjects number
sixteen. That title, however, would serve, it being understood
that it covers all the subjects, as the title *French Overture* covers a
suite as well as the overture, and the title *Partita* a prelude as well
as a suite.

Bach and his pupils played the work at a sitting. It is of the
proportions of a mass or a Passion, and so could not be included
as an entity in a modern organ recital. But it can be appre-
hended and played by a performer to and for himself, with rare
musical and poetical pleasure, and with a sense of sharing something in secret with one of the spiritually wisest men the world
has known.

CHAPTER XIII

ORGAN MUSIC

I

It was perhaps in the great decade of the 1740s, when he had practically given up composition for the church and was with-drawing into the heights and solitudes where such works as the 'Prussian Fugue' and *The Art of Fugue* awaited him, that Bach wrote his last three works for the organ. They are things worthy of the decade, whether written in it or not. As preludes and fugues they are perfectly companioned: the prelude is complete in itself, the fugue is the same; yet the fugue rises from the prelude, and the prelude ascends into the fugue, with the natural move-ment of the art which in modern times is called symphonic; and growth or sequence of this kind is rare, even with Bach. Each of the six movements having its own character, the works express the composer's varying qualities, as these were developed in the last phase of his life. The works are the C major (Breitkopf, No. 3), the E minor (No. 5) and the B minor (No. 6).

At Leipzig Bach continued his revision of some of the organ preludes and fugues that he had written during his last years at Weimar or when at Cöthen. (His earlier organ pieces in the free forms he left alone, because in them he had already brought idea and expression as near to unity as was possible: though he did at some period in his life make drastic changes in the brilliant D major Fugue.) He removed the original prelude from the C minor Fugue (No. 2) and substituted for it the prelude now con-nected with it. The original prelude—the Fantasia in C minor (No. 40)—is a lovely, exquisitely intimate piece of music; the new prelude is of symphonic proportions, and it is in a modified con-certo form, in that its contrasted subjects have the character of solo and *tutti* elements. He did not change the prelude of the A minor Fugue (No. 4), but he worked on it again and again until he had

effected a kind of transfiguration of the music.   He also worked a
good deal on two preludes and fugues that for many students
stand 'like sister and like brother' because of their common
spiritual tone of festivity: the C major (No. 1) and the G major
(No. 8).   In the C major it is as if the soul stood rapt, gazing at
the sky beyond which are the celestial regions, calm and secure.
In the G major the spirit dances with joy.   (The fugue subject of
the G major is a version, in the major, of the G minor theme of the
first movement of the cantata 'Ich hatte viel Bekümmerniss.')

These six works are sometimes called the 'Six Grand Preludes
and Fugues,' because in contemporary manuscripts they were
brought together and so named.

II

The toccata of the Toccata and Fugue in F major (No. 17) was
written either at Leipzig or at Cöthen, the fugue at Weimar.
This critical conclusion is arrived at by the following process of
reasoning.   There is no affinity, musical or spiritual, between the
two movements, yet each is characteristic: therefore it is unlikely
that they were conceived as a pair.   The fugue is overshadowed
by the toccata.   The toccata does not need a fugue to follow it.
The toccata is an example of musical virtuosity—virtuosity of the
highest artistic order, yet still virtuosity; while the fugue inclines
to the pure type of chorale music.   It is this quality of the fugue
that causes it to be allocated to the latter portion of the Weimar
period, because at that particular time Bach wrote a set of organ
fugues of the same style and spirit, abandoning the brilliance and
dash of the north German school (as this is apparent in the D
major Fugue) for the restraint and calm of the Italian, which last
was then his chief delight.   The other fugues of the set are the
C minor (No. 2), the F minor (No. 12) and, in modified degree,
the C minor (No. 15), which is known to British concert-goers
by an orchestral arrangement by Elgar.   The Canzona in D
minor is to be added to them (No. 37).

The 'Dorian' Toccata and Fugue (No. 19) differs from the

Toccata and Fugue in F in the respect that the two movements live in the same world. This work was probably written at Cöthen, or in the first of the Leipzig years, for performance on a visit to some town. Its fugue is unique in that a phrase, constructed in Buxtehudean manner in invertible counterpoint, recurs perpetually between the appearances of the subject. (The subject, by the by, is fashioned like the independent pedal subject of the *Clavierübung* chorale 'Wir glauben all': it climbs mightily up the course of an octave, and then descends to the starting-place. Therefore if the semiquaver descent of the 'Wir glauben all' subject represents a giant tumbling down the stairs, the slower, smoother descent here should be taken as representing the giant, or it may be his brother, descending by sliding on the banister rail.)

It occasionally happens that in a work otherwise great and complete an inorganic passage occurs. The passage is inorganic because it differs from the rest of the piece, is inferior and does not develop into a characteristic interlude or episode. Its presence proves that Bach has not finally revised the work—in other words, has not thoroughly finished the composition; for with him to revise was to bring all elements to the level they should be on. Its presence proves also that in an act of original composition he might let anything serve for the time being at a point that was relatively of secondary importance. The matter can be studied by help of the two versions of the organ arrangement in B flat major of 'Valet will ich dir geben' (No. 134). The first version (which is in vol. 10 of the Augener edition of Bach's organ works) is radically defective in the first half-dozen bars of the working of the last line of the tune. The music added to the melody here is such as would be conspicuously poor even in one of the chorale partitas written by Bach at Lüneburg. It is as if a boy were copying from a score which at this point was smudged and had put down something out of his own head for what he could not decipher. Now in two of the great fugues spoken of above such inorganic passages exist. One is the F minor (No. 12), the other the C minor (No. 2); and the defective passages are bars

69–72 and 93–5 of the F minor, and bars 122–39 of the C minor. Their existence proves that Bach never finally revised the two pieces. And this in turn suggests that it was in the last phase of his life that he gave some at least of his time and thought to the task of perfecting his earlier organ works in the free forms; and that death took him from it before it was completed.

III

Death perhaps interrupted the revision he made of his greater organ chorales, since the collection of revised pieces omits some of equal and in a few instances even superior interest, significance and beauty. The collection contains eighteen works. Two on 'Allein Gott in der Höh'' (No. 75, A major, *adagio*, and No. 72, G major, 3–2) are early writing, and it is surprising that Bach did not strengthen the last section of the second of them. The sequence of three arrangements of 'Nun komm, der Heiden Heiland' (Nos. 128, 129, 130) is like the essence of a cantata of the great Weimar days: the exquisite final phrase in the first piece is a direct borrowing from Buxtehude's piece on this Advent hymn. One of the arrangements of 'Jesus Christus, unser Heiland' (No. 109, E minor, with a chromatic counterpoint to the third line) is marked *sub communione*, which means that it was designed in the first place for performance during the partaking of the elements. The F major piece on 'Komm heiliger Geist' is probably the most sheerly brilliant organ chorale in existence. The G major on the same Whitsun hymn instances Bach's calm pursuance of a design, whatever the cost in the way of length and serial uniformity; but at the end he breaks suddenly into a brilliant coda that would have thrilled Tunder, Buxtehude, Böhm and Bruhns—though it would have shocked Pachelbel. The 'An Wasserflüssen Babylon'—a piece of unsurpassed lyrical charm—comes here to its third condition (No. 76). 'Schmücke dich, o liebe Seele' is the piece Mendelssohn played to Schumann, saying when he had finished: 'If I had lost all my religious faith, this thing alone would be sufficient to restore it.' [1] The remaining numbers of the set are 'Herr Jesu Christ, dich zu uns wend' (No. 100, trio), 'O Lamm Gottes, unschuldig,' 'Nun danket alle Gott,' 'Von Gott will ich nicht lassen,' 'Allein Gott' (No. 74, trio, A major), 'Jesus Christus, unser Heiland' (No. 110, chiefly for manuals only) and 'Wenn wir in höchsten Nöten sind' (No. 144). This last is based upon the arrangement of the hymn in the *Orgelbüchlein*, but it is in all chief respects a new composition. This is the piece that Bach dictated—blind and dying—to Altnikol. It is his last recorded musical thought.

IV

It may be that if he had lived longer he would have completed the *Orgelbüchlein*. He planned the book to contain 164 short arrangements of hymns; mostly in forms that kept the chorale tune plain and eliminated free interludes between the lines. The work was artistic in Bach's finest manner and poetic in the way only he could effect. But it was also practical. Bach and his fellow organists made the giving out of a tune a very individual feature of the service. For the chief seasonal hymns, and for the hymns sung during the communion, they put forth the best that was in them. But there was always the danger that their 'preamble' might be too long. Also it might not express in true poetic manner the exact spirit of the occasion. For himself and for his pupils Bach therefore set out to provide for this important purpose what in effect are a series of musical poems—such musical poems in his style as in a free modern style would be called Album Leaves. He did not finish the work. The autograph contains forty-six pieces only. There has been much speculation why he abandoned the task, which was one peculiarly after his own heart. But it is to be assumed that he started it towards the end of

---

[1] 'Schmücke dich,' and another of the 'Eighteen,' 'Komm, Gott Schöpfer, heiliger Geist,' exist in orchestral arrangements by Schoenberg, and the arrangements are recorded for the gramophone.

his years at Weimar.[1]   Going to Cöthen, where he was not an
organist, he had no need for such a set of pieces.   New interests
surrounding him and occupying his attention as a composer, the
Little Organ-Book ceased to attract him.   He therefore put it aside.
At Leipzig things were the same: he was not a church organist.
Moreover, he was busier there as an official composer than ever
before.   He certainly had many organ pupils; but in the portion
of the book already written there was enough for them in this
particular direction.   Thus there was no *occasion* for him to finish
it.   Not until the last decade of his life were his conditions, personal and external, such that he could have set about writing a
hundred and more pieces in this style.   During those years his
pen was as busy as it could be; and if he contemplated finishing
the book, the book had to wait its turn.   It happened that its
turn never came.   It perhaps would have come, if Bach had lived
to be seventy.   We should then have had in full the supply of these
treasures that was originally planned, since every hymn included
in the scheme was suitable for poetic treatment in the *Orgelbüchlein*
manner, as Bach proved by his treatment in cantatas and elsewhere
of so many of them.   There would have been no rehandling of
the old pieces on the lines adopted for the 'Wenn wir in höchsten
Nöten sein,' for those lines are radically different from those of the
book: they represent in most complete degree the form of fugal
preparation, in which every individual line of the tune is preluded
by a short fugal working of a subject made from the melody of
the line—as in the 'Aus tiefer Not' of the *Clavierübung*.   Each
new piece would have been brief, as brief in most instances as the
tune itself, and compact of harmony and counterpoint that expressed the essential spirit of the hymn in the way the music of a
lyrical song expresses the essential spirit of its poem.   But this was
not to be, any more than was Beethoven's tenth Symphony.

[1] On the title-page he names himself as one connected with the court
at Cöthen.

CHAPTER XIV

FURTHER CLAVIER MUSIC AT LEIPZIG

I

THE energy, impetuosity, far-ranging imaginativeness and high romance of much of the music produced at Weimar and Cöthen were qualities that never faded entirely from Bach's art. But from the time he turned forty they modified themselves, until it was rather an elevated, steady glow of the spirit that shone out through his music. The difference was that which is brought about by development and growth, however, and there is consequently no essential temperamental contrast between true Weimar and Cöthen works and true Leipzig ones.

This great truth can be tested by the Chromatic Fantasia and Fugue and the Fantasia and Fugue in A minor (Peters, No. 208, p. 22). The former is well described by Spitta as 'an emotional *scena*.' The latter is a pure *calmato* in its *alla breve* first movement, and in its second it is like a serene yet very strong choric ode. It can be tested further by two A minor clavier works of the earlier period and the Leipzig Fantasia in C minor. The first of the A minors is a *moto perpetuo* fugue (Peters, No. 207, p. 36) and the second (Peters, No. 211, p. 14) is a prelude in applied concerto form and a fugue in 12–16. The Leipzig Fantasia (Peters, No. 207, p. 36) makes use of the then modern Italian technique of crossing hands, with results as charming as anything of the kind in Mozart.

Attached to this Fantasia in the autograph is two-thirds of a fugue (Peters, No. 212, p. 26). The manuscript is a fair copy, which is proof that the fugue was finished. The connection of fantasia and fugue might suggest that the two pieces were written together. But that they may not have been can be gathered from the case of certain of the organ works mentioned above. And the music of the fugue is actually not only less good than that of the fantasia, but less good than anything we know Bach to have done after he entered his twenties. The piece consists of a fugue (on an inflected chromatic subject) which is quite un-Bachian in its stiff crotchet rhythm, and of a free middle section of primitive north German kind, which is remarkable only for a canon-like reflection of the fugue subject in a single line of semiquavers. The manu-script breaks off at the point where the fugue returns: let the fugue as written be repeated, let a cadence be added, and the piece is complete. The union of two such pieces—the first the product of one of Bach's finest hours in the finest period of his life, the other something that may be called student's work—presents us with a problem which it is interesting and profitable to attempt to solve.

The second set of preludes and fugues through all the keys (universally conceived now as Part II of *The Well-tempered Clavier*) was made about 1740. Some of the numbers are revisions of pieces written originally at Weimar or Cöthen. The English Suites belong to the 1720s. These two works, with those in the *Clavierübung*, represent Bach's main activities in the matter of clavier music during his years at Leipzig. The fugues in *The Musical Offering* and *The Art of Fugue* are playable on the clavier, even the one in six parts; but they do not live in the world of the instrument.

II

For performance at the concerts of the Telemann Musical Union —which he conducted for an unknown number of years, but which were for certain in the 1730s—Bach turned a number of his Cöthen violin concertos into clavier concertos. He took the music down a tone: the well-known violin Concerto in E major, for example, becomes the clavier concerto in D major. There are seven of these works, of which the originals of more than half are lost. The only one familiar to modern concert audiences is the D minor, a work that every one loves who has heard it or played in it with understanding. Bach himself thought highly of it, since he worked over it several times, and used its first movement for the sinfonia of the cantata 'Ich habe meine Zuversicht' (1730 or 1731) and its slow movement for the chorus in 'Wir müssen durch viel Trübsal.' The first movement is also the sinfonia in 'Wir müssen.' But he made church use of the E major Concerto as well: the first movement here is the sinfonia of 'Gott soll allein mein Herze haben' (1731), the second is the basis of the alto aria in the same cantata, while the third is the sinfonia of 'Ich geh' und suche mit Verlangen' (1731); and another cantata, 'Geist und Seele wird verwirret,' incorporates an entire concerto—the first and third movements as sinfonias and the second as an aria. The original of this Concerto is, however, lost. The fourth of the Brandenburg Concertos, by the by, is an adaptation of the violin Concerto from which comes the F major number of these seven clavier concertos.

It was in the same period of the late 1720s and early 1730s that Bach made his concertos for several claviers and orchestra. These include three for two claviers, two for three claviers and one for four. The four-clavier work is an arrangement of a Vivaldi composition for four violins. Two of the two-clavier works are from violin concertos: they are both in C minor. Their companion, which is in C major, is regarded as a work composed directly in its existing form. A family tradition says that Bach wrote the three-clavier concertos for performance at home by himself and his sons Wilhelm Friedemann and Carl Philipp Emanuel, who were then in their teens or, in the case of Wilhelm Friedemann, just out of them. The performances must have been things to remember, especially of the regal C major.[1]

Belonging to this important and interesting department of the Leipzig creations is the concerto for flute, violin, harpsichord and orchestra. It was made out of the powerful A minor Prelude and Fugue mentioned above (Peters, No. 211, p. 14), of which the fugue is in 12–16 time, and the slow movement of the organ Trio-Sonata in D minor. It is a work that towers high, and if it were

[1] The C major has been arranged by Adolph Lotter for a string band in ten parts.

known to the concert-going public it might win for itself some suggestive nickname.

During his last years, when he was collecting and revising his Weimar organ chorales, Bach gathered these various concertos together and worked over them again. His Italian Concerto of the *Clavierübung* (1735) was a direct issue of them: it inherited their many fine qualities and exercised these in its one exquisite individuality—much as Bach himself did in respect of all that had gone before him in the art of music.

CHAPTER XV

THE CANTATAS

I

BACH wrote at Leipzig between 250 and 275 church cantatas and some 25 to 30 secular ones. He disposed his church cantatas into five annual cycles; and since a cycle contained 59 works (the number required in an ecclesiastical year), his total production in this department was at least 295. The cantatas that survive number 206, and so not less than 89 are lost. The German Bach Society (Bachgesellschaft) published the church cantatas during the second half of the nineteenth century. They could not publish them in even the most roughly approximate chronological order, because not all the material was immediately available. Thus the number attached to a cantata indicates only its place in the Bach Society's edition.

Bach's standard form became (1) a chorus, (2) a series of recitatives and arias and (3) a chorale. The chorus was on the grand scale. The chorale, which consisted of one verse of the hymn, was mostly in the simple congregational condition. Thus cantata form is like that suite form in which a very spacious prelude or symphony is followed by a set of short dance movements. The chorale, however, was big in effect, though small of size: the full organ accompanied it, and all the instruments of the orchestra.

There is no word from the seventeenth or eighteenth century to say whether or not the congregation joined in the concluding chorale, and modern critics cannot come to agreement on the matter. If the congregation did join in, they must have been confused when, as not infrequently happened, Bach chose to set the chorale in a fantasia construction. Moreover, a simple chorale occasionally appeared in the body of a cantata. If the people sang at the end, they could also sing here. And many simple chorales appear in a Passion.

Cantatas are free, chorale or solo. A solo work is one in which there is no chorus, except perhaps in a concluding chorale; and it may be for one and the same singer throughout. A chorale cantata has for text the material of a hymn. A free one is free only in the sense that it has not such a text. Throughout the twenty-one years in which he wrote cantatas at Leipzig (1723–44) Bach used both free and chorale forms—more of the free in the first ten years and more of the chorale in the second.

A Passion differs from a cantata only in size and in containing a Bible narrative, which is expressed partly by the solo recitative of the narrator and partly by dramatic choruses. It consists otherwise of the same kinds of lyrical numbers—recitatives, arias and choruses—and of the same simple chorales. These lyrical numbers and chorales are all thoughts and meditations upon pregnant elements of the story, just as in a cantata they are thoughts and meditations upon the gospel teaching of the day for which the cantata is intended: or rather they should be that, for librettists often lacked the ability to make the teaching flower into poetry suitable for music; and they had then to fall back on conventional pious ejaculations. When a librettist thus failed him, Bach found inspiration either in the spirit of the day or in the fine essential truth that lay beneath and beyond what the librettist had put down for him.

When into what would otherwise be an ordinary cantata Bible narrative enters, the work is called an oratorio. The Christmas Oratorio is a set of six cantatas thus modified; the Ascension Oratorio, 'Lobet Gott in seinen Reichen,' is simply one. The Easter Oratorio, 'Kommt, eilet und laufet,' has no actual narrative, but its style is quasi-dramatic. A Passion is therefore an oratorio, as the oratorio existed for Bach.

He called a cantata a concerto, because it was concerted (that is, vocal and instrumental) music. The church called it merely 'the music': the reference was to the band of instrumentalists, which in those days was still called 'the music.' in sacred and secular quarters alike.

II

Bach's first cantatas were, naturally, in the form and style of the seventeenth century. Their text was made up of sentences from the Bible, verses of hymns and occasional passages of free reflective poetry. Their musical forms were the arioso for solo movements and a kind of simple partsong (called *aria* then) for the choral. The *da capo* aria for solo song rarely appeared. The recitative was practically unknown in cantata composition until after 1700.

'Denn du wirst meine Seele nicht in der Hölle lassen' is a Leipzig creation from two, perhaps three, cantatas Bach wrote in 1704. One of them had for text a poem in six somewhat tumultuous and headlong stanzas. Other works in the old manner, but characterized by some fugal numbers, are 'Der Herr denket an uns,' 'Aus der Tiefe,' 'Nach dir, Herr, verlanget mich,' 'Gott ist mein König' and 'Gottes Zeit ist die allerbeste Zeit.' All these can be regarded as written before 1710, and so while Bach was still not more than twenty-five. The recitative in 'Denn du wirst' was added to the old material for the Leipzig revival.

In these works Bach begins the mighty and inexhaustible employment of chorales that was to occupy him for the whole of his life. In 'Gott ist mein König,' for example, he uses the chorale duet, which consists of an arioso for one singer and a chorale for another. Here the singers are a tenor, whose text is:

I now am fourscore years. Wherefore should thy servant [Knecht] himself more burden? I will return then, and will die there in mine own place, there by my father's and by my mother's grave (2 Sam. xix. 35),

and a soprano, whose text is a verse of the hymn 'O Gott, du frommer Gott.' The voice sings the tune of the hymn, but the notes are embellished here and there, and certain words are expressed by special inflections. The simple tune therefore acquires a lyrical quality.

A chorale number in 'Gottes Zeit' contains three elements, and could be called a chorale trio. The first is a fugue for chorus on a passage from Ecclesiasticus xiv. 17 ('All flesh waxeth old as a garment: and this is the condition of all times, Thou shalt die the death'), which appears as:

It is the bond of old:
'Man, thou must perish.'

The second element is from Revelation xxii. 20, and it is sung by the soprano:

Yea, yea come, Lord Jesus, come!

The third is the chorale 'Ich hab' mein' Sach' Gott heimgestellt.' But the chorale element is inarticulate. That is to say, it appears without words, being played by the instruments. Bach uses the inarticulate chorale many times in his cantatas, and always with a profound mystical significance.

III

The new form of cantata was established by Erdmann Neumeister, a clergyman-poet, in a book of libretti published in 1700. Neumeister's object was to make possible the use in church music of two expressive elements of opera—the *da capo* aria and the 'dry' recitative (*recitativo secco*, the adjective signifying plain, or unadorned, or declamatory). Each element required verse of a special construction. Recitative required that it should not be cast in a regular stanzaic construction, but had lines of arbitrarily varying length. The *da capo* aria, in which the first section is repeated after the second, required that the text of the first section should be a self-contained sentence, and that the text of the second section should be such, in thought or idea, that the first could follow it reasonably well. The following, which is from Bach's 'Meine Seele rühmt und preist,' illustrates the form:

I. { Now my spirit doth extol
     God's dear grace and plenteous goodness:

II. { And my heart,
      Mind and sense, and my whole being
      Is in Him, my God, made glad,
      Who my Health and Helper is.

III. *da capo* { Now my spirit doth extol
                 God's dear grace and plenteous goodness.

Other librettists at once followed Neumeister's lead. The most gifted was Salomo Franck, ducal librarian at Weimar when Bach was organist there.

Bach adopted the new form shortly after 1710, when he had completed the contract with himself to master thoroughly the old form and to bring it to perfection—all in accordance with his life-long custom. He rapidly extended the scope of the *da capo*, which in its primitive condition has to end its first section in the key in which it begins: that is, in the tonic. Bach made it end in some other key, generally the dominant, or in the case of a piece in the minor, in the relative major. He then so arranged the repeat that at the point where in the first section the music turned towards the new key, it remained in the tonic. The construction thus created is, of course, that of the classical sonata form.

In the matter of recitative Bach rapidly developed a kind of music which, even at its 'driest,' is highly emotional, indeed thrillingly so. And in it he incorporated arioso, which is rhythmical melody, but not formal melody—melody not developed as it is in aria. It is applied sometimes to single words

that are intrinsically significant, and sometimes to entire sentences; and this makes it necessary that in a translated text such
words and sentences shall come exactly in their original places,
since otherwise there is an absurd conflict between music and
text. Early examples of Bach's perfected recitative are in the
cantatas 'Meine Seele rühmt,' 'Gleich wie der Regen' and the
Easter work 'Ich weiss dass mein Erlöser lebt.' The last-named
is a remarkable and conspicuous achievement. It shows the
young composer with the finished instrument of recitative already
in his hand, and his hand already capable with a finished technique. The poem is the longest for recitative he ever set, but the
flow of his particular melodic movement for recitative never flags.
The poet, Neumeister, tells how he has lived within his soul
through Christ's agony, and Bach in his setting tells of the same

experience. The only touch of arioso is at the word 'Freuden-
tränen' ('tears of gladness').

Equally soon, that is, before he was thirty, Bach perfected
accompanied recitative. In this the instruments play music that
is expressive of some idea which illuminates the subject of the
text. The process is metaphorical: the speech is concrete, the
thought abstract, as is proper with realistic or pictorial composition. An example of such music is in the 1714 cantata
'Nun komm, der Heiden Heiland' (No. 61). The text is
Christ's words, 'See thou, see thou, I stand before the door and
knock thereon' (Revelation iii. 20). The accompaniment is a
series of *pizzicato* chords, in crotchet rhythm. The concrete
subject is not, however, what at first fancy it might seem to be,
namely, the *knocking*, for that is a subject that could not be applied
mystically. It is rather the conception of a swinging pendulum

of time, that marks with awful solemnity the movement of creation to the Second Coming.[1]

The music in this piece of accompanied recitative moves from E minor to G major.   The voice ends on an interrupted cadence. The instruments complete the cadence with four chords: musically the chords are like those of the interlude in the working of the first subject of the E flat major organ Prelude, spoken of above on page 140; symbolically they seem expressive of some such thought as 'The elder brother found, the younger melts with fondness in His arms.'

The aria preceding this recitative—a piece for tenor, unison strings and bass—is an ideal example of the *da capo* aria in primitive form, and of Bach's practice of working one musical subject throughout a movement and in all the parts.   The subject itself, which is sixteen bars long, is an example of his extended melody,

[1] The technical device of reiterated chords was used by the north Germans in connection with such subjects as the bearing of the cross. Bach employs it in the organ prelude in C minor he wrote when between seventeen and nineteen (Breitkopf, No. 26) and in the organ chorale 'Erbarm' dich mein, O Herre Gott.'   And Kuhnau employs it in the chorale 'Aus tiefer Not' in his 'David and Goliath' Sonata.

of the kind familiar through the setting of the second verse in the Leipzig cantata 'Wachet auf.'

Komm, Je-su, komm zu dei-ner kir - che

The chorale that ends the same cantata is equally an ideal example of the use of a chorale to finish a work.   It is a portion of 'Wie schön leuchtet der Morgenstern' ('How fair doth shine the morning star'), which is one of the most beautiful and appealing of German hymns and hymn-tunes.   It rises into being here much as the Passion chorale does in the Matthew Passion.

Elementary arioso song is illustrated by two numbers in 'Denn du wirst': the bass solo of the opening and the soprano solo 'Auf,

Denn du wirst mei-ne See-le nicht in der Höl - le — lass-en

freue dich, Seele.'   Arioso trying to make its way to a clear musical form is illustrated by the soprano solo in 'Nach dir, Herr, verlanget mich.'

IV

'Nun komm, der Heiden Heiland' (1714: No. 61) is regarded as Bach's first perfect achievement in the new form.   It is the work he selected for performance on the occasion of a visit he made to Leipzig, when he played the organ at a St. Thomas's Church service.   This was, almost for certain, during his Cöthen period. The cantatas he wrote at Weimar during the time of his official appointment as church composer to Duke Wilhelm are Nos. 31, 132, 152, 161, 162, 163, 182 and 185 for 1714; Nos. 59, 70, 147, 155 and 80 for 1715.   Only a portion of No. 80, however, is of Weimar origin: the first and fifth movements were written for a Leipzig revival in 1730; and so the cantata 'Alles was von Gott geboren' became the cantata 'Ein' feste Burg ist unser Gott.'

Others of the Weimar cantatas were revised at Leipzig, and some were enlarged: thus No. 70, 'Wachet, betet, seid bereit,' received the addition of its present recitatives. The librettists in the thirteen works were Neumeister and Franck. During the nineteenth century the most popular of Bach's sacred compositions was 'Ich hatte viel Bekümmerniss' (1714: No. 21).

These creations of the last part of Bach's life at Weimar have qualities of their own, in the way of beauty, imaginativeness, novelty and variety of form, range of feeling and so forth, by which they can be distinguished from the majority of the corresponding works written at Leipzig. This is because at that time the composer was entirely a poet in his art, spontaneously, unreservedly and radiantly. He is as a youth rejoicing in his youth. His vision enraptures him. His power of expression thrills him. He is as an artist carefree, he knows no weariness, he is not stale with perpetual official duties and he is not pressed for time. He has but one person to consider, himself. He has but one object, which is to capture and apply this energy and inspiration that have come to him along with this splendid opportunity to realize, in adequate performance, what he has created. The latterday student consequently goes through the pages as through the cave of a magician. He alights on this, that and the other treasure and is enriched as Bach himself was when he found them in the realms of gold that were the sphere of his art. Such treasures are the aria 'Lift up your heads on high, Be comforted, ye faithful,'

in 'Wachet, betet' (No. 70); the opening solo of 'Bereitet die Wege' ('Prepare ye the highways, Prepare ye the road, Messiah comes on,' No. 132); and the recitative in 'Komm, du süsse Todesstunde' ('Come, thou moment sweet of dying,' No. 161), in which, at the words 'Then strike indeed, thou final moment's stroke,' realism enters with instrumental imitation of the funeral bells, to awaken feelings that the bells themselves awaken.

It was an excellent thing that here in Weimar Bach had at his disposal good singers and good bandsmen, not boys from a school and weary men from a municipal employment. He had a *basso profondo*, for example, of exceptional character, both musical and intellectual, as is shown by the curious bass aria in 'Bereitet die Wege,' and by the downward‚plunging and mightily ascending melodic movement in the bass recitative of 'Tritt auf die Glau‚ bensbahn' (No. 152), at the words 'The Saviour He is set in

Der Heil-and ist ge - setz   in Is - ra-el zum   Fall   und Auferstehen

Israel for *fall* and *rise* of many.' Having highly capable violinists, he could write in a register rarely ventured on at that time, as in the last bars of 'Wie schön leuchtet der Morgenstern,' where comes a note of which a listener, ignorant of the text, once said: 'It pierces as a star does the darkness of the night!'

In the recitative just mentioned the voice drops a third, and then a tenth, plunging to low D♯ for the word *Fall*. It then climbs a tenth and a fourth for the first two syllables of *Auferstehen*. Spitta remarks that this is 'almost a joke.' Schweitzer condemns it by implication when he says that it represents 'Bach's deter‚ mination to be characteristic.' It is not a joke, however, and the principle at work is one deeper than that of mere characterization: it is the principle of what may be called elocutionary music—the delivery of words with regard to tone and pitch. As operative here, it creates a kind of gesture of the voice, by which Hamlet's advice to the player is followed and the word is suited to the action, the action to the word. The proceeding is therefore natural, and it is adopted by all composers in all kinds of music. Buxtehude, for example, adopts it in his cantata 'Jesu, meine Freude,' when he sends his basses to their lowest notes at the point where the text speaks of 'Erd' und Abgrund' ('earth and the abyss'), by which is meant the inimical powers of darkness. And he adopts it in his organ arrangement of 'Durch Adams Fall ist ganz verderbt,' when he works a falling figure into his pedal bass in his setting of the first line. Bach also adopts it in *his* arrange' ment of the same chorale. But Bach gets more into his figure. He continues it past the element that is expressive of the fall to a cadence that is expressive of the main subject of the hymn, which is recovery from the effects of the fall. And he works his com' pound figure all through the piece. He can joke, even in his church music. But his jokes are grim and confined chiefly to such a theme as scorn of Satan. Thus in verse 4 of the cantata 'Christ lag' he has a kind of humour in his music to the words 'Ein Spott' ('a mockery'). He could not joke in this present recitative, where his theme is the 'stone of stumbling,' 'the rock of offence' that shall cause many 'to stumble, and fall and be broken,' or in the more immediate reference, 'The Child that is set for the fall and rising again of many in Israel.' The profound note for 'fall', and the high ringing notes for 'resurrection,' are elements of expressive oral delivery, not elements merely of material imitation and realism. They are picturesque, but to the end of de' picting something behind the things pictured, and they require therefore in their performer the imagination of the poet and the art of the actor and the orator. Otherwise they are like the actions of a preacher who would crouch in the pulpit when saying the word 'fall' and leap to tiptoe when saying 'resurrection.' More' over, if the passage is on the way to being a musical joke, or if it is just characterization ('at any cost'), similar passages must be the same: for example, this from the late cantata 'Jesu, der du meine Seele':

The wounding,   nail-ing,   crown   and   grave

V

Nearly 200 of the cantatas Bach wrote at Leipzig are on the Weimar model. The rest are based on chorales.

A local librettist, whose pen-name was Picander, served him for many years. He was a poor poet, but he could take directions from Bach and give him what he asked for, whether in a work like the Matthew Passion, in an ordinary cantata or in such a task as fitting fresh words to a piece already written and now wanted for another purpose. He therefore served him well. He is certainly guilty at times of 'exceeding the bounds of good taste,' as it is phrased. Thus in 'Es ist nichts gesundes an meinem Leibe' he writes a recitative that begins 'Now all the world is but a hospital,' and it contains passages like 'The other lieth sick, To proper honour an offensive stench' (which is altered for modern singers to 'The other lieth sick, since proper honour forced him to the ground'). But he is guilty with the Bible, which in the passage Picander had particularly in mind when writing this has the expression 'My wounds stink and are corrupt.'

The chorale-cantata differs in no formal respect from the free. It still consists, in the main, of an opening chorus, a string of arias and recitatives and a simple end-chorale. It differs textually in the respect that its verbal material is the hymn, or something based on or derived from the hymn. And it differs musically in the respect that its first and last movements use the tune of the hymn, and that its middle movements may, if the composer so wishes, use the tune or have subjects that derive from the tune.

Bach began the composition of chorale-cantatas within a year of his settling at Leipzig. His first work of the kind, 'Christ lag in Todesbanden,' incorporates the whole of the hymn, and it employs the tune in every number. But its forms are those of the seventeenth century, and so far as we know Bach wrote no other cantata like this, though in the motet 'Jesu, meine Freude' he came near to copying it.

The text of 'Jesu, meine Freude' consists of the hymn and of verses from Hebrews: the scriptural sentences alternate with the verses of the hymn—now one of the latter, with the tune, now one of the former, set in free chorus. In the cantata 'Wachet auf' (1731) a similar construction obtains: between one verse of the hymn and the next come a free recitative and a free duet. A similar construction appears in 'Ein' feste Burg' (1730), but the cause now is accidental: as already remarked, the work was originally an ordinary cantata entitled 'Alles was von Gott geboren.' It appears also in 'Warum betrübst du dich, mein Herz' (1740 or earlier).

In 'Wachet auf' and in 'Ein' feste Burg' the tune and the hymn are present, and the treatment is that of the chorale fantasia. What Bach wanted to have, immediately after writing 'Christ lag,' was not this, but chorale-cantatas of the modern style and design. But he doubted at first if he could create them with a text each part of which was cast in a strict metrical mould, and he therefore got his librettist to reshape the middle verses of a hymn, so that the material should become suitable for aria and recitative. In Bach criticism the process is called paraphrasing—incorrectly but conveniently. Words, phrases and sometimes whole sentences of the hymn are retained in the paraphrase, and fresh material is added of the kind used by librettists in their ordinary free texts.

The first cantata created on this plan is 'O Ewigkeit, du Donnerwort' (1725: No. 20), and the first recitative is the first paraphrase to be treated by Bach. The verse of the hymn, literally reproduced, runs thus:

> There's no mischance in all the world
> That does not fall at last with time,
>   And is abolished wholly:
> Alone th' eternal has no term;
> It carries on and on its sport,
>   Leaves off its fury never:
> Yea, as my Saviour saith Himself,
> Deliverance from it there is none.

The paraphrase, translated in the same way, runs:

> *There's no mischance in all the world for finding*
> *That e'er-enduring is;*
> *With time it must indeed at last*
> *Pass off and vanish.*
> *Ah yea, but ah!*
> *Eternal anguish has alone no term;*
> *It carries on and on its torment-sport:*
> *Yea, as Christ saith Himself,*
> *Deliverance from it there is none.*

Other cantatas with paraphrases are 'Es ist das Heil' (1731) and 'Was Gott tut' (No. 99, perhaps 1733).

A bold experiment in the blending of chorale and modern cantata form was made in 1728, in 'Wer nur den lieben Gott lässt walten.' Some of the features of the work are as follows:

(1) The first movement combines the chorale-fantasia and the arrangement with thematic preparation. The chorale-fantasia (which, it will be remembered, is a fantasia-accompaniment of the hymn-tune) is on a free subject, and it is in the orchestra. The quasi-fugal prelude to each line, its subject formed of the melody of the coming line, is of course in the voices.

(2) For the tenor aria (verse 3) the original text is paraphrased. The musical form is the two-part, or binary, that is so frequently used in clavier suites. But each part has its own subject: the subject for the first part is derived from the melody of the opening line of the chorale; that for the second is derived from the melody of the fifth line. Thus thematically the piece is like such organ chorales as 'Schmücke dich, o liebe Seele.' And if the tune were present, in a voice or in an instrument, the piece would be a chorale-fantasia.

(3) For the soprano aria (verse 6) the text is a paraphrase, and the musical subject reflects in its first three notes the opening of the tune. The form is again two-part, or binary. Into the second part is brought now the melody of the last two lines of the tune. This is given to the voice, and it is worked alternately

with the musical subject. Thus this portion of the aria actually is a modified type of chorale-fantasia.

(4) For the duet (verse 4) the text is not paraphrased. Again the form is two-part. And again there are—as in the tenor aria —two musical subjects, one for each part, and these are formed again from the melodies of the first and fifth lines of the hymn. And now the full tune of the chorale is present, the instruments playing it being the strings in unison. Thus the piece is a true and proper chorale-fantasia, and it is one of the six that Bach transcribed for the organ and published through Schübler. The chief point to notice about this number, however, is that a verse of a hymn, in its original condition, is sung, not to the tune of the hymn, but to freely composed music.

(5) For the recitatives (verse 2, the bass, and verse 5, the tenor) the original text is retained, and with it the tune. But passages of free recitative are set between the lines, in this manner:

> Think not in heat of thy oppression
> *When flash and thunder crack,*
> *And sultry tempest maketh thee afraid,*
> That thou forsaken art by God,
> *He standeth by in deepest need,*
> *Yea, even unto death,*
> *There with His grace beside His chosen.*
>
> *Thou dar'st not hold it*
> That this one in God's lap remaineth
> *Who daily as the wealthy man*
> *Can live in gladness and in joy.*
> Who is with constant fortune fed
> *Mid naught but pleasant moments,*
> *Must oft at last,*
> *After he hath enjoyed an empty pleasure,*
> *Cry out, 'Death in the goblet!'*

This construction, which Bach generally calls 'Chorale with Recitative,' is an adaptation of the chorale-fantasia: the recitative represents the interludes between the phrases of the tune, in which the fantasia follows its course of development and (like the interludes or episodes in a fugue) makes things ready for the next phrase to enter. Cantatas in which Bach uses it again are Nos. 3, 27, 73, 91, 92, 94, 101, 113, 125, 126, 138 and 178.

(6) In the tenor recitative (from which the above text is taken) Bach handles the tune in a way that is perhaps unique in all chorale music: it is to have each individual line in a different key, the line of keys being (1) E flat minor, (2) F minor, (3) B flat minor, (4) C minor, (5) C major (harmonized in A minor) and (6) G minor. In an insignificant and very early organ arrange⁄ ment of 'In dulci jubilo' (Peters, No. 2067) Bach gives the tune once in G, and then gives it again in D as far as the sixth line, when without warning he switches back to G for the seventh and eighth lines. In the cantata 'Aus tiefer Not' (about 1740) the tune forms the bass of the soprano recitative: the first two phrases are in A minor, the rest in D minor. Johann Walther occa⁄ sionally did things like this; but in general all composers kept a chorale wholly in one key. The progression to the new keys in the 'Wer nur den lieben Gott' recitative is, of course, effected by the recitative passages.

VI

During the first half of the 1730s Bach wrote chorale⁄cantatas according to varying schemes, as indicated above. A set of nine were written (mostly in 1732) on another scheme, which was to keep the hymn unchanged, and to have not the tune, but free music, for the setting of the middle verses. He had already tried out the idea in the vocal part of the duet of 'Wer nur den lieben Gott lässt walten' (1728) and had found it practicable. He was to create in these nine works some of his finest and loveliest arias and a few excellent recitatives. But he did not continue along the line. Instead, he abandoned it entirely, taking up the form with paraphrased middle verses; and this proves that he did not find complete ease and satisfaction in this process.

His chief problem was the moulding into aria of strict and recurrent metrical forms. He solved it so well that the student reading the pieces does not suspect that any problem existed; and this was because he had so many aria forms at command, and because he had such keen intellectual perception of the varying syntactical structure of the verses. The stanza of 'Sei Lob und Ehr,' for example, is a seven-line metre, of which the last is the refrain 'Give to our God the glory.' The tenor aria is cast in the sectional form that Bach generally calls a fantasia: there are four sections, each concerned with two lines except the last, which has the refrain. The alto aria is cast in that modified *da capo* which makes it like the Beethoven sonata form: the first section has lines 1–4, the second has lines 5–7 and the third (a shortened reprise of the first) has a further treatment of 5–7. The bass aria starts with the same form as the alto: lines 1–4 are given to the first section, lines 5–6 to the second, and then, with a delightful casualness, the form is abandoned—there is no proper third section, but instead a resumption of the arioso which in the immediately preceding recitative had been occupied with the refrain.

As in 'Wer nur den lieben Gott' the tune sometimes generates the subject of an aria. This takes place in the soprano number of 'Was willst du dich betrüben,' in the bass of 'Was Gott tut'

Was Gott thut, das ist wohl-ge-than   Was Gott thut, das ist   wohl-ge-than

(No. 100) and in the duets of 'Lobe den Herrn' and 'Nun danket.'

Also as in 'Wer nur den lieben Gott,' the tune is sometimes worked into an aria. In 'Lobe den Herren' the voice sings it in the alto aria, the violin playing the counterpoint, and in the tenor aria the trumpet proclaims it, with the voice now making the counterpoint. (The alto number is one of the Schübler chorales.) But this feature of composition recurs so frequently in Bach's cantatas, whatever their form, that it has no special significance here.

Again as in 'Wer nur den lieben Gott,' phrases from the tune may enter into the free music of an aria. The most moving, most

subtle example of this is in the tenor aria of 'Ich ruf' zu dir, Herr
Jesu Christ.' The phrase concerned is the last of the tune. The

Die uns er - rett't vom Ster-ben

last line of the verse has been sung to the free music, 'Thy
grace, that rescues us from dying,' with an expressive modulatory
treatment (B flat major to E flat minor), in a sudden *piano*, of the
final word ('sterben'), which for beauty and significance is rare
even for Bach; and then the words are unexpectedly repeated to a
decorated version of the chorale phrase. The perception of this

Die uns er-rett't vom Ster - - ben,die uns er - rett't vom ster - ben

element of the tune is like the vision of a flower partly hidden in
a rich undergrowth, or the discovery of the special contemporary
meaning a powerful word has in a passage of Shakespeare.
Another instance, this one as open as the day, occurs in the
soprano aria of 'Was willst du dich betrüben.' The aria is ended,
and the orchestra starts the concluding ritornello. But over the
opening phrase of the ritornello floats, in unaltered notes, and
with the words just sung, the last phrase of the tune. It is now
as though the singer were transported for a moment to the gates
of the mystery that is the spiritual subject of the hymn; and all the
nature of *Choral-Bearbeitung* as an art is made apparent.[1]

Recitative is used in four of the nine cantatas. The *secco* with
bare continuo accompaniment comes but three times. It comes
another three times with the accompaniment of sustained chords
in the strings, and once with an *a tempo* accompaniment of oboes.

[1] Something similar to this exists at the end of the first movement of
'Herr, wie du willst,' which was written soon after Bach went to
Leipzig. And something similar to what occurs in the tenor aria
exists in pedal passages in the *Clavierübung* arrangement in G major
of 'Allein Gott in der Höh' sei Ehr',' the line worked being the first
of the tune.

The two *secco* passages in 'In allen meinen Taten' are very conventional indeed.   They might even be called perfunctory.   But
there is probably a material reason for this.   The aria music seems
to be an adaptation from some work written in the first days at
Weimar, or perhaps still earlier.   Bach had perhaps to produce a
cantata in great haste and had perforce (as happened quite a
number of times) to make use of some old material that was lying
by.   In such conditions he would have only a minute or two for
the recitatives and could bring no thought to their composition.
The passages of dry recitative in 'Der Herr ist mein getreuer Hirt,'
'Was willst du dich betrüben' and 'Sei Lob und Ehr' dem
höchsten Gut' are, on the contrary, expressive poetically and rich
musically, and in every way most excellent examples of this phase
of Bach's art.   The metre does not obstruct the composer in the
slightest degree.

The recitative in 'Der Herr ist mein getreuer Hirt' ('The Lord
is my [faithful] Shepherd') and two of the three in 'Sei Lob und
Ehr'' are each in two sections, one of dry recitative, the other of
arioso.   These likewise are excellent examples of Bach's endlessly
varied art of the arioso.   The first-named, which has for text the
psalm passage about walking through the valley of the shadow of
death, and fearing no evil, is little less than a sketch for an heroic
march.

When considering the fitness of hymn verses for recitative, the
student should bear in mind that specially written recitative verse
is sometimes cast in a strict metre, and that Bach does not object
to it, nor has any trouble with it.   An example is in 'O ewiges
Feuer' (1740), where the metre is, syllabically, 8 6, 8 6 6, 8 6, and
the rhyming scheme is *a a, b b b, c c.*

Seven of the nine cantatas in this batch have already been named.
The remaining two are 'Nun danket alle Gott' and 'Gelobet sei
der Herr.'   The batch can be increased to ten by the addition of
'Gott fähret auf' (1735), because a portion of the text of that
cantata is a hymn beginning 'Mein Jesus hat nunmehr das
Heilandswerk vollendet,' of which four verses are set as arias
and two as recitatives.

VII

Some libretti Bach came across in 1735 pleased him so much that he set nearly a dozen of them in a few months. Spitta had felt in a number of cantatas written in this year the presence of a new poet, because the words expressed 'a deeper and purer spirit' than was usual. Then in 1892 he discovered a little book of texts, written by a Marianne von Ziegler of Leipzig, and published in 1728, and found in the book the texts of these cantatas and of several others. Their numbers are 68, 74, 87, 103, 108, 128, 175, 176 and 183.

Of special interest in the nine works is a deeply moving treatment of scriptural passages in accompanied solo song. The style is the arioso; but it is the arioso with a measure of development and form, and with an accompaniment, not simply of the figured bass of the continuo, but of concerted instruments. These modifications of simple arioso style open the way to music of a quite singular beauty and expressiveness. The piece in 'Bisher habt ihr' is, for example, as lovely as anything in the whole of Bach. The text is 'Ye have in my name asked nothing yet of the Father,' and the subject, which belongs to both voice and instruments, is:

The mood of the music is that essence of the *calmato* of which

Bach alone knew the secret, and in comparison with which all other music of his time seems restless.

This mood, and the power to express it, are of course native to him; but it was his assimilation of Italian art that first gave him full opportunity for their exercise, first in works like the organ Fugue in B minor on a theme from Corelli, and then in works like the organ Canzona in D minor. Here, in this arioso-quasi-aria, and in its companions in other cantatas, what is generally spoken of as the Italian element in his art comes to final flower and fruit. Buxtehude's attempts in the same direction can be examined in such organ pieces as those which he wrote on the Magnificat.

VIII

During the years centring immediately upon 1740 Bach wrote a few free cantatas and a large number of chorale-cantatas. The former are chiefly Nos. 13, 17, 30, 32, 34, 45, 48, 57, 90, 151 and 197. The latter are Nos. 1, 2, 3, 4, 7, 10, 14, 26, 33, 38, 41, 62, 78, 91, 92, 94, 96, 101, 111, 113, 114, 115, 116 ('Du Friedefürst, Herr Jesu Christ,' 1744: assumed to be Bach's last cantata), 121, 122, 123, 124, 125, 126, 127, 130, 133, 135, 139, 178 and 180.

All the chorale-cantatas have paraphrased texts for the middle movements. If a verse of the hymn happens to be kept in its original condition, it is set to the tune of the hymn, though the tune may be richly embellished: this is the case with the soprano solo in 'Schmücke dich, o liebe Seele.' It is rare for even the

odd lines that may be incorporated in a paraphrase to be set to free music: an occasion in which it is so set is the tenor recitative of 'Jesu, der du meine Seele,' where the first two lines and the last two of the text are in the original. Fragments of the tune are often brought into a recitative at the point where in ordinary recitatives the style leaves the *secco* for the arioso. The fragment is melted into lyric melody, as in the following example from 'Ach Herr, mich armen Sünder':

There is, of course, at this late time nothing new in respect of form and style in these chorale-cantatas. But there are striking selections from what is familiar, and some notable combinations. A case in point is afforded by the duet in 'Herr Jesu Christ, du höchstes Gut.' The musical subjects are the first and fifth lines of the tune. These are given out in the subject-and-answer manner of a fugue. After each pair of utterances of a subject the voices continue with florid phrases of free music. Thus the piece is like the thematic preparations in the first movement of 'Wer nur den lieben Gott.' Again: the bass aria in 'Herr Jesu Christ, wahr'r Mensch und Gott' is a mixture of four elements—the chorale-fugue, the *vivace* arioso, the *basso ostinato* and the *da capo*; it contains six sections that are alternately fugato and arioso. Yet again: the bass aria of 'Nimm von uns, Herr' begins with a mixture of chorale phrase and aria that reminds one of the recitatives with chorales in 'Wer nur den lieben Gott'; but after a while the instruments take up the chorale and play it in full against the counterpoint of voice and accompaniment; and one is reminded now of such organ pieces as those on the Magnificat (Breitkopf, No. 124), 'Herr Jesu Christ, dich zu uns wend'' (trio, G major, 4-4) and 'Allein Gott' (trio, A major, 4-4) and in particular of one of Bach's most amazing creations on a chorale, the first movement of the cantata 'Du sollst Gott, deinen Herren, lieben' (1725), in which the chorale is the commandments hymn, 'Dies sind die heil'gen zehn Gebot'.' In 'Nimm von uns, Herr,' by the by, the tune is present in every section but one, as it is in 'Wer nur.'

In the alto aria of 'Ach Gott, vom Himmel sieh darein' a use is made of a detached chorale phrase like that made in the tenor aria of 'Ich ruf' zu dir' and the soprano of 'Was willst du dich betrüben,' but under different conditions and to the production of an impression that is perhaps unique. The text speaks of the incredible intrepidity of blasphemers, false prophets and the like. The voice is pronouncing the words in the free music of the aria, when suddenly, in the midst of the passage, it breaks off and delivers them to the last phrase of the tune, in the original simple notes. It is as if the spirit of the song, shocked and bewildered, fled for a moment into the refuge of the arms of faith.

One more of the many sublimities of these last cantatas may be mentioned. It exists in the first movement of 'Herr Jesu Christ, wahr'r Mensch und Gott.' The composition is a chorale-fantasia, on the chorale of the work. But into its fabric is worked another chorale, which is the Agnus Dei hymn 'Christe, du Lamm Gottes.' The total resultant form is that of the opening chorus of the Matthew Passion, except that there only one chorale is present, which is this same Agnus Dei hymn, though in another version ('O Lamm Gottes, unschuldig'). The hymn symbolizes Christ before the sacrifice. Its presentation is therefore dramatic. But the issue of the drama—its *application*—is spiritual.

IX

A full study of Bach's cantatas could begin profitably with those written at Weimar in 1715 and 1716, because these embody, in freshness, simplicity and variety, nearly all that goes to the making of cantatas. It could continue with the works written around 1732 on original hymns, because these teach what chorales are, what they meant for Bach and how he expressed their meaning.

Study reduced to the finest point could concern itself with 'Christ lag in Todesbanden' (1724), 'Nun komm, der Heiden Heiland' (No. 61: 1714), 'Ich hatte viel Bekümmerniss' (1714), 'Wer nur den lieben Gott' (?1728), 'Ich ruf' zu dir' (1732), 'Schmücke dich' (1740) and 'Du Friedefürst, Herr Jesu Christ' (1744).

Texts and hymns should be studied in the German original, or in precise literal translations. Few translations available for the student preserve the substance of the originals or reflect their spirit.

Tunes should be studied along with their hymns, so that the two together may become part of the 'inward experience' of the student. Otherwise what Bach does with them cannot make the appeal he expects it to make. How readily tunes and hymns can be thus wrought into the consciousness is shown, absolutely and beyond dispute, by the chorale 'O Haupt, voll Blut und Wunden,' which is employed so conspicuously in the Passions that it is called the Passion Chorale. The thrill we receive when this chorale arises in the performance, and the thrill we experience when, knowing it thus, we hear it in such an organ piece as 'Herzlich tut mich verlangen' (one of the several hymns for which the tune was used), is the authentic thrill of chorale music; and it should affect us, in one degree or another, in every work.

CHAPTER XVI

THE B MINOR MASS AND MAGNIFICAT

I

THE Mass in B minor is a work of which little can be said to help the student unless a big space is available and unless the writer goes into all the vast ramifications of the total subject, as these have been traced through the centuries the office of the mass has existed. It is also a work which in performance overwhelms and wearies the listener who brings to the performance no thought of the 'idea' it expresses, but goes as to a musical entertainment: it seems to him an arbitrary string of pieces, and to threaten to go on for ever. But for the listener who is prepared for it the whole work comes and goes as if in a single flash, the hours thought down to minutes (to adapt Cowper), and he is so uplifted and refreshed that he feels that only an immediate repeat of the performance can content him.

The Kyrie and the Gloria were sung at certain times in the Lutheran service in the Latin, and Bach composed suitable settings of them, which for convenience are called 'short masses.' The ideas are consciousness of sin in the Kyrie and atonement in the Gloria. The other numbers of the office were excluded in the Latin, except occasionally the Sanctus. The Credo has for idea the conception of Christ operative in the creation of the church. The other numbers have ideas directly associated with the act of celebration. Bach apparently did not intend to produce in the B minor setting more than a 'short mass'; but the subject so caught him up into itself that he had to change his mind and set the whole. His thought was of the church universal, in contrast with the church protestant that he served in his cantatas and in the five 'short masses,' and he could not leave the task half finished, as it would have been if he had not realized all the numbers in music.

The work is not, of course, intended for use in the church. It is suitable only for concert performance, as if it were an oratorio. Such performance was not possible in Bach's time. Therefore, here with the Mass, as elsewhere with *The Musical Offering* and *The Art of Fugue*, he wrote as an abstract artist, with no thought of gain or glory.

His plan is that of self-contained movements within the grand frame of each major section of the text that admits of such treatment. And as the words of a movement change, so does the music. Thus there is in this Mass a differentiation not known before him, nor to be known again after him until Beethoven produced *his* Mass. The contrasts are indeed tremendous. Mighty choruses are followed by solo songs. Sublimity that can be rendered only by musical architecture is followed by passages of extreme humanity that vibrate with personal feeling. This last is always present when Christ as suffering man is contemplated, as in the close of the Crucifixus:

The end of this movement comes properly at the cadence in E minor; but Bach cannot at once leave the matter: as in a hundred similar conditions in his church music (for example, in the recitative 'Siehe, siehe' spoken of on page 158) he must say what man, Christ's brother, feels and he says it in the freely added further phrase that cadences itself in G major. And from this he leaps into:

This differentiation in the treatment of ideas is very strikingly effected in the Kyrie. The first number is a prayer to God the Father, its theme being:

The second is a prayer to God the Son, with the theme:

The last is a prayer addressed to God the Holy Ghost:

Bach alone has distinguished in this manner the ideas of the Kyrie; and he has done it again, in the Kyrie chorale arrangements of the Catechism Hymns of the *Clavierübung*.

II

Bach's other great work with a Latin text is the *Magnificat*. This is older than the Mass: the general critical opinion is that it was written for the composer's first Christmas at Leipzig—that is in 1723. Embodied in it are some of the results of the long practice he had given himself at Cöthen in Italian styles, forms and (so far as they meant anything to him) moods. This does not mean that the *Magnificat* is after an Italian style. The work is still Bach. It is still of Protestant Germany. Two or three movements are, indeed, as characteristically Teutonic as anything Bach ever wrote, except the cantatas 'Christ lag in Todesbanden,' 'Gottes Zeit' and a few others. But it does mean that the *Magni-*

ficat differs in technique, style and spirit from, say, the typical cantatas of the Weimar period. The differences are partly in the direction of touch and partly in that of immediacy of idea or poetic subject. Thus there is lightness and clarity in the music. And in its local inspirations there is little, if any, of that quality of allusion and association which, as said here in another place, is in music much the same as metaphor is in spoken language.

This makes the work a good thing for students starting to learn about the complete and essential Bach. Another feature that has the same virtue is the shortness of the numbers. The service (vespers on Christmas Day) contained a cantata and a sermon, and so less than forty-five minutes could be allowed for the figured setting of the canticle. Bach therefore could not let himself go in the matter of length, just as in writing his Inventions (or Sinfonias) for clavier students he could not do other than consider what young pupils needed and what they could sustain. The fugue *Sicut locutus est* ('As he promised to our forefathers'), for example, consists of only a double exposition of the subject and a coda on the counter-subject. Everything propounded is adequately rendered, of course, but never in proportions that might weary or confuse a beginner in the essential study of Bach.

A third matter that makes the *Magnificat* particularly instructive for the student is that the text abounds in highly significant words and phrases, which Bach—as was his custom—sets conspicuously, so that they stand up in their full likeness in the music. Such words are *humilitatem* ('lowliness'), *dispersit* ('He hath scattered'), *superbos* ('the proud'), *misericordia* ('mercy,' that is, pity for the miserable and wretched out of one's heart, which is the prime literal meaning of the Latin word). The musical expression of the innermost significance of words and phrases is effected sometimes by the melody which is the subject of the movement, sometimes by a special, self-contained passage, but it is effected always, because the composer was always alive to reality; and in this work it is effected with the precision and energy that the conditions of the occasion required of him.

The *Magnificat* was written originally in E flat major, and since it was designed in the first place for Christmas, it has in several places a kind of sentiment that has a Christmas flavour. We determine what this is, and where it is manifested, by study of Bach's Christmas cantatas and his arrangements of Christmas chorales. Also it had, in its E flat form, four interpolated numbers: the hymn 'Vom Himmel hoch,' which had previously been sung by the congregation; another hymn, 'Freut euch und jubilirt,' which speaks of the holy child in Bethlehem; the song of the angels, 'Gloria in excelsis'; and some lines from a special kind of hymn in which Latin and German sentences appeared— 'Virga Jesse floruit' ('The stem of Jesse hath flourished'). These were all proper to the day. Kuhnau had actually used them as the text of a Christmas vespers cantata. The congregation expected them, holding them to be indispensable units of the service. Therefore Bach, with his perfect sense of the fitness of things, and in accordance with his custom when writing music for his church, made them part of his *Magnificat*. They enter at properly spaced intervals, as chorales do in the Passions and in many of the cantatas. His action seems to have been of his own thinking out: it certainly does not appear that any composer of magnificats before him had ever done anything like it. But since his *Magnificat* was to be sung at Easter and Whitsuntide as well as at Christmas, he did not write these four extraneous pieces in the body of his score: he ran them in on bottom staves, giving directions where they were to be taken up. Subsequently he revised the work, transposed it to D major and removed the Christmas hymns.

The story of the four hymns makes it clear that Bach's setting is Teutonic in conception. This is made clear again by the circumstance that in one of the numbers he introduces the chorale tune which was used for a metrical version of the canticle ('Meine Seel' erhebt den Herren'), and which he had already worked up in an organ arrangement. The tune is a version of the *tonus peregrinus* (the 'stranger' or 'foreign' tone) which since the establishment of the Christian church was used for the psalm *In exitu Israel* ('When Israel came out of Egypt'), and which tradition says was used for that poem in the Temple itself a thousand years before.[1]   The movement into which Bach brings it is the 'Suscepit Israel' ('He hath holpen His servant Israel').   The words are sung by a trio of solo singers.   The chorale is given in the inarticulate form.   In the E flat version of the *Magnificat* it was given in the silver-toned trumpet of Bach's time.   In the version in D it is given by the oboes.   The only accompaniment is the continuo, which is played on the organ.   The strings do not play an accompaniment; nor could they in any such piece of Bach's as this.

For the 'Omnes generationes' chorus ('All generations') a style of perpetual imitation is adopted that Bach learnt first from Buxtehude, in whose music it leads to a sense of what may be called the intoxication of the dance.   For twenty-one bars the subject strikes in at every half-bar, except at two sectional cadences.   At first the imitation is on the octave.   Then it is by the steps of the ascending scale, each entry a second higher: F♯, G♯, A, B, etc.:

After eight of these steps the imitation is alternately on the octave and the fifth.   Then the step-by-step motion is resumed.   The finish of the piece is a brilliant canon five in one, on the unison and octave, at two quavers' distance, rounded off by two harmonic presentations of the subject.   It was in the Weimar cantata 'Nach dir, Herr, verlanget mich' that Bach practised in church music

---

[1] The Arnstadt church council use the term *tonus peregrinus* in their complaint to their organist about his hymn accompaniments. But they do not use it in the above historical sense. This is shown by their following use of the opposed term, *tonus contrarius* (see page 45). Their language can only be an example of the Latin jargon of the time.

this closely interwoven style, in which vigour and concentration of purpose are carried to the final condition of power. Critical interpretations of this movement, like those of Handel's 'All we like sheep,' show how diverse ideas may be, and consequently how performances may vary. Robert Franz considered that Bach's poetic subject was 'Christianity driving the nations against one another in deadly battle.' The music therefore is wild and vehement. Spitta considered it was 'the entrance of an innumer-able company of people moved by one and the same idea.' There-fore for him the music was something 'grave and mighty in its rush and flow.' Herman Roth thought that the music was expressive of 'the profound shadows of a dark and gloomy world seen by a visionary.' The practical musician, proud of his free-dom from such things as poetry, spiritual purpose, metaphysical concepts and psychology, no doubt regards it as a bit of rattling quavers and semiquavers.

There is a grand opening chorus and a similar closing one (on 'As it was in the beginning'). The two numbers have the same subject. There is a chorus in the middle of the work, on 'Fecit potentiam' ('He hath shewed strength'). The chorus 'Omnes generationes' is a sequel to the preceding aria, 'Quia respexit' ('For he hath regarded'). There is the further chorus, 'Sicut locutus' ('As he promised to our forefathers'). All the rest are pieces for solo singers—one a duet, another, as noted above, a trio.

An interesting feature of the 'Fecit potentiam' chorus is the way the word *dispersit* ('He hath scattered') enters amid the text of 'He hath shewed strength with his arm.' It enters first singly, in one

[di] - sper   -   sit, di-sper-sit

voice; then in two voices, with repetitions; then in three, with more repetitions; and so on until at last all five voices have it, and it alone: all to lead into a single abrupt and overwhelming ejaculation of *superbos* ('the proud'):

Music has few such shouts of scorn of a defeated enemy as this. The music then changes to a broad and slow passage for *mente cordis suae* ('in the imagination of their hearts'), which is pronounced twice, once in B minor, once—with that awful solemnity that the major key possesses at times like this—in D major. The duet 'Et misericordia' ('His mercy is on them') is characterized by restless harmonic oscillations for the words *timentibus eum* ('that fear him'): the music goes a score of times into and out of the minor keys of E, A and D.

The Magnificat has for two thousand years lost its original personal significance. It is the song, not of the girl-mother of Christ, but of the church. But Spitta sees in the aria 'Quia respexit' ('For he hath regarded') 'a German picture of the Madonna':

CHAPTER XVII

THE END

I

JOHANN SEBASTIAN and his people lived the twenty-seven years
in their home in the Thomas School, except for a period when
the old place was being enlarged and partly rebuilt. The first
family grew up, became middle-aged; the second kept itself in
manageable proportions by frequent and regular deaths. Pupils
came and went, one or more always resident in the apartments.
Visitors were many, because few musicians entered Leipzig
without calling on the famous man: it frequently happened,
indeed, that musicians went to the town for no other purpose than
to see him. He was always willing to play to them, it might be
for several hours on end. There does not seem to have been
much in the way of social life for the Bachs. Perhaps there were
few people there they wanted to know. Or it might be that there
were few who wanted to know them, because of the continued
unpleasantness between the cantor and the town council, the
University and the rector—to which group was eventually to be
added the superintendent of the churches, Bach's ecclesiastical
head. Always work went on, and on and on, for every individual
in the establishment. And work was about all that such persons
as these wanted.

One son brought disgrace into the home and deep sorrow to the
father. He was Johann Gottfried Bernhard, born in 1715, and
so a year younger than Philipp Emanuel. He became organist at
Mühlhausen, where Johann Sebastian had been for a year before
removing to Weimar. There he made some shady acquaintances.
He got into debt, failing to pay even for his board and lodging.
Then when matters approached a climax he slipped out of the
town and returned home. His father paid his debts, managed to
hush the business up locally, and got him an organist's post at

Sangerhausen, where some thirty years before he had himself won a post, though without the appointment materializing. But Bernhard remained Bernhard. Again he lived an irregular life. Again he got into debt. And again he ran away, this time from his family as well as from his responsibilities. Johann Sebastian begged the authorities at Sangerhausen to be lenient. He assured them that he had done all a father could to keep his son straight, and said that he felt that if he had another opportunity he would succeed in his endeavours. He asked them for help in the search for the young man and promised to pay his debts as soon as he had been able to check them. Bernhard was in the end found at Jena, where he had entered himself in the University as a student of law. But a few months later he died, shortly after his twenty-fourth birthday.

Not long before Bernhard's death a Bach came into the household whose name was Johann Elias. He hailed from Schweinfurt, in Franconia, where a first cousin of Johann Sebastian's had settled. This cousin being his father, Johann Elias was first cousin once removed, which counted as a very near relationship with the Bach clan. He was thirty-three, and established as a professional musician; yet he came here to study. He remained a number of years, and Johann Sebastian so admired and appreciated him that he put the education of his younger children in his charge.

Many letters written by Johann Elias have survived. We learn from one of them that in August 1741 Anna Magdalena was ill, and that the family thought Johann Sebastian, who was from home, ought to come back at once. They did not know what was the matter with her. But we do. She was in the third month of the pregnancy that resulted in her thirteenth child, after the break of four years in her serial child-bearing, and the condition did not suit her, especially in the August air of Leipzig. We learn further from Johann Elias that Anna Magdalena loved flowers, and that her great joy was her little garden, to the care of which she gave all her spare time.

In October 1748 Johann Elias sent his cousin a small cask of wine from Schweinfurt. Writing to acknowledge the gift, Johann Sebastian said that the cask had leaked on the journey, and only about a quart of the contents remained. He remarked that he regretted one single drop 'of such a noble gift of God should be wasted.' Then in a postscript he asked his cousin not to do what he had said he would, which was to repeat the gift. He explained that the various charges he had had to pay on this first cask—for freight, for delivery to the house, to the inspector, to the town excise and to the general excise—amounted to more than 3*s*.; which, he said, 'makes of it too expensive a present.' And this it certainly did, since at this time a quart of good wine could be bought for about 5*d*.

The first marriage in the family took place in 1744, when Philipp Emanuel, aged thirty, was married in Berlin. Wilhelm Friedemann, though older than Philipp Emanuel by four years, did not marry until 1751, when he was forty-one. The second marriage in the family, and the only one from the home, took place in January 1749: it was of Elisabeth Juliane Friederica, eldest daughter of the second family, to Christoph Altnikol, organist at Naumburg. The Altnikols had a son the following October. They named him Johann Sebastian. But he died before the end of the year.

II

Bach got about freely until 1747. That was the year of his meeting with King Frederick II at Potsdam, and that visit to Prussia seems to have been his last excursion. In the spring of 1749 it became apparent that his health was breaking up. In the May he had a paralytic stroke. At once the town council selected his successor, one Gottlob Harrer. But Bach made a partial recovery. His mind was unaffected. He went on with his revision of his Weimar organ works. He even took part in a dispute with a rector named Biedermann who, like his own Leipzig rector years earlier, had spoken disparagingly of music and musicians. Indeed, he brought his *Phoebus and Pan* to performance again, with alterations in the text to make it point more exactly to this new conflict of opinions. He also went on with his work on *The Art of Fugue* and with his supervision of the engraving of that vast and intricate work.

Towards the end of the summer his eyes, which had been ailing for a long while, grew weaker, until at last they ceased to function altogether. Now Bach was blind. At the end of the year an eye specialist operated. The operation was unsuccessful. The patient sat in a darkened room. The drugs he had to take in connection with the operation depressed him. But still his mind worked well, and he dictated the music he could not write. Lissgen (as Elisabeth's family name was) came over with her husband from Naumburg, and Altnikol acted as amanuensis, among the pieces he wrote down being the 'Jesus Christus, unser Heiland' and the 'Komm, Gott Schöpfer, heiliger Geist' of the 'Eighteen' chorale preludes. On 18th July Bach suddenly said 'I can see!' But the restored sight did not last long. He took to his bed, dictated one more piece of music to Altnikol, suffered a second stroke and died. He died at a quarter to eight, on Tuesday 28th July 1750, and was buried at St. John's Church on the 31st.

That last piece of music was the new treatment of the little *Orgelbüchlein* piece, 'Wenn wir in höchsten Nöten sein' (When we are in our deepest need And know not where to turn for aid'), which is mentioned above, on page 147. The tune was associated with another hymn, 'Vor deinen Tron tret' ich hiermit' ('Before Thy throne herewith I walk'). It was this hymn that occupied Bach's mind in his closing hours. And so he told his son-in-law to put its title at the head of the piece. Always, always, Bach knew the truly fitting chorale for a thought, an event, a condition or a situation, in cantata, Passion or motet. And here, in the final issue of his earthly life, his knowledge, his genius and his poetic susceptibility served him faithfully and to perfect purpose.

The town council met on the 29th and settled Harrer's appointment. No expression of regret was made and no vote of condolence was passed. No memorial was set up in school or church. Rector Ernesti did not refer to the dead cantor in his rectorial speech the next year. The periodical musical press had a few obituary lines of a conventional character. Telemann, however, was moved to express himself in a sonnet, which runs thus in literal translation:

> Let other lands speak on and praise their virtuosi,
> Who win themselves renown by instrumental art:
> Likewise on German soil 'tis to be found by asking
> How we do deem ourselves for plaudits fit no less.
> Bach, pale in death! thy organ peal alone did bring thee
> That precious word of merit, *Great*, most long while since:
> And what the art thy quill bore to the page of music,
> That was with loftiest joy, oft too with envy, viewed!
>
> So sleep! Thy name is free from downfall, free indeed:
> The pupils of thy brood, their pupils in their file,
> Do for thy head prepare posthumous crowns of glory;
> Also thy children's hands their ornament set there,—
> Yea truly, what can make thee precious over all
> In one all-worthy son Berlin to us revealeth.

Great organist, great composer, great teacher, great father, says Telemann, in capable accents and in earnest tones; but assured of continuing fame not as a performer, naturally, nor as a composer, but as a teacher, and especially as the father of notable sons. Hence his reflection of the psalmist's declaration, 'As arrows are in the hand of a mighty man, so are the children of the youth. . . . Happy is the man that hath filled his quiver with them.' But Telemann was mistaken, along with the rest of his generation. It is not the sons who keep the father's name alive. It is the father who keeps theirs alive; for without him none, not even the one eminent then in Berlin, would be much more than an item in the general historical record of the art.

In 1885 Leipzig put a tablet to Bach's memory on the wall of St. John's Church near where his grave was supposed to be, its exact position not being known. A monument to him had been erected at Leipzig in 1843, through the efforts of individuals like Mendelssohn and Schumann; and at its inauguration had appeared a forgotten grandson of Johann Sebastian in the person of Wilhelm Friedrich Bach, son of the Bückeburg Bach, aged then eighty-four—the master's last male descendant.   On October 1894, during some building work to the church, old graves were disturbed and coffins were opened to see if one might contain the remains of Bach.   The search was successful.   A skeleton was found which was proved scientifically to be his.   It was coffined afresh and put in a vault beneath the altar.

III

Bach made no will.   He therefore gave no thought to his wife's financial position after his death: if he had, and if he had willed his estate to her, she would possibly have escaped life in an alms-house and a pauper's grave.   The eldest sons, Wilhelm Friede-mann and Philipp Emanuel, descended and claimed as theirs by gift some of the more valuable items of the estate.   Chief of these was the vast accumulation of manuscripts, which included the whole of their father's works.   They did not want these for sentimental reasons.   They had, indeed, but little respect for the music.   They wanted them for commercial ones.   Possession of an original manuscript carried with it the right to make and sell copies.   The demand for Bach's music was not great, but there was still some demand, and all through their lives the two men found it profitable to supply it, though towards the end Wilhelm Friedemann sold the autographs and so brought about the loss of many of them.   Indeed, Emanuel's wife and daughter carried on this business after his death.   And in the second or third year of her widowhood Anna Magdalena got about £4 5s. from the town council, partly as a charitable contribution, but partly as a return for her handing to them a few scores that had remained in her possession.

Johann Christian, son of the second marriage, claimed three claviers as his by gift.   The two elder sons were suspicious, but they gave way when the rest of the family supported the boy.

The estate, less what was thus taken from it, was valued for probate at about £126. The widow received one-third. The nine children each received a ninth of the balance. The inventory is full of interesting particulars. A dozen black leather chairs were valued at 4s. 6d. the lot, a writing-table at 6s. 6d., a cloth coat at 13s. and a mourning coat at 11s. There were a silver court sword and a court coat of silk, valued respectively at £1 6s. and 17s. 6d. No other of the dead man's garments appear. A quantity of things in silver plate (candlesticks, cups, coffee pots and the like) were set down at £22. There was a snuff-box of agate, set in gold, priced at £4 7s.: this would be a gift from some nobleman. The clavier that was priced at £8 14s. must have been a fine instrument. Four other claviers totalled £18 10s. Two lute-harpsichords (Bach's invention) were worth £3 5s. each. Ten stringed instruments were worth £4 5s. Six tables were itemed at 4s. 6d. the lot, and seven wooden bedsteads (for which there were no sheets or blankets) at 6s. About eighty volumes or theological literature were valued at £4 3s. 6d. Cash in hand amounted to £30. The only investment was a share in a mine, worth £6 10s. A sister-in-law owed on bond the sum or £6 6s.

When Bach died, Wilhelm Friedemann, aged forty, was working at Halle; Carl Philipp Emanuel, aged thirty-six, in Berlin and Johann Christian Friedrich, aged eighteen, at Bückeburg. The household contained two middle-aged women, Anna Magdalena, forty-nine, and Catharina Dorothea, forty-two (one wonders how they got on together); Gottfried Heinrich, twenty-six, the idiot son; Johann Christian, fifteen, known in history as the Milanese or English Bach; Johanna Carolina, thirteen; and Regine Susanna, eight. These daughters all died unmarried. It seems that the Altnikols took Gottfried Heinrich back to Naumburg with them. Philipp Emanuel took Johann Christian to Berlin. Thus when the family moved from the rooms in the Thomas School it consisted of four females—two elderly women and two children. Anna Magdalena announced that she would not marry again, but would devote herself to bringing up the two

girls. Guardians were appointed to help her. But the arrangement did not last long. The widow went into the almshouse, on
the way to her pauper's grave. Catharina Dorothea may have
got work in the town. The girls may have passed into the sole
charge of their guardians. But no one knows anything of this
matter.

Thus Bach was. And at Leipzig his music was as if it had
never been, for his successors put it aside, except for an occasional
performance of a motet. It was chiefly in Berlin that it was used,
mostly by teachers; and some of these loved and cherished it.
There the Austrian diplomat, Baron van Swieten, encountered it,
was drawn to it and first filled his friend Mozart with admiration
for it before striving to make the amateurs of Vienna accept it.
There among the teachers was Carl Friedrich Zelter, who taught
it to every one of his pupils for sixty years, introduced it to his friend
Goethe, who uttered the first wise remarks about it, and finally to
one of his latest pupils, Mendelssohn, from whom proceeded the
great Bach revival of the nineteenth century.

The revival is not yet complete, since the music still waits for
the discovery of the right way to perform it. But there are English
music-lovers who were caught up in the spirit by it in their first
days, when they did not know how to pronounce the composer's
name, and could not have said whether he was alive or dead.
They have lived with it unbrokenly all their lives (but in private,
not in public), finding more and more contentment in it as the
years pass, until in their old age, when so many things fade, it
becomes very nearly all they want in the way of music, and is
certainly the kind they hope to discover in whatever next world
they may be destined for.

APPENDICES

APPENDIX A

CALENDAR

(Figures in brackets denote the age reached by the person mentioned during the year in question.)

Year	Age	Life	Contemporary Musicians
1685		Johann Sebastian Bach born March 21, at Eisenach, son of Johann Ambrosius Bach (40), a violinist and town musician.	Handel born, Feb. 23; Scarlatti (D.) born, Oct. 26. Abaco aged 10; Albinoni 11; Ariosti *c*. 25; Blow 37; Böhm 24; Bononcini 13; Buxtehude 48; Caldara *c*. 15; Campra 25; Charpentier *c*. 50; Clarke *c*. 25; Corelli 33; Couperin 17; Croft 7; Desmarets 23; Destouches, *c*. 13; Durante 1; Eccles *c*. 22; Fux 25; Geminiani 5; Keiser 11; Kerl 57; Kuhnau 25; Lalande 28; Legrenzi *c*. 60; Lotti 18; Lully 53; Muffat (sen.) *c*. 40; Pachelbel 32; Pepusch 18; Purcell 26; Rameau 2; Reinken 62; Scarlatti (A.) 26; Steffani 31; Telemann 4; Vivaldi *c*. 15; Walther 1.
1686	1		Marcello born, July 31/ Aug. 1; Porpora born, Aug. 19.
1687	2		Graupner born, Feb.; Lully

Year	Age	Life	Contemporary Musicians
			(55) dies, March 22; Senaillé born, Nov. 23.
1688	3		Fasch (J. F.) born, April 15; Foggia (84) dies, Jan. 8.
1689	4		
1690	5		Legrenzi (c. 65), dies, July 26; Muffat (jun.) born, April; Vinci born.
1691	6		d'Anglebert (56) dies.
1692	7		Tartini born, April 8; Vitali (G. B.) (c. 48) dies, Oct. 12.
1693	8		Kerl (65) dies, Feb. 13; Locatelli born; Sammartini (G.) born (approx.).
1694	9	Death of B.'s mother, née Elisabeth Lämmerhirt (50), May 3.	Daquin born, July 4; Leo born, Aug. 5.
1695	10	Death of B.'s father, Johann Ambrosius Bach (50), Feb. 24. B. goes to live at Ohrdruf with his eldest brother, Johann Christoph (24), under whom he studies music.	Greene born; Purcell (36) dies, Nov. 21.
1696	11	Makes astonishing progress in music and goes to school at the Lyceum.	
1697	12	Has become too advanced for his brother's tuition.	Leclair born, May 10; Quantz born, Jan. 30.
1698	13	Elias Herda becomes cantor at the Lyceum, Jan., and teaches B.	Francœur born, Sept. 28.
1699	14	Is now a very versatile musician and takes part as soprano in his brother's church services.	Hasse born, March 25.

Year	Age	Life	Contemporary Musicians
1700	15	His brother's family increasing, B. is obliged to earn his own living. He becomes a singer at St. Michael's at Lüneburg.	Strungk (60) dies, Sept. 23.
1701	16	His voice breaks, but he is retained as violinist. He hears Böhm (40) at St. John's Church, (?) takes organ lessons from him and composes for the organ.	Graun born, May 7; Sammartini (G. B.) born.
1702	17	Walks more than once to Hamburg to hear Reinken (79) play and visit the Opera; also goes to Celle, where he hears the French court band.	
1703	18	Leaves Lüneburg for Weimar, where he is engaged as violinist in Duke Johann Ernst's orchestra, April 8. Leaves Weimar for Arnstadt, where he becomes organist at the New Church, Aug, 14.	
1704	19	Easter Cantata composed.	Biber (60) dies; Charpentier (c. 60) dies, March; Muffat (sen.) (c. 50) dies, Feb. 23.
1705	20	Is granted four weeks' leave to go to Lübeck, where he meets and hears Buxtehude (68), Oct. He much outstays his leave.	
1706	21	Return to Arnstadt, Feb. He is summoned before the consistory to answer for his prolonged absence, also for	Galuppi born, Oct. 18; Martini born, April 24.

Year	Age	Life	Contemporary Musicians
		his elaborate manner of accompanying the chorales. Another summons, Nov., for making music in church with his cousin, Maria Barbara Bach (22). Organ music composed.	
1707	22	Appointed organist at the church of St. Blasius, Mühlhausen, June 15. Marriage to Maria Barbara Bach (23), Oct. 17.	Buxtehude (70) dies, May 9; Clarke (*c.* 47) dies, Dec. 1.
1708	23	Cantata, *Gott ist mein König* (No. 71), Feb. B. leaves Mühlhausen and returns to Weimar as court organist and chamber musician to Duke Wilhelm Ernst of Saxe-Weimar (46). His kinsman, Walther (24), is town organist there. First child, Catharina Dorothea, born, Dec. 29.	Blow (60) dies, Oct. 1.
1709	24	Visit to Mühlhausen with Walther (25) to inaugurate the new organ at St. Blasius's. Much organ music composed.	Benda (F.) born, Nov. 25; Colasse (60) dies, July 17; Duni born, Feb. 9; Richter (F. X.) born, Dec.
1710	25	Son, Wilhelm Friedemann, born, Nov. 22.	Arne born, March 12; Avison born (approx.); Boyce born, Feb. 7; Pasquini (73) dies, Nov. 22; Pergolesi born, Jan. 3.
1711	26		Holzbauer born; Terradellas born, Feb.
1712	27		Zachau (49) dies, Aug. 14.
1713	28	Visit to Halle, end of year,	Corelli (60) dies, Jan. 10;

Year	*Age*	*Life*	*Contemporary Musicians*
		to test a new organ; he offers himself for the post of organist vacated by the death of Zachau, Handel's (28) former master, but the salary is too small.	Dauvergne born, Oct. 4; Krebs born, Feb. 10.
1714	29	Second son, Carl Philipp Emanuel, born, March 8. Cantata, *Ich hatte viel Bekümmerniss* (No. 21), June. Visit to Cassel, end of year, at the invitation of the hereditary prince (38), later King Frederick, of Sweden.	Gluck born, July 2; Homilius born, Feb. 2; Jommelli born, Sept. 10
1715	30	Third son, Johann Gottfried Bernhard, born, May 11. Cantatas: *Himmelskönig, sei willkommen* (No. 182), Palm Sunday; *Der Himmel lacht* (No. 31), Easter; *Komm, du süsse Todesstunde* (No. 161); *Ach, ich sehe* (No. 162); *Bereitet die Wege* (No. 132), etc.	Wagenseil born, Jan. 15.
1716	31	Secular cantata, *Was mir behagt*, performed on the birthday of Duke Christian of Saxe-Weissenfels, Feb. 23. B., with Kuhnau (56) and other organists, plays at the opening of the new organ at Halle, May. On the death, Dec. 1, of Drese (72), the conductor of the court orchestra, the post is given to his son in preference to B., who decides to leave as soon	

Year	Age	Life	Contemporary Musicians
		as possible. Church Cantatas Nos. 70 and 155.	
1717	32	Church Cantata No. 160, Easter. Visit to Dresden, where he plays the organ at court, autumn. A contest with Marchand (48) is arranged, but the French organist has left hastily. B. put under arrest by the duke for wishing to accept an appointment at Cöthen, Nov. 2. He is released and reluctantly allowed to resign, Dec. 2. Visit to Leipzig to test the new organ at St. Paul's Church, Dec. 16.	Nichelmann born, Aug. 13; Stamitz (J. W.) born, June 19.
1718	33	In the service of Prince Leopold of Anhalt-Cöthen (24), B. finds only a small orchestra and an inferior organ, but a more dignified and agreeable position. Birthday cantata, *Durchlaucht'ster Leopold*.	Vitali (T. A.) (*c.* 53) dies (approx.).
1719	34	Visit to Halle, where he wishes to meet Handel (34), who, however, has just left. Clavier and chamber music composed.	
1720	35	On returning from a visit to Carlsbad with Prince Leopold, July, B. finds that his wife, *née* Maria Barbara Bach (36), was buried July 7. Visit to Hamburg, autumn, where he hopes to obtain the organistship at St. Jacob's	Agricola (J. F.) born, Jan. 4.

Year	Age	Life	Contemporary Musicians
		Church. Though he cannot wait for the contest, the praise of Reinken (97) gains him the offer of the post. He then decides to decline it. Mattheson (39) severely criticizes the Church Cantata No. 21.	
1721	36	Six Concertos for orchestra dedicated to the Margrave Christian Ludwig of Brandenburg (44). B. marries his second wife, Anna Magdalena Wilcken (21), Dec. 3.	Kirnberger born, April.
1722	37	*Clavierbüchlein* for Anna Magdalena Bach (22). Part I of *Das wohltemperierte Clavier* finished. On the death of Kuhnau (62) B. applies for the post of Cantor at St. Thomas's in Leipzig.	Benda (G.) born, June 30; Kuhnau (62) dies, June 25; Nardini born; Reinken (99) dies, Nov. 24.
1723	38	Performance of St. John Passion at St. Thomas's Church in Leipzig, March 26, as a trial of his skill. B. is unanimously elected cantor, May 13. Cantata, *Die Elenden sollen essen* (No. 75), performed in St. Nicholas's Church, May 30. *Magnificat* produced, Dec. 25. Motet, *Jesu, meine Freude.* Cantatas Nos. 22, 24, 40, 63, 64, 76, 119, 186, 194.	Gassmann born, May 4; Telemann (42) competes with B. at Leipzig.
1724	39	Finds St. Thomas's School in a deplorable condition, which nothing is done to	Theile (78) dies, June.

Year	Age	Life	Contemporary Musicians
		improve. Church Cantatas Nos. 4, 12, 16, 23, 65, 69, 81, 83, 153, 154, 165, 172, 179.	
1725	40	*Notenbuch* for Anna Magdalena Bach (25). A large number of church cantatas. Secular cantata, *Der zufriedengestellte Aeolus*, composed for the University.	Krieger (J. P.) (76) dies, Feb. 6; Scarlatti (A.) (66) dies, Oct. 24.
1726	41	Finds it difficult to secure adequate performances at St. Thomas's and at the other Leipzig churches under his supervision. First Partita for clavier published. Secular cantata, *Vereinigte Zwietracht* and church cantatas.	Krebs (13) and Nichelmann (9) become B.'s pupils. Lalande (69), dies, June 18; Philidor born, Sept. 7.
1727	42	Visit to Hamburg. Funeral ode performed at the memorial ceremony for the Electress Christiane Eberhardine of Saxony, Oct. 17. A number of church cantatas.	Croft (49) dies, Aug. 14; Traetta born, March 30.
1728	43	On the death of Prince Leopold of Anhalt-Cöthen (32) B. compiles music for the funeral from portions of the St. Matthew Passion, which is in progress. His earlier patron, Duke Wilhelm Ernst (66) at Weimar has also died and B. resumes relations with that court, now	Hilier (J. A.) born, Dec. 25; Marais (72) dies, Aug. 15; Piccinni born, Jan. 16; Steffani (74) dies, Feb. 12.

Year	Age	Life	Contemporary Musicians
		under Duke Ernst August (40).	
1729	44	First performance of St. Matthew Passion, Good Friday (April 15). Quarrel with the council of St. Thomas's, who admit un- musical scholars that have not been examined by B., Easter. During an illness, June, B. sends Wilhelm Friedemann (19) to Halle to invite Handel (44), who is unable to come. B. ap- pointed conductor of the Telemann Musical Society. Motet, *Der Geist hilft unsrer Schwachheit auf,* composed for the memorial service for Johann Heinrich Ernesti the Rector of St. Thomas's.	Monsigny born, Oct. 17 Sarti born, Dec. 1.
1730	45	Quarrel with the St. Thomas council reaches its height, Aug. B. addresses to the council a memoran- dum concerning the require- ments and decline of church music. Conditions at St. Thomas's much improved by the appointment of Johann Matthias Gesner (40) as rector. Various church cantatas composed.	Senaillé (43) dies, Oct. 15.
1731	46	Visit to Dresden, Sept., where he makes friends with Hasse (32) and his wife, Faustina Bordoni (38).	Cannabich born.

Year	Age	Life	Contemporary Musicians
		Clavierübung, Part I, published. Church cantatas Nos. 29, 84 and many others.	
1732	47	Cantata, *Froher Tag*, performed at the opening of the rebuilt Thomas School, June 5. Birth of son, Johann Christoph Friedrich, June 23. Visit to Cassel to examine an organ, Sept. Church cantatas and orchestral chamber music composed.	Haydn born, March 31/April 1.
1733	48	Visit to Dresden, July, where he presents the Elector Frederick Augustus of Saxony (37) with the *Kyrie* and *Gloria* of the B minor Mass, with a petition for the title of court composer, which is for the moment ignored. Church and secular cantatas composed.	Couperin (65) dies, Sept. 12.
1734	49	First performance of the Christmas Oratorio during the Christmas season.	Gossec born, Jan. 17; Sacchini born, July 23.
1735	50	Son, Johann Christian, born, Sept. 5. *Clavierübung*, Part II, published. About 30 church cantatas composed and composition of organ music, neglected since Weimar, resumed.	Eccles (*c.* 72) dies, Jan. 12; Krieger (J.) (83) dies, July 18.
1736	51	Dispute between B. and the rector, Johann August Ernesti (29), over the appoint-	Anfossi born (approx.); Caldara (*c.* 66) dies, Dec. 28; Fasch (C. F. C.) born,

Year	*Age*	*Life*	*Contemporary Musicians*
		ment of prefects, summer. Conditions at the school grow worse. B. is appointed court composer by the Elector of Saxony, Nov., before whom he brings the quarrel. B. plays the new organ at the Frauenkirche in Dresden, Dec. 1. B. edits and contributes to Schemelli's (*c.* 58) *Musicalisches Gesangbuch.* About 30 church cantatas written.	Nov. 18; Pergolesi (26) dies, March 17.
1737	52	Scheibe's (29) attack on B. appears in *Der critische Musicus*, May 14. Secular cantata, *Angenehmes Wiederau*, Sept.	Mysliveček born, March 9.
1738	53	Quarrel with Ernesti (31) settled by a visit of the Elector of Saxony, April; the council grow more respectful towards B. Carl Philipp Emanuel Bach (24) enters the service of the Crown Prince Frederick of Prussia (26) in Berlin. Church cantata No. 30. Agricola (J. F.) (18) becomes B.'s pupil.	Murschhauser (75) dies, Jan. 6.
1739	54	Death of his son, Johann Gottfried Bernhard (24), at Jena, where he studied law, May 27. *Clavierübung*, Part III, published. Kirnberger (18) becomes a pupil of B.	Dittersdorf born, Nov. 2; Keiser (65) dies, Sept. 12; Marcello (53) dies, July 24; Rust born, July 6; Wanhal born, May 12.
1740	55	B.'s eyesight, which has for	Böhm (79) dies (approx.);

Year	*Age*	*Life*	*Contemporary Musicians*
		some time deteriorated, is now seriously impaired.	Lotti (73) dies, Jan. 5.
1741	56		Desmarets (79) dies, Sept. 7; Fux (81) dies, Feb. 13; Grétry born, Feb. 8; Naumann born, April 17; Paisiello born, May 9.
1742	57	Secular cantata, *Mer hahn en neue Oberkeet,* Aug. *Clavierübung,* Part IV, published.	Abaco (67) dies, July 12.
1743	58		Boccherini born, Feb. 19; Vivaldi (*c.* 73) dies.
1744	59	Part II of *Das wohltemperierte Clavier* finished. Church cantata No. 116.	Campra (84) dies, June 29; Leo (50), dies, Oct. 31.
1745	60	Scheibe (37), in *Der critische Musicus,* withdraws the attack he made on B. in 1737.	Albinoni (71) dies (approx.).
1746	61	Six chorale preludes published by Schübler of Zella (approx.).	Stamitz (C.) born, May 7.
1747	62	Visit to Frederick the Great (35) and to his son Carl Philipp Emanuel (33) at Potsdam in company of his eldest son, Wilhelm Friedemann (37), who is now organist at Halle. The king gives B. a theme to improvise on, April. On his return to Leipzig, B. composes the *Musicalisches Opfer* on the king's theme and dedicates it to him, July 7.	
1748	63	Composition of *Die Kunst der Fuge* begun (approx.).	Walther (64) dies, March 23.
1749	64	Marriage of his daughter, Elisabeth Juliane Friede-	Cimarosa born, Dec. 17; Destouches (*c.* 77) dies

Year	Age	Life	Contemporary Musicians

rike (23), to J. C. Altnikol, organist at Naumburg. The failure of B.'s eyesight is now so serious that the council considers appointing a successor.

(approx.); Vogler born, June 15.

1750 65 Unsuccessful operation on his eyes, end of March. His sight almost gone. Fantasy on the chorale, *Wenn wir in höchsten Nöten sind*, sung to the tune of *Vor deinen Tron tret ich hiermit*, dictated to Altnikol, July. Son, Johann Christoph Friedrich (18), enters the service of Count Schaumburg at Bückeburg. Bach dies, July 28.

Bononcini (78) dies (approx.); Salieri born, Aug. 18; Sammartini (G.) (*c.* 57) dies (approx.); Veracini (*c.* 65) dies.
Agricola (J. F.) aged 30; Anfossi *c.* 14; Arne 40; Bach (C. P. E.) 36; Bach (J. C.) 15; Bach (W. F.) 40; Benda (F.) 41; Benda (G.) 28; Boccherini 7; Boyce 40; Cannabich 19; Cimarosa 1; Dittersdorf 11; Duni 41; Durante 66; Fasch (C. F. C.) 14; Fasch (J F.) 62; Filtz *c.* 25; Galuppi 44; Gassmann 27; Geminiani 70; Gluck 36; Gossec 16; Graun 49; Graupner 63; Greene 55; Grétry 9; Handel 65; Hasse 51; Haydn 18; Hiller (J. A.) 22; Holzbauer 39; Homilius 36; Jommelli 36; Kirnberger 29; Krebs 37; Leclair 53; Locatelli 57; Martini 44; Monsigny 21; Muffat (jun.) *c.* 30; Mysliveček 13; Nardini 28; Naumann 9; Nichelmann 33; Paisiello 9; Pepusch 83; Philidor 24; Piccinni 22; Porpora 64; Quantz 53;

Year	Age	Life	Contemporary Musicians
			Rameau 67; Richter (F. X.) 41; Rust 11; Sacchini 16; Sammartini (G. B.) *c.* 49; Sarti 21; Scarlatti (D.) 65; Stamitz (C.) 4; Stamitz (J. W.) 33; Tartini 58; Telemann 69; Terradellas 39; Traetta 23; Vogler 1; Wagenseil 35; Wanhal 11.

APPENDIX B

A. *VOCAL*

LITURGICAL WORKS

Ascension Oratorio (Cantata No. 11, *Lobet Gott in seinen Reichen*) (*c.* 1735).
Christmas Oratorio (6 Cantatas) (1734).
Easter Oratorio (Cantata, *Kommt, eilet und laufet*) (*c.* 1736).
Magnificat, D major (? 1723).
Mass in B minor (1733–? 1738).
Missa (*Kyrie* and *Gloria*): A major (*c.* 1739); F major; G major (*c.* 1739); G minor.
Passion according to St. John (1723).
Passion according to St. Matthew (1729).
Sanctus: C major, 4 voices; D major (*c.* 1723), 8 voices; D major, 4 voices; D minor, 4 voices; G major, 4 voices.

CHURCH CANTATAS [2]

(Numbers in brackets are those of the Bach Society Edition.)

Ach Gott, vom Himmel sieh' darein (2). Second Sunday after Trinity (*c.* 1740).
Ach Gott, wie manches Herzeleid (3). Second Sunday after Epiphany (1740).
Ach Gott, wie manches Herzeleid (58). Sunday after Circumcision (1733).
Ach Herr, mich armen Sünder (135). Third Sunday after Trinity (*c.* 1740).
Ach, ich sehe itzt (162). Twentieth Sunday after Trinity (1715).
Ach, lieben Christen, seid getrost (114). Seventeenth Sunday after Trinity (*c.* 1740).
Ach wie flüchtig, ach wie nichtig (26). Twenty-fourth Sunday after Trinity (*c.* 1740).

---

[1] Not including works known to be lost or of doubtful authenticity.
[2] Nos. 1–3, 5, 7, 10, 16, 26, 33, 38, 41, 62, 91, 92, 94, 101, 111, 113–16, 121–7, 133, 135, 139, 17?, 178, 180 are chorale cantatas.

Allein zu dir, Herr Jesu Christ (33). Thirteenth Sunday after Trinity
(*c.* 1740).

Alles nur nach Gottes Willen (72). Third Sunday after Epiphany (*c.*
1726).

Also hat Gott die Welt geliebt (68). Whit Monday (? 1735).

Am Abend aber desselbigen Sabbaths (42). First Sunday after Easter (1731).

Ärg're dich, o Seele, nicht (186). Seventh Sunday after Trinity (1723).

Auf Christi Himmelfahrt allein (128). Ascension Day (? 1735).

Aus der Tiefe rufe ich, Herr, zu dir (131). For a Funeral (1707).

Aus tiefer Not schrei' ich zu dir (38). Twenty-first Sunday after Trinity
(*c.* 1740).

Barmherziges Herze der ewigen Liebe (185). Fourth Sunday after Trinity
(1715).

Bereitet die Wege (132). Fourth Sunday in Advent (1715).

Bisher habt ihr nichts gebeten in meinem Namen (87). Fifth Sunday after
Easter (? 1735).

Bleib' bei uns, denn es will Abend werden (6). Easter Monday (1736).

Brich dem Hungrigen dein Brot (39). First Sunday after Trinity (1732).

Bringet dem Herrn Ehre (148). Seventeenth Sunday after Trinity
(*c.* 1725).

Christ lag in Todesbanden (4). Easter Day (1724).

Christ unser Herr zum Jordan kam (7). St. John's Day (*c.* 1740).

Christen, ätzet diesen Tag (63). Christmas (? 1723).

Christum wir sollen loben schon (121). Second Day of Christmas (*c.* 1740).

Christus, der ist mein Leben (95). Sixteenth Sunday after Trinity (? 1732)

Das ist je gewisslich wahr (141). Third Sunday in Advent (*c.* 1721).[1]

Das neugebor'ne Kindelein (122). First Sunday after Christmas (*c.* 1742).

Dazu ist erschienen der Sohn Gottes (40). Second Day of Christmas
(? 1723).

Dem Gerechten muss das Licht (195). Wedding Cantata (? 1726).

Denn du wirst meine Seele nicht in der Hölle lassen (15). Easter Day (1704).

Der Friede sei mit dir (158). Purification (*c.* 1708–16).

Der Herr denket an uns (196). Wedding Cantata (1708).

Der Herr ist mein getreuer Hirt (112). Second Sunday after Easter (1731).

Der Himmel lacht, die Erde jubiliret (31). Easter Day (1715).

Die Elenden sollen essen (75). First Sunday after Trinity (1723).

Die Himmel erzählen Ehre (76). Second Sunday after Trinity (1723).

---

[1] Not by Bach (Whittaker, *Collected Essays*, p. 137).

Du Friedefürst, Herr Jesu Christ (116). Twenty-fifth Sunday after Trinity (1744).

Du Hirte Israel, höre (104). Second Sunday after Easter (*c.* 1725).

Du sollst Gott, deinen Herren, lieben (77). Thirteenth Sunday after Trinity (*c.* 1725).

Du wahrer Gott und Davids Sohn (23). Quinquagesima (1724).

Ehre sei dir, Gott, gesungen. Part V of Christmas Oratorio.

Ehre sei Gott in der Höhe. Christmas. Incomplete (? 1728).

Ein' feste Burg ist unser Gott (80). Reformation Festival (1730, composed mainly 1716).

Ein Herz, das seinen Jesum lebend weiss (134). Easter Tuesday (*c.* 1717–22).

Ein ungefärbt Gemüte (24). Fourth Sunday after Trinity (1723).

Er rufet seinen Schafen (175). Whit Tuesday (? 1735).

Erforsche mich, Gott, und erfahre (136). Eighth Sunday after Trinity (*c.* 1725).

Erfreut euch, ihr Herzen (66). Easter Monday (1731).

Erfreute Zeit im neuen Bunde (83). Purification (? 1724).

Erhalt' uns, Herr, bei deinem Wort (126). Sexagesima (*c.* 1740).

Erhöhtes Fleisch und Blut (173). Whit Monday (*c.* 1718).

Erschallet, ihr Lieder (172). Whit Sunday (*c.* 1724).

Erwünschtes Freudenlicht (184). Whit Tuesday (? 1724).

Es erhub sich ein Streit (19). Michaelmas Day (1726).

Es ist das Heil uns kommen her (9). Sixth Sunday after Trinity (? 1731).

Es ist dir gesagt, Mensch, was gut ist (45). Eighth Sunday after Trinity (*c.* 1740).

Es ist ein trotzig und verzagt Ding (176). Trinity Sunday (? 1735).

Es ist euch gut, dass ich hingehe (108). Fourth Sunday after Easter (? 1735).

Es ist nichts Gesundes an meinem Leibe (25). Fourteenth Sunday after Trinity (*c.* 1731).

Es reifet euch ein schrecklich Ende (90). Twenty-fifth Sunday after Trinity (*c.* 1740).

Es wartet Alles auf dich (187). Seventh Sunday after Trinity (1732).

Fallt mit Danken. Part IV of Christmas Oratorio.

Falsche Welt, dir trau' ich nicht (52). Twenty-third Sunday after Trinity (*c.* 1730).

Freue dich, erlöste Schaar (30). St. John's Day (1738).

Geist und Seel wird verwirret (35). Twelfth Sunday after Trinity (? 1731).

Gelobet sei der Herr, mein Gott (129). Trinity Sunday (1732).

Appendix B—Catalogue of Works

Gelobet seist du, Jesus Christ (91). Christmas (*c.* 1740).
Gleich wie der Regen und Schnee (18). Sexagesima (*c.* 1714).
Gloria in excelsis Deo (191). Christmas (*c.* 1733).
Gott, der Herr, ist Sonn' und Schild (79). Reformation Festival (? 1735).
Gott fähret auf mit Jauchzen (43). Ascension Day (1735).
Gott ist mein König (71). Council Election (1708).
Gott ist uns're Zuversicht (197). Wedding Cantata.
Gott, man lobet dich in der Stille (120). Council Election (1730).
Gott soll allein mein Herze haben (169). Eighteenth Sunday after Trinity
 (*c.* 1731).
Gott, wie dein Name, so ist auch dein Ruhm (171). Circumcision (? 1730).
Gottes Zeit ist die allerbeste Zeit (106). (Actus tragicus.) For a Funeral
 (? 1707 or 1711).
Gottlob! nun geht das Jahr zu Ende (28). First Sunday after Christmas
 (*c.* 1736).
Halt' im Gedächtnis Jesum Christ (67). First Sunday after Easter (*c.* 1735).
Herr Christ, der ein'ge Gottes-Sohn (96). Eighteenth Sunday after
 Trinity (*c.* 1740).
Herr, deine Augen sehen nach dem Glauben (102). Tenth Sunday after
 Trinity (? 1731).
Herr, gehe nicht in 's Gericht (105). Ninth Sunday after Trinity (*c.* 1725).
Herr Gott, Beherrscher aller Dinge. Wedding Cantata. Incomplete
 (*c.* 1740).
Herr Gott, dich loben alle wir (130). Michaelmas Day (*c.* 1740).
Herr Gott, dich loben wir (16). Circumcision (? 1724).
Herr Jesu Christ, du höchstes Gut (113). Eleventh Sunday after Trinity
 (*c.* 1740).
Herr Jesu Christ, wahr'r Mensch und Gott (127). Quinquagesima (*c.* 1740).
Herr, wenn die stolzen Feinde schnauben. Part VI of Christmas Oratorio.
Herr, wie du willst, so schick's mit mir! (73). Third Sunday after Epiphany
 (*c.* 1725).
Herrscher des Himmels. Part III of Christmas Oratorio.
Herz und Mund und Tat und Leben (147). Visitation B.V.M. (1716).
Himmelskönig, sei willkommen (182). Palm Sunday (1715).
Höchsterwünschtes Freudenfest (194). Trinity Sunday (1723).
Ich armer Mensch, ich Sündenknecht (55). Twenty-second Sunday after
 Trinity (*c.* 1731).
Ich bin ein guter Hirt (85). Second Sunday after Easter (1735).
Ich bin vergnügt mit meinem Glücke (84). Septuagesima (1731).

Ich elender Mensch, wer wird mich erlösen (48). Nineteenth Sunday after Trinity (*c.* 1740).

Ich freue mich in dir (133). Third Day of Christmas (*c.* 1735).

Ich geb' und suche mit Verlangen (49). Twentieth Sunday after Trinity (*c.* 1731).

Ich glaube, lieber Herr, hilf meinem Unglauben (109). Twenty-first Sunday after Trinity (*c.* 1731).

Ich habe genug (82). Purification (*c.* 1731).

Ich hab' in Gottes Herz und Sinn (92). Septuagesima (*c.* 1740).

Ich habe meine Zuversicht (188). Twenty-first Sunday after Trinity (*c.* 1730).

Ich hatte viel Bekümmerniss (21). Third Sunday after Trinity (1714).

Ich lasse dich nicht, du segnest mich denn (157). Purification (1727).

Ich liebe den Höchsten von ganzem Gemüte (174). Whit Monday (*c.* 1731).

Ich ruf' zu dir, Herr Jesu Christ (177). Fourth Sunday after Trinity (1732).

Ich steh' mit einem Fuss im Grabe (156). Third Sunday after Epiphany (? 1730).

Ich weiss, dass mein Erlöser (160). Easter Day (1717).

Ich will den Kreuzstab gerne tragen (56). Nineteenth Sunday after Trinity (*c.* 1731).

Ihr, die ihr euch von Christo nennet (164). Thirteenth Sunday after Trinity (*c.* 1723).

Ihr Menschen, rühmet Gottes Leben (167). St. John's Day (*c.* 1725).

Ihr Pforten zu Zion (193). Council Election. Incomplete (*c.* 1740).

Ihr werdet weinen und heulen (103). Third Sunday after Easter (? 1735).

In allen meinem Taten (97). For no special season (1734).

Jauchzet, frohlocket. Part I of Christmas Oratorio.

Jauchzet Gott in allen Landen (51). Fifteenth Sunday after Trinity (*c.* 1731).

Jesu, der du meine Seele (78). Fourteenth Sunday after Trinity (*c.* 1740).

Jesu, nun sei gepreiset (41). Circumcision (? 1736).

Jesus nahm zu sich die Zwölfe (22). Quinquagesima (1723).

Jesus schläft, was soll ich hoffen? (81). Fourth Sunday after Epiphany (1724).

Komm, du süsse Todesstunde (161). Sixteenth Sunday after Trinity (1715).

Kommt, eilet und laufet. Easter Oratorio (1736).

Leichtgesinnte Flattergeister (181). Sexagesima (*c.* 1725).

Appendix B—Catalogue of Works

Liebster Gott, wann werd' ich sterben (8). Sixteenth Sunday after Trinity (*c.* 1725).

Liebster Immanuel, Herzog der Frommen (123). Epiphany (*c.* 1740).

Liebster Jesu, mein Verlangen (32). First Sunday after Epiphany (*c.* 1740).

Lobe den Herren, den mächtigen König der Ehren (137). Twelfth Sunday after Trinity (? 1732).

Lobe den Herrn, meine Seele (69). Twelfth Sunday after Trinity (? 1724).

Lobe den Herrn, meine Seele (143). Circumcision (1735).

Lobet Gott in seinen Reichen (11). Ascension Day (Ascension Oratorio) (*c.* 1735).

Mache dich, mein Geist, bereit (115). Twenty-second Sunday after Trinity (*c.* 1740).

Man singet mit Freuden vom Sieg (149). Michaelmas Day (1731).

Mein Gott, wie lang' (155). Second Sunday after Epiphany (1716).

Mein Herze schwimmt im Blut. Eleventh Sunday after Trinity (*c.* 1714).

Mein liebster Jesus ist verloren (154). First Sunday after Epiphany (1724).

Meine Seel' erhebt den Herren (10). Visitation B.V.M. (*c.* 1740).

Meine Seele rühmt und preist (189). Visitation B.V.M. (*c.* 1707–10).

Meine Seufzer, meine Tränen (13). Second Sunday after Epiphany (*c.* 1736).

Meinen Jesum lass' ich nicht (124). First Sunday after Epiphany (*c.* 1740)

Mit Fried' und Freud' ich fahr' dahin (125). Purification (*c.* 1740).

Nach dir, Herr, verlanget mich (150). ? For a Funeral (*c.* 1710).

Nimm von uns Herr, du treuer Gott (101). Tenth Sunday after Trinity (*c.* 1740).

Nimm was dein ist, und gehe hin (144). Septuagesima (*c.* 1725).

Nun danket alle Gott (192). ? Reformation Festival. Incomplete (? 1732).

Nun ist das Heil und die Kraft (50). Michaelmas (*c.* 1740).

Nun komm, der Heiden Heiland (61). First Sunday in Advent (first version, A minor) (1714).

Nun komm, der Heiden Heiland (62). First Sunday in Advent (second version, B minor) (*c.* 1740).

Nur Jedem das Seine (163). Twenty-third Sunday after Trinity (1715).

O ewiges Feuer. Wedding Cantata. Incomplete (*c.* 1730).

O ewiges Feuer, o Ursprung der Liebe (34). Whit Sunday (*c.* 1740).

O Ewigkeit, du Donnerwort (20). First Sunday after Trinity (*c.* 1725).

O Ewigkeit, du Donnerwort (60). Twenty-fourth Sunday after Trinity (1732).

O heil'ges Geist~ und Wasserbad (165).   Trinity Sunday (? 1724).

O Jesu Christ, mein's Lebens Licht (118).   For a Funeral (*c.* 1737).

Preise Jerusalem den Herrn (119).   Council Election (1723).

Schau, lieber Gott, wie meine Feind' (153).   Second Sunday after Christ~mas (1724).

Schauet doch und sehet (46).   Tenth Sunday after Trinity (*c.* 1725).

Schlage doch, gewünschste Stunde (53).   Funeral Cantata (1723–34).

Schmücke dich, o liebe Seele (180).   Twentieth Sunday after Trinity (*c.* 1740).

Schwingt freudig euch empor (36).   First Sunday in Advent (*c.* 1730).

Sehet welch' eine Liebe (64).   Third Day of Christmas (? 1723).

Sehet, wir geb'n hinauf gen Jerusalem (159).   Quinquagesima (? 1729).

Sei Lob und Ehr' dem höchsten Gut (117).   For no special season (*c.* 1733).

Selig ist der Mann (57).   Second Day of Christmas (*c.* 1740).

Sie werden aus Saba alle kommen (65).   Epiphany (1724).

Sie werden Euch in den Bann tun (44).   Sunday after Ascension Day (*c.* 1725).

Sie werden Euch in den Bann tun (183).   Sunday after Ascension Day (second version) (? 1735).

Siehe ich will viel Fischer (88).   Fifth Sunday after Trinity (1732).

Siehe zu, dass deine Gottesfurcht nicht Heuchelei sei (179).   Eleventh Sunday after Trinity (? 1724).

Singet dem Herrn ein neues Lied (190).   Circumcision (*c.* 1725).

So du mit deinem Munde bekennest Jesum (145).   Easter Tuesday (*c.* 1729).

Süsser Trost, mein Jesus kommt (151).   Third Day of Christmas (*c.* 1740).

Tritt auf die Glaubensbahn (152).   First Sunday after Christmas (*c.* 1715).

Tue Rechnung, Donnerwort (168).   Ninth Sunday after Trinity (*c.* 1725).

Und es waren Hirten in derselben Gegend.   Part II of Christmas Oratorio.

Uns ist ein Kind geboren (142).   Christmas (*c.* 1714).[1]

Unser Mund sei voll Lachens (110).   Christmas (after 1734).

Vernügte Ruh', beliebte Seelenlust (170).   Sixth Sunday after Trinity (? 1732).

Wachet, auf, ruft uns die Stimme (140).   Twenty~seventh Sunday after Trinity (*c.* 1731).

Wachet, betet, seid bereit allezeit (70).   Twentieth Sunday after Trinity (1716).

Wahrlich, ich sage euch (86).   Fifth Sunday after Easter (*c.* 1725).

---

[1] Not by Bach (Whittaker, *Collected Essays*, p. 137).

Appendix B—Catalogue of Works

Wär' Gott nicht mit uns diese Zeit (14). Fourth Sunday after Epiphany (1735).

Warum betrübst du dich, mein Herz (138). Fifteenth Sunday after Trinity (c. 1740).

Was frag' ich nach der Welt (94). Ninth Sunday after Trinity (? 1735).

Was Gott tut, das ist wohlgetan (98). Twenty-first Sunday after Trinity (c. 1732).

Was Gott tut, das ist wohlgetan (99). Fifteenth Sunday after Trinity (c. 1733).

Was Gott tut, das ist wohlgetan (100). Fifteenth Sunday after Trinity (? 1735).

Was mein Gott will, das g'scheh' allzeit (111). Third Sunday after Epiphany (c. 1740).

Was soll ich aus dir machen (89). Twenty-second Sunday after Trinity (c. 1730).

Was willst du dich betrüben (107). Seventh Sunday after Trinity (? 1735).

Weinen, klagen, sorgen, zagen (12). Third Sunday after Easter (c. 1724).

Wer da glaubet und getauft wird (37). Ascension Day (c. 1727).

Wer Dank opfert, der preiset mich (17). Fourteenth Sunday after Trinity (c. 1737).

Wer mich liebet der wird mein Wort halten (59). Whit Sunday (1716).

Wer mich liebet der wird mein Wort halten (74). Whit Sunday (second version) (? 1735).

Wer nur den lieben Gott lässt walten (93). Fifth Sunday after Trinity (? 1728).

Wer sich selbst erhöhet, der soll erniedriget werden (47). Seventeenth Sunday after Trinity (? 1720).

Wer weiss wie nahe mir mein Ende (27). Sixteenth Sunday after Trinity (1731).

Widerstehe doch der Sünde (54). For no special season (1723–34).

Wie schön leuchtet der Morgenstern (1). Annunciation (c. 1740).

Wir danken dir, Gott, wir danken dir (29). Council Election (1731).

Wir müssen durch viel Trübsal (146). Third Sunday after Easter (c. 1740).

Wo gehest du hin (166). Fourth Sunday after Easter (c. 1725).

Wo Gott der Herr nicht bei uns hält (178). Eighth Sunday after Trinity (c. 1740).

Wo soll ich fliehen hin (5). Nineteenth Sunday after Trinity (1735).

Wohl dem der sich auf seinen Gott (139). Twenty-third Sunday after Trinity (c. 1740).

Bach

FUNERAL MUSIC

Trauer-Ode, for the death of the Electress Christiane Eberhardine (1727).

MOTETS

Der Geist hilft uns'rer Schwachheit auf. 8 voices with accompaniment (1729).
Fürchte dich nicht. 8 voices (? 1726).
Jesu, meine Freude. 5 voices (1723).
Komm, Jesu, komm. 8 voices.
Lobet den Herrn, alle Heiden. Psalm 117. 4 voices.
Singet dem Herrn ein neues Lied. Psalm 149. 8 voices.

CHORALES

3 Chorales for Weddings: *Was Gott tut*; *Sei Lob und Ehr'*; *Nun danket alle Gott.*
185 Chorales, harmonized by Bach (from Carl Philipp Emanuel Bach's collection).
75 Chorales, harmonized by Bach (from Anna Magdalena Bach's *Notenbuch,* 1725, and [69 numbers] from Schemelli's *Gesangbuch,* 1736).

SECULAR CANTATAS

Amore traditore.
Angenehmes Wiederau (adapted from Church Cantata No. 30, *Freue dich, erlöste Schaar*) (1737).
Auf schmetternde Töne (adapted from *Vereinigte Zwietracht*) (1733).
Der Streit zwischen Phöbus und Pan (1731).
Der zufriedengestellte Aeolus (1725).
Die Freude reget sich (adapted from *Schwingt freudig euch empor*) (1726).
Die Wahl des Herkules, or *Herkules am Scheidewege* (opening chorus adapted from the *Christmas Oratorio*) (1733).
Durchlaucht'ster Leopold (1718).
Ich bin in mir vergnügt (c. 1730).
Mer hahn en neue Oberkeet (Peasant Cantata) (1742).
Mit Gnaden bekröne der Himmel die Zeiten (? 1721).
Non sa che sia dolore.

Appendix B—Catalogue of Works

O angenehme Melodei (adapted from *O holder Tag*) (? 1749).
O holder Tag (? 1749).
Preise dein Glücke, gesegnetes Sachsen (1734).
Schleicht, spielende Wellen (1734).
Schweiget stille, plaudert nicht (*Coffee Cantata*) (c. 1732).
Schwingt freudig euch empor (1726).
Tönet, ihr Pauken! (1733).
Vereinigte Zwietracht der wechselnden Saiten (1726).
Vergnügte Pleissen-Stadt (1728).
Was mir behagt, ist nur die muntre Jagd (1716).
Weichet nur, betrübte Schatten (c. 1730).

VOICE AND CLAVIER

5 Songs from Anna Magdalena Bach's *Notenbuch: So oft ich meine Tabakspfeife; Bist du bei mir; Gedenke doch; Gieb dich zufrieden; Willst du dein Herz mir schenken* (1725).

FOUR VOICES AND CONTINUO

Quodlibet (? 1705).

B. INSTRUMENTAL

ORCHESTRAL WORKS

Brandenburg Concertos: No 1, F major, for *violino piccolo*, 3 oboes, 2 horns, bassoon and strings (1721); No. 2, F major, for violin, flute, oboe, trumpet and strings (1721); No. 3, G major, for strings (1721); No. 4, G major, for violin, 2 flutes and strings (1721); No. 5, D major, for clavier, violin, flute and strings (1721); No. 6, B flat major, for strings (without violins) (1721).

Ouvertures (Suites): No. 1, C major, for woodwind and strings; No. 2, B minor, for flute and strings; No. 3, D major, for oboes, bassoons, trumpets, drums and strings; No. 4, D major, for oboes, bassoons, trumpets, drums and strings.

CONCERTOS [1]

A minor, for violin (1717–23).

---

[1] All accompanied by strings and continuo only, unless otherwise mentioned.

E major, for violin (1717–23).
D minor, for 2 violins (1717–23).
A major, for clavier (1729–36).
D major, for clavier (identical with violin Concerto in E major) (1729–36).
D minor, for clavier (1729–36).
E major, for clavier (1729–36).
F major, for clavier with 2 flutes, strings and continuo (identical with *Brandenburg Concerto* No. 4) (1729–36).
F minor, for clavier (1729–36).
G minor, for clavier (identical with violin Concerto in A minor) (1729–36).
C major, for 2 claviers (1727–36).
C minor, for 2 claviers (identical with the Concerto for 2 violins in D minor) (1727–36).
C minor, for 2 claviers (probably identical with a lost Concerto for violin and oboe) (1727–36).
C major, for 3 claviers (*c.* 1733).
D minor, for 3 claviers (*c.* 1733).
A minor for 4 claviers (transcription of a Concerto for 4 violins by Vivaldi) (*c.* 1733).
A minor, for clavier, flute and violin (*c.* 1730).

Sinfonia, D major, for violin, with 2 oboes, 3 trumpets, drums, strings and continuo (incomplete).

CHAMBER MUSIC

Unaccompanied

6 Sonatas (Partitas) for violin alone. A minor, B minor, C major, D minor, E major, G minor (*c.* 1720).
6 Suites (Sonatas) for violoncello alone. C major, C minor, D major, D minor, E flat major, G major (*c.* 1720).

One Instrument with Continuo

Fugue, G minor, for violin (1717–23).
3 Sonatas for flute. C major, E major, E minor (1717–23).
2 Sonatas for violin. E minor, G major (1717–23).

Appendix B—Catalogue of Works

Two Instruments with Continuo

Canon, C minor, for flute and violin (added to *Das musicalische Opfer*).
Musicalisches Opfer, Das, for flute and violin (1747).
Sonatas: G major, for 2 flutes (1717–23); C minor, for flute and violin (added to *Das musicalische Opfer*); G major, for flute and violin (1717–23); C major, for 2 violins (1717–23).

Clavier and One Instrument

3 Sonatas for clavier and flute. A major, B minor, E flat major (1717–23).
6 Sonatas for clavier and violin. A major, B minor, C minor, E major, F minor, G major (1717–23).
3 Sonatas for clavier and *viola da gamba*. D major, G major, G minor (1717–23).
Suite for clavier and violin, A major (1717–23).

Organ Music

Alla breve pro organo pleno, D major (1708–17).
Canzona, D minor (*c.* 1714).
143 Chorale Preludes: Catechism Preludes (21) (*Clavierübung,* vol. iii) (1739); Eighteen Preludes (*c.* 1747–50); Kirnberger's collection (24); Miscellaneous Preludes (28); *Orgelbüchlein* (46) (1717); Schübler's book (6) (*c.* 1747–50).
4 Concertos (after Vivaldi and others). A minor, 2 C major, G major (1708–17).
6 Fantasies. B minor, C major, C minor, 2 G major (1700–8); C minor (1708–17).
3 Fantasies and Fugues. A minor (1700–8); C minor, G minor (1708–17).
7 Fugues. C minor, D major, G major (1700–8); B minor, C minor, G major, G minor (1708–17).
Passacaglia, C minor (1708–17).
Pastorale, F major (1708–17).
4 Preludes. A minor, 2 C major, G major (1700–8).
26 Preludes and Fugues. A minor, C major, C minor, E minor (Short) (1700–8); A major, A minor (Great), C major, C minor (Great), D major, F minor, G major (Great), G major, G minor, 8 Short Preludes and Fugues (1708–17); B minor (Great), C major

(Great), D minor, E flat major (*Clavierübung*, vol. iii), E minor (Great) (1723-39).

6 Sonatas (Trios). C major, C minor, D minor, E flat major, E minor, G major (1727-33).

5 Toccatas and Fugues. E major (1700-8); C major, D minor ('Dorian'), D minor, F major (1708-17).

3 Trios. C minor, D minor, F major (Aria) (1708-17).

4 Variations on Chorales (Partitas). *Christ, der du bist der helle Tag*; *O Gott, du frommer Gott*; *Sei gegrüsset, Jesu gütig* (1700-8); *Vom Himmel hoch, da komm' ich her* (1723-50).

CLAVIER MUSIC
Original Works

Aria variata, A minor (*c.* 1708-12).

Aria with 30 Variations (Goldberg Variations, *Clavierübung*, vol. iv) (1742).

Capriccio in honorem Joh. Christoph. Bachii (*c.* 1704).

Capriccio sopra la lontananza del suo fratello dilettissimo (1704).

Chromatic Fantasy and Fugue, D minor (1720-3).

Clavierbüchlein vor Wilhelm Friedemann Bach, including 2 *Allemandes*, *Applicatio* in C major, Fugue in C major, 15 Inventions, Minuets, Minuet-Trio, 15 Preludes, Symphonies (1720).

Concerto in the Italian Style, F major (*Clavierübung*, vol. ii) (1735).

Duet for 2 claviers, F major.

4 Duets (*Clavierübung*, vol. iii) (1739).

Fantasies. C minor (1700-8), G minor (1708-17).

Fantasy (on a Rondo), C minor (1700-8).

Fantasy (Prelude), A minor (1708-17).

Fantasy (with unfinished Fugue), C minor (*c.* 1738).

Fantasy and Fugue. A minor (1717-23), A minor (after 1723).

Fughetta, C minor (1700-8).

Fugues. C major, C minor, 2 D minor, E minor (1700-8); 2 A major, A major (on theme by Albinoni), A minor, B minor (Albinoni) (1708-17).

12 Little Preludes (1717-23).

Notenbuch vor Anna Magdalena Bachin contains only Marches, Minuets, a *Musette*, Polonaises and a *Cembalo solo* by Bach (1725).[1]

---

[1] Anna Magdalena's *Clavierbüchlein* of 1722 contains no music not found elsewhere, and listed here, except a fragment of an Air in E minor.

Partita (*Ouverture*), B minor (*Clavierübung*, vol. ii) (1735).

6 Partitas (*Clavierübung*, vol. i). A minor, B flat major, C minor, D major, E minor, G major (1731).

Prelude (Fantasy), C minor (1700–8).

4 Preludes and Fughettas. D minor, E minor, F major, G major (1700–8).

3 Preludes and Fugues. A minor (1700–8); A minor (1717–23); E flat major (after 1723).

6 Preludes for Beginners (1717–23).

2 Sonatas. A minor (one movement) (1700–8); D major (*c.* 1704).

Suite, D minor (1717–23) (possibly not by Bach).

Suite (*Ouverture*), F major (1708–17).

Suite (unfinished), F minor (1717–23).

2 Suites (originally for lute), B flat major, C minor.

2 Suites. A minor, E flat major (1708–17).

6 Suites (English). A major, A minor, D minor, E minor, F major, G minor (*c.* 1725).

6 Suites (French). B minor, C minor, D minor, E major, E flat major, G major (*c.* 1722).

7 Toccatas. D major, D minor, E minor, G major, G minor (1700–8); C minor, F sharp minor (1717–23).

Wohltemperierte Clavier, Das (24 Preludes and Fugues), Part I (1722).

Wohltemperierte Clavier, Das (24 Preludes and Fugues), Part II (1744).

Arrangements

Adagio, from the third Sonata for solo violin, G major.

16 Concertos, after Vivaldi and others (1708–12).

Fugue, B flat major, after Reinken (1708–17).

Fugue, B flat major, after Erselius (1708–17).

Sonata, from the second Sonata for solo violin, D minor.

2 Sonatas, after Reinken, A minor, C major (1708–17).

Suite, from the third Partita for solo violin, E major.

Probably intended for Clavier

Die Kunst der Fuge (1748–50).

APPENDIX C

Able, Johann Georg (1650–1706), composer, organist at the church of St. Blasius at Mühlhausen. Son of

Able, Johann Rodolph (1625–73), composer, appointed organist at Erfurt in 1646 and to the church of St. Blasius at Mühlhausen in 1654.

Altnikol, Johann Christoph (died 1759), clavier player, organist and composer, pupil of Bach at Leipzig from 1744. Appointed organist at Niederwiesa near Griefenberg, 1747, and at Naumburg, 1748. Married Bach's daughter, Elisabetha Juliane Friederica (1726–81), in 1749.

Bach. For all members of the Bach family see Appendix E, p. 228.

Böhm, Georg (1661–1773), composer, organist at Hamburg before 1698, then at St. John's Church, Lüneburg.

Bruhns, Nikolaus (c. 1665–97), organist, string player and composer, first employed at Copenhagen, then town organist at Husum, Slesvig-Holstein, his native country.

Buxtehude, Dietrich (1637–1707), Swedish [1] composer and organist, settled in Denmark and from 1668 organist of St. Mary's Church at Lübeck.

Drese, Johann Samuel (1644–1716), musical director to the court of Weimar.

Erich, Daniel (17th–18th cent.), German organist and composer, pupil of Buxtehude and organist at Güstrow, Mecklenburg, early in the eighteenth century. He wrote organ preludes and probably pieces for harpsichord.

Forkel, Johann Nikolaus (1749–1818), writer on music, organist and musical director at the University of Göttingen. Bach's first biographer.

Franz, Robert (1815–92), German composer. Studied with Schneider at Dessau, and later became organist, choral conductor and lecturer

---

[1] Always regarded as a Dane, but proved by Pirro to have been born at Helsingborg in Sweden.

at Halle. He is especially distinguished as a composer of songs, and as conductor he did much to promote performances of Bach and Handel.

Gabrieli, Giovanni (1557–1612), Italian composer, pupil of his uncle, Andrea Gabrieli, at St. Mark's in Venice, where he succeeded him as first organist in 1585. He had many famous Italian and foreign pupils, and specialized in music laid out antiphonally, to be sung and played from opposite galleries in St. Mark's.

Gerber, Heinrich Nikolaus (1702–75), organist and composer, pupil of Bach in Leipzig, court organist at Sondershausen from 1731. Invented the *Strohfiedel*, a kind of xylophone.

Goldberg, Johann Gottlieb (born *c.* 1720), clavier player and organist, pupil of Bach 1733–46.

Görner, Johann Gottlieb (1697–1778), organist and composer in Leipzig. Founded a *Collegium Musicum* in 1723. Organist at St. Paul's (University) Church 1721; at St. Nicholas's and St. Thomas's Churches 1729.

Gräser, Wolfgang (1906–28), Swiss mathematician, physicist, philologist and writer on music, who wrote a book on Bach's *Art of Fugue* and scored it for orchestra.

Graupner, Christoph (1683–1760), composer, studied under Schelle and Kuhnau at St. Thomas's School in Leipzig and was harpsichordist at the Hamburg Opera under Keiser 1706–9, afterwards musical director at Darmstadt.

Harrer, Gottlob (died 1755), composer and collector of music, succeeded Bach as cantor of St. Thomas's Church in Leipzig in 1750.

Kuhnau, Johann (1660–1722), organist, clavier player, composer and writer on music, cantor at Zittau, went to Leipzig in 1682, became organist at St. Thomas's Church in 1684, musical director of the university and the churches of St. Nicholas and St. Thomas in 1700, and cantor of St. Thomas's in 1701, in which post he preceded Bach. His Biblical Sonatas for clavier are early examples of programme music.

Loewe, Johann Jakob (1628–1703), organist and composer, pupil of Schütz at Dresden, held appointments at Brunswick from 1655 and Zeitz from 1663, became organist of St. Nicholas's Church at Lüneburg in 1682.

Lübeck, Vincentius (1654–1740), organist and composer for his instrument, organist at Stade until 1702, when he was appointed organist to St. Nicholas's Church at Hamburg. One of the exponents of the chorale prelude before Bach.

Marchand, Louis (1669–1732), French organist and composer for his instrument, held various organist's posts in Paris and became court organist at Versailles, but was exiled in 1717 and went to Dresden, returning to Paris, his banishment being withdrawn, after his flight before the contest with Bach.

Mattheson, Johann (1681–1764), writer on music, organist and composer, first sang female parts at the Hamburg Opera, then composed two operas (1699 and 1704), went to Lübeck with Handel to investigate the chances of succeeding to Buxtehude's organ appointment, became cantor of Hamburg Cathedral in 1715. Wrote several books on music, the most important being *Das neu eröffnete Orchester* (1713), *Der vollkommene Capellmeister* (1739), and *Grundlage einer Ehrenpforte* (1740), remarkable for the inadequate entry given to Bach.

Mizler, Lorenz Christoph (1711–78), musical writer and editor, was one of Bach's scholars at St. Thomas's School in Leipzig, founded the Association for Musical Science there in 1738 and edited a periodical, *Die neu eröffnete Musik-Bibliothek*, 1739–54.

Pachelbel, Johann (1653–1706), organist and composer, went to Vienna as pupil of Kerl and his deputy organist in the imperial chapel. Subsequently organist at Eisenach, Erfurt, Stuttgart and Gotha. Appointed organist of St. Sebaldus's Church at Nuremberg, his native city. Anticipated several of Bach's forms of organ music, especially the chorale prelude.

Reinken (or *Reincken*), *Johann Adam* (1623–1722), organist and composer for his instrument, was appointed organist at St. Catherine's Church in Hamburg, where he remained until his death.

Scheibe, Johann Adolph (1708–76), writer on music and critic, studied law at Leipzig and settled in Hamburg as music teacher in 1736. Began to publish the weekly, *Der critische Musicus*, in 1737. He was also a prolific composer.

Scheidt, Samuel (1587–1654), organist and composer, pupil of Sweelinck in Amsterdam, held several organist's posts at Halle, his native city.

Schweitzer, Albert (born 1875), French (Alsatian) theologian, medical missionary, organist and writer on music. He studied the organ at

Strasbourg Cathedral and with Widor in Paris, and later became lecturer in theology at Strasbourg University and undertook medical mission in Central Africa. He wrote an important book on Bach and often gave recitals of that master's organ music in many countries.

Sebastiani, Johann (1622–83), composer, studied probably in Italy, went to Königsberg about 1650, where he held various appointments and retired in 1679. He composed a Passion according to St. Matthew.

Silbermann, Gottfried (1683–1753), instrument maker and organ builder at Freiberg(Saxony)and Dresden. He made famous clavichords and was the first German to make a pianoforte after the model of Cristofori.

Spitta, Philipp (1841–94), German musicologist, studied at Göttingen University and in 1875 became professor of musical history at Berlin University. He was joint editor with Adler and Chrysander of the *Vierteljahrsschrift für Musikwissenschaft*, edited the complete works of Schütz and Buxtehude's organ music, and wrote a work in two volumes on Bach, which is still one of the standard authorities.

Swieten, Gottfried van, Baron (1734–1803), Dutch diplomat and musical amateur, who was brought to Vienna in 1745, when his father became court physician there. In 1771 he became Austrian ambassador to Prussia, and after 1778 held various official posts in Vienna, where he gave choral and orchestral Sunday morning concerts.

Telemann, Georg Philipp (1681–1767), studied at the University of Leipzig from 1700 and in 1704 was appointed organist to the New Church there and founded a *Collegium Musicum*. After holding various posts at Sorau, Eisenach and Frankfort, he was appointed cantor of the Johanneum and musical director to the five principal churches at Hamburg, posts which he held until his death.

Terry, Charles Sanford (1864–1936), English historian and musical biographer, was professor of history at Aberdeen University, but devoted much of his time to the study of Bach, on whom he wrote a definitive biography which he himself translated into German, as well as several works on various aspects of Bach's music.

Tunder, Franz (1614–67), organist and composer, pupil of Frescobaldi in Rome, became organist of St. Mary's Church at Lübeck, his native city, predecessor there of Buxtehude.

Vivaldi, Antonio (c. 1670–1743), Italian violinist and instrumental composer, appointed *maestro de' concerti* at the Ospedale della Pietà in

Bach

Venice, his native city. The creator of a new, definitely instrumental style.

Walther, Johann Gottfried (1684–1748), organist, composer and writer on music, a kinsman of Bach's, became organist of St. Thomas's Church at Erfurt in 1702 and town organist at Weimar in 1707. Compiled a *Musicalisches Lexicon*.

Weckmann, Matthias (1621–74), German organist and composer, pupil of Schütz at Dresden and of J. Praetorius at Hamburg. After service in Denmark he settled as organist at Hamburg, where he organized a *Collegium Musicum*.

Wilhelmj, August (1845–1908), German violinist, studied with David at Leipzig, and later travelled extensively as a virtuoso.

Zachau, Friedrich Wilhelm (1663–1712), composer, theorist and organist at Halle, first teacher of Handel.

Zelter, Carl Friedrich (1758–1832), German conductor, teacher and composer, friend of Goethe, on whose poems he wrote songs. He did much useful work as choral conductor in Berlin, where he allowed Mendelssohn to conduct Bach's St. Matthew Passion in 1829, the first performance within living memory.

APPENDIX D

BIBLIOGRAPHY

Bach-Jahrbuch. Published by the Neue Bachgesellschaft. (Leipzig, 1904 and annually.)

Bitter, C. H., 'Johann Sebastian Bach' (in German). 4 vols. (Berlin, 1881.)

Boughton, Rutland, 'John Sebastian Bach.' (London, 1928.)

Dahms, Walter, 'Johann Sebastian Bach: ein Bild seines Lebens.' (Munich, 1924.)

Danckert, Werner, 'Beiträge zur Bachkritik.' (Cassel, 1934.)

Dickinson, A. E. F., 'The Art of Bach.' (London, 1936.)

Forkel, Johann Nikolaus, 'Johann Sebastian Bach: his Life, Art and Work.' Translated from the German by Charles Sanford Terry. (London, 1920.)

Fuller-Maitland, J. A., 'The Brandenburg Concertos.' (Oxford and London, 1929.)

——, 'The Forty-eight' (*Well-tempered Clavier*). 2 vols. (Oxford and London, 1928.)

——, 'The Keyboard Suites.' (Oxford and London, 1925.)

Gérold, Th., 'J.-S. Bach: biographie critique.' (Paris, 1925.)

Grace, Harvey, 'The Organ Works of Bach.' (London, 1922.)

Gray, Cecil, 'The Forty-eight Preludes and Fugues of J. S. Bach.' (Oxford and London, 1938.)

Hannam, W. S., 'Notes on the Church Cantatas of John Sebastian Bach.' (Oxford and London, 1928.)

Hilgenfeldt, C. L., 'Johann Sebastian Bachs Leben, Wirken und Werke: ein Beitrag zur Kunstgeschichte des achtzehnten Jahrhunderts.' (Leipzig, 1850.)

Hitzig, Wilhelm, 'Johann Sebastian Bach.' (Leipzig, 1935.)

Iliffe, F., 'The Forty-eight Preludes and Fugues of J. S. Bach analysed.' (London, 1902.)

Johnston, H. F. H., 'Passion Music.' (London, 1858.)

Kemmerling, Franz, 'Die Thomasschule zu Leipzig, 1212-1927.' (Leipzig, 1927.)

Kinsky, Georg, 'Die Originalausgaben der Werke Johann Sebastian Bachs.' (Vienna, 1937.)

Kretzschmar, Hermann, 'Bach-Kolleg: Vorlesungen über Johann Sebastian Bach.' (Leipzig, 1922.)

Mizler, L. C., 'Bibliothek,' vol. iv, part i, pp. 158–76. Article compiled by C. P. E. Bach and J. F. Agricola. (Leipzig, 1754.)

Moser, Hans Joachim, 'Johann Sebastian Bach.' (Berlin-Schöneberg, 1935.)

Parry, C. Hubert H., 'Johann Sebastian Bach: the Story of the Development of a Great Personality.' (London, new ed., 1934.)

Pirro, André, 'J. S. Bach' (in French). (Paris, 1913.)

——, 'Johann Sebastian Bach: the Organist and his Works for the Organ.' Translated by Wallace Goodrich. (New York, 1902.)

——, 'L'Esthétique de Jean-Sébastien Bach.' (Paris, 1907.)

Reimann, Heinrich, 'Johann Sebastian Bach' (in German). (Berlin, 1921.)

Schweitzer, Albert, 'J. S. Bach.' Translated by Ernest Newman. 2 vols. (London, 1911.)

Spitta, Philipp, 'Johann Sebastian Bach: his Work and Influence on the Music of Germany.' Translated by Clara Bell and J. A. Fuller-Maitland. 3 vols. (London, 1899.)

Steglich, Rudolf, 'Johann Sebastian Bach.' (Potsdam, 1935.)

Taylor, Stainton de B., 'The Chorale Preludes of J. S. Bach.' (Oxford and London, 1942.)

Terry, Charles Sanford, 'Bach: a Biography.' Second edition, revised. (Oxford and London, 1933.)

——, 'Bach: the Historical Approach.' (Oxford and London, 1930.)

——, 'Bach's Chorals.' 3 vols. (Cambridge, 1915–21.)

——, 'Bach's Orchestra.' (Oxford and London, 1932.)

——, 'Joh. Seb. Bach, Cantata Texts Sacred and Secular: with a Reconstruction of the Leipzig Liturgy of his Period.' (London, 1926.)

——, 'The Cantatas and Oratorios.' 2 vols. (Oxford and London, 1925.)

——, 'The Four-part Chorals of J. S. Bach: with German Text of the Hymns and English Translation, Historical Introduction, Notes and Appendices.' 2 vols. (Oxford and London, 1927.)

Terry, 'The Magnificat, Lutheran Masses and Motets.' (Oxford and London, 1929.)

——, 'The Mass in B Minor.' (Oxford and London, 1924.)

——, 'The Music of Bach: an Introduction.' (Oxford and London, 1933.)

——, 'The Origin of the Family of Bach Musicians.' (Oxford and London, 1929.)

——, 'The Passions.' 2 vols. (Oxford and London, 1926.)

Tovey, *Donald Francis,* 'A Companion to *The Art of Fugue* of J. S. Bach.' (Oxford and London, 1931.)

——, 'The Chamber Music,' in Cobbett's 'Cyclopedic Survey of Chamber Music.' (Oxford and London, 1929.)

Wesley, *Samuel,* 'The Bach Letters: relating to the Introduction into England of the Works of Bach.' Edited by E. Wesley. (London.)

Whittaker, *W. G.,* 'Fugitive Notes upon some Cantatas and the Motets of J. S. Bach.' (Oxford and London, 1925.)

Wolfrum, *Philipp,* 'Johann Sebastian Bach' (in German). 2 vols. (Leipzig, 1910.)

Zulauf, *Max,* 'Die Harmonik Johann Sebastian Bachs.' (Berne, 1927.)

APPENDIX E

1. VEIT BACH, 155—1619.

    Sons of Veit:

2. HANS, d. 1626.   3. LIPS (PHILIPPUS), d. 1620.

    Sons of Hans:

4. JOHANN, 1604–1673.   5. CHRISTOPH, 1613–1661.   6. HEIN-
    RICH, 1615–1692.

    Sons of Johann (No. 4):

7. JOHANN CHRISTIAN, 1640–1682.   8. JOHANN AEGIDIUS,
    1645–1716.   9. JOHANN NICOLAUS, 1653–1682.

    Sons of Christoph (No. 5):

10. GEORG CHRISTOPH, 1642–1697.   11. JOHANN AMBROSIUS,
    1645–1695.   12. JOHANN CHRISTOPH, 1645–1693.

    Sons of Heinrich (No. 6):

13. JOHANN CHRISTOPH, 1642–1703.   14. JOHANN MICHAEL,
    1648–1694.   15. JOHANN GUNTHER, 1653–1683.

    Sons of Johann Christian (No. 7):

16. JOHANN JACOB, 1668–1692.   17. JOHANN CHRISTOPH, 1673–
    1727.

    Sons of Johann Aegidius (No. 8):

18. JOHANN BERNHARD, 1676–1749.   19. JOHANN CHRISTOPH,
    1685–1740.

    Son of Johann Nicolaus (No. 9):

20. JOHANN NICOLAUS, 1682–174–.

    Sons of Georg Christoph (No. 10):

21. JOHANN VALENTIN, 1669–1720.   22. JOHANN CHRISTIAN,
    1679–1707.   23. JOHANN GEORG, 16——17—.

    Sons of Johann Ambrosius (No. 11):

24. JOHANN CHRISTOPH, 1671–1721.   25. JOHANN JACOB, 1682–

1712. 26. JOHANN SEBASTIAN, 1685–1750.

Sons of Johann Christoph (No. 12):

27. JOHANN ERNST, 1683–1739. 28. JOHANN CHRISTOPH, 1689–1740.

Sons of Johann Christoph (No. 13):

29. JOHANN NICOLAUS, 1669–1753. 30. JOHANN CHRISTOPH, b. 1676. 31. JOHANN FRIEDRICH, d. 1730. 32. JOHANN MICHAEL, b. 1685.

Children of Johann Michael (No. 14):

33. JOHANN LUDWIG, 1677–1730. MARIA BARBARA (first wife of Johann Sebastian), 1684–1720.

Sons of Johann Christoph (No. 17):

34. JOHANN SAMUEL, 1694–1720. 35. JOHANN CHRISTIAN, b. 1696. 36. JOHANN GÜNTHER, 1703–1756.

Son of Johann Bernhard (No. 18):

37. JOHANN ERNST, 1722–1777.

Sons of Johann Christoph (No. 19):

38. JOHANN FRIEDRICH, 1706–1743. 39. JOHANN AEGIDIUS, 1709–1746. 40. WILHELM HIERONYMUS, b. 17—.

Sons of Johann Valentin (No. 21):

41. JOHANN LORENZ, 1695–1773. 42. JOHANN ELIAS, 1705–1755. 43. JOHANN HEINRICH. . . .

Sons of Johann Christoph (No. 24):

44. TOBIAS FRIEDRICH, 1695–1768. 45. JOHANN BERNHARD, 1700–1743. 46. JOHANN CHRISTOPH, 1702–1756. 47. JOHANN HEINRICH, 1707–1783. 48. JOHANN ANDREAS, 1713–1779.

Children of Johann Sebastian (No. 26) and his first wife, Maria Barbara:

49. WILHELM FRIEDEMANN, 1710–1784. 50. JOHANN CHRISTOPH and a twin sister, 1713, d. same year. 51. CARL PHILIPP EMANUEL, 1714–1788. 52. JOHANN GOTTFRIED BERNHARD, 1715–1739. 53. LEOPOLD AUGUST, 1718–1719. (And one daughter.)

Children of Johann Sebastian (No. 26) and his second wife, Anna Magdalena:

54. GOTTFRIED HEINRICH, 1724–1763. 55. CHRISTIAN GOTTLIEB, 1725–1728. 56. ERNST ANDREAS, 1727, d same year. 57. JOHANN CHRISTOPH FRIEDRICH, 1732–1795. 58. JOHANN AUGUST ABRAHAM, 1733, d. same year. 59. JOHANN CHRISTIAN, 1735–1782. (And 7 daughters.)

INDEX

INDEX

Index

Catalog

If you are interested in a list of fine Paperback
books, covering a wide range of subjects
and interests, send your name and address,
requesting your free catalog, to:

McGraw-Hill Paperbacks
1221 Avenue of Americas
New York, N.Y. 10020